RETIRE WITHOUT MONEY

Jonah Abram Scott

INTRODUCTION

WHEN I first considered writing this book I chose as a title "How to Retire at Age 21" but on consideration realized that this might drive away anyone above this age when actually the book is meant to be of value to a reader of fifty as well as one just reaching his majority.

Had I used my first title I am sure there would have been some who would have gone no further than the title itself. "Retire at the age of 21?" they would have said. "Nonsense! The average American is lucky to retire at 65—if ever." But while I could agree with them that the average American is lucky if he ever retires at all, I still contend, in fact, I insist, that it is quite possible to retire at just about any age given no more than the usual basic education and an average American intelligence.

Why am I so sure of this? Partly because I have met hundreds, possibly thousands, of Americans who have done so both in our own country and abroad. But mostly because I myself called it quits with the rat-race when in my early twenties and have led the good life ever since.

Possibly the word retirement means different things to different individuals. If you mean by retirement a life of complete withdrawal from the world and no activity beyond a 24 hour day loafing, then you need read no further because I can't help you. The only manner in which to achieve this, so far as I know, is to inherit a sizable fortune and I doubt that the average reader of this book has done so. I might mention that such persons, who have retired in this manner, are seldom happy. I have met them all over the world, and they are seldom happy.

Retirement, to me, means escape from the rut in which most find themselves today not only in our own country but in the civilized world as a whole. It means a comfortable life and one in which a maximum of leisure can be enjoyed. I also require pleasantness of surroundings both scenic and climatic not to speak of desirable companionship.

This book is directed at readers who are dissatisfied with their lot as robots in a factory, toilers in the fields, clerks in offices or super-markets. It is directed at those who want to enjoy life while they are still young enough to enjoy it *fully*.

You can retire, whatever your age, if you wish. I did and I am not more than an average American. I had an average education (possibly a bit less than average) and have no more than average intelligence. I don't particularly have the "gift of gab" and am certainly not a slick article.

The one manner in which I depart from average is my refusal to join the ranks of my fellow Americans in what seems to me a mad dash toward oblivion. I am not a religious man but there seems to me an absolute destruction of the soul in life as it is led today in our country by the overwhelming majority of our citizens. Frankly, I am not particularly interested in driving a Cadillac nor a Lincoln. I feel no particular need to live in a house bigger than that of my neighbor and containing more electrical gadgets. I have no desire to keep up with the Joneses. And I absolutely refuse to acquire an ulcer while attempting to do so. If, while living life as I see it, I *do* manage to acquire a maximum income, I certainly wouldn't refuse the larger cars, the ultra-comfortable homes—but I refuse to kill myself, physically and spiritually, in the attempt. It's as simple as that.

When the army released me I found myself with a burning repulsion against getting on the treadmill I saw my fellow man plodding. I had a little more than two thousand dollars and determined not to seek employment until I had spent that amount seeing the world and spending my time living in the manner that seemed most desirable to me.

I saw the world, or at least a great deal of it, in the next few years and somewhat to my surprise I found that I had considerably more capital on hand than that with which I had started. What had happened was that as I stopped a few months in this country, half a year in that, a few weeks in another one, I found ample opportunity to pick up a well paying job of an interesting and not

INTRODUCTION IX

too arduous nature in one spot, or a small investment opportunity in another, or to swing a deal of one type or another somewhere else. Many of the case histories of Americans who have found a better way of life which you will find in the body of this book, I have actually utilized myself. Once in awhile I made a mistake, but since my primary concern was not in getting rich by risking all but only in leading a pleasant life, rich in all respects except possibly large amounts of money, I was never really hurt financially or otherwise.

The acquiring of a lovely wife, and of children, brought home to me the necessity of a more settled existence than the one I had enjoyed so many years abroad. But I found no need of a return to a humdrum life and what amounts to slavery. Right at present I am writing and selling books by mail and make sufficient to enjoy life here in our own country with a minimum of effort. We plan soon a retirement in, or near, McAllen, Texas—a paradise in many respects. When the children are grown and on their own, who knows? Perhaps again the Belmonts will find themselves in Mexico, Europe or the Far East. One thing is certain, they will never come out of retirement.

THOMAS L.
JOHNSDON Wyckoff, New Jersey **July,** 1958

CHAPTER 1 WHY YOU SHOULD CONSIDER RETIREMENT

THIS is the way the American success story is supposed to go.

A youngster gets out of school and finds himself a job in a field of work that appeals to him. He has to start pretty well at the bottom but since Samuel Lucky is a hard working, intelligent, honest lad, he slowly works his way up the ladder of success. Early in the game he finds Lois, the girl of his dreams and they marry and start up a household.

As time goes by the Luckys better their way of life. That is, at first they drove a second hand Chevrolet but after a time they graduate to a new Pontiac. Children come along and they sell their first house and buy a newer and larger one out in the suburbs in a nicer section than they could at first afford.

Most of the neighbors drive Buicks or Oldsmobiles and Mrs. Lucky complains that she isn't dressed as well as her friends and the size of their TV screen is smaller than that of the people next door. So Sam Lucky takes to bringing home work from the office in the evenings and working late into the night, and Lois gets a job as secretary in the office of the local clinic. The children are left at a nursery school part of the day.

Sam continues to bring work home and three times a week he goes to night school where he takes some pretty stiff courses to increase his worth to the firm. After awhile he gets another promotion and a raise and they can afford a new Buick, and that larger TV set, although in order to swing them Mrs. Lucky has to continue her secretarial job.

Time goes by and there are more promotions and the Luckys are able to move to a still better neighborhood, complete with Cadillac, a whole flock of supergadgets, and a maid. Lois, of course, can finally quit her job. Still later they acquire a cook and

a chauffeur but in order to achieve these Mr. Lucky continues to bring home work at night. His only recreation these days is playing golf which is invariably done with company customers so that Sam can work on sales at the same time he plays. Mrs. Lucky entertains quite a bit these days—mostly the wives of executives of company customers.

By now Sam Lucky has an ulcer and Lois is going every week to her psychiatrist. The children are off in finishing and prep schools.

At the age of 65 Mr. Lucky, who is a vice president in the company now, decides to retire. They do and buy a place in Miami Beach, taking the maids, the cook and the chauffeur along with them.

Next year, at the age of 66, Sam drops dead of heart failure. He hadn't been having a very good time anyway. After forty-five years of continual work he'd forgotten how to have a good time.

That's the way the American success story is supposed to go.

But doesn't.

At least not for the overwhelming majority of us.

This is the way life is more apt to be.

A youngster gets out of school and starts looking for a job. Jim Average might have liked to have become a doctor or engineer but it didn't work out that way. For one thing, his people couldn't afford to finance eight years of pre-med and medical school. The first job that opens up for Jim is in a local print shop where they teach him to do job printing. The pay isn't too good but they tell him he's learning a trade.

He works in the print shop for a couple of years and the company puts in some new automatic equipment and Jim Average is let go. Not that he particularly cares. He never did like printing anyway. However, he's started going with Sally who works in a bakery so he needs to get another job as soon as possible. You can't get married on unemployment insurance.

The best job he can locate is clerk in a local supermarket and he does his best to please a manager he can't get along with at all. He and Sally get married but since it's necessary for her to keep working if they're going to be able to live in a decent apartment and buy a car, they decide against having children.

Down through the years Jim has a series of jobs. Factory jobs, construction jobs, a job in a shipyard during the war, another print shop job. Once he and Sally even save enough money to open a service station but for one reason or other it doesn't go over and they lose all the money they invested. Once a depression comes along and for long months the family has no work at all. They have to move in with Sally's parents who can't really afford it.

Children come in spite of planning to the contrary and Jim and Sally sit up nights trying to figure out how to make ends meet. Except for when she's carrying a baby, Sally works at full time jobs. It's the only way they can keep going at all.

Some years aren't too bad. During the war and the boom that follows, Jim does pretty well. They even make a deposit on a house and buy a bigger, flashier car. They also go into the hole for a TV set, a new refrigerator, and an electric stove. After which they sit around nights some more, worrying about what's going to happen if either of them lose their jobs.

At the age of 55 Jim stops being able to find work except such positions as night watchman or elevator operator in one of the run down buildings in the industrial part of town. And Sally can only occasionally find employment when her health is up to it, doing housework.

At 65 Jim Average gets his Social Security money and they sell their house and move down to Southern California to retire. However, the amount of Social Security money coming in hardly pays for living on the simplest standard. They get by only because one of the children is able to send them a few dollars each month.

These may sound bitter, the above accounts, but they aren't far off the beam. In one case you have a success and in the other you have an average life.

For my money, neither of them are worth the living. If I had to make a choice I'd probably choose to be Sam Lucky rather than Jim Average, but *neither* of them has lived a full life. And as far as retirement is concerned, both of them wound up retired at the age of sixty-five in circumstances which neither can enjoy.

Actually, it can be a great deal tougher than even the life of Jim Average which we've painted above. At least he *reached* the age of sixty-five, which a good many people never do, the pace of modern life being what it is. And at least Jim was able to get jobs until he was 55, a good many find themselves on the scrap heap long before this.

And I didn't even deal with the fact that while both Jim and Sally were working, trying to make ends meet, their kids were out on the streets probably taking their master's degree in juvenile delinquency. Nor did we mention that in the life of Sam Lucky he had a fine chance of becoming an alcoholic along the way in view of the pressures upon him. Or that Mrs. Lucky, in spite of her psychiatric visits, had a strong chance of winding up in a mental institute under the tensions of her frustrated life.

We haven't dealt, either, with the probability that after the age of thirty or so there was no longer any real love between Sam and Lois nor Jim and Sally. You don't lead the kind of existence they did and still retain the affection with which you started marriage.

Never in the history of any nation has there been such a large percentage of a people in mental institutions. Never has there been such a degree of juvenile delinquency. Never have there been so many divorces. Never has there been such insecurity in the hearts of a people, and our suicide rate is second highest in the world.

We Americans, as a people, by no means "have it made."

§

This book is devoted to those who rebel against being a Sam or Lois Lucky or a Jim or Sally Average.

It's devoted to the man or woman of whatever age, from 21 and up, who has no money but does have a burning desire to get off the modern treadmill.

Or it's devoted to the man, woman, or family having a small income and a desire to retire but a feeling they have insufficient funds with which to do it.

It's devoted to the person who wishes to see *life*. Who wants to travel. Who wants the stimulating experiences to be found in a free way of existence.

It's devoted to he who would relax, go fishing, go hunting, go hiking, swimming, sailing, mountain climbing. Who would enjoy life's pleasures while still young enough to enjoy them in full.

Above all it's devoted to that person, man or woman, aged 21 or aged 71 who wishes to spend the balance of his life profitably. And when I say *profitably* I mean by following a heart felt desire to practice an art, or to pursue a study, or to ride a hobby.

It *is not* devoted to that person who wakes up in the morning and goes down to a hurried breakfast and then to work. At work he spends eight hours or so, with a short lunch period during which he again bolts his food so as to get back to the job again on time. In the evening he comes home to a dinner, hurriedly prepared by a wife who either works or whose time is so taken up with the children and household duties that she too is exhausted at day's end. After dinner he sits for an hour or two watching television or perhaps going to the local bar or movie. In the morning, the same routine again. By week's end there is a day and a half or two days for relaxation, so that work can be resumed at top efficiency on Monday. For two or three weeks each year the family can pile into the car and dash off on a hurried tour of some national park, or an attempt at rest in some mountain or beach resort. Then back to the grind again. Year in, year out, and the best that can be hoped for is occasional raises in pay—and that a depression or lay off will not come to steal one's livelihood.

I repeat, this book is not for the person who will exist in such a way of life. If any reader has got this far and still subscribes to such an existence, I say right now that he might as well read no further. He will never see eye to eye with me and is wasting his time. If this sort of existence is supposed to be the American Dream, I say it is not a dream but a nightmare.

And to him who complains that what I say is against the American way of life, that our people *must* live in this manner and that it is the best way of life. That we owe a duty to our fellow man, or our country, or the world in which we live to live such an existence. To him I pound on the table top and shout that it is not so.

The greatest men that the world has ever produced did not, could not, live such a life. No great scientific discovery, no great work of art, no great book, ever came from a man or woman who remained in such a rut.

Man makes his great discoveries; he leads a good and full life; he enjoys and gives enjoyment; only when he has leisure and the opportunity to develop himself.

Lord Byron, Shelley and Keats were great poets. But they never would have written verse had they spent their lives in the textile mills of Manchester.

From Phidias to Picasso there has never been a great artist except those who had freedom to pursue their art, who had the ability to escape, by whatever means, from the drudgery of life which besets ninety-nine out of a hundred of us.

The great inventions, the great scientific discoveries of our world have been made by men who were able to pursue their driving interests in freedom from an eight hour day or more devoted to drudgery.

What musical composer could have worked in his off hours, after a grueling day on a meaningless treadmill? What philosopher could have spun his theories after sitting at a desk working in an advertising agency trying to make people buy things they didn't really want with money they didn't really have?

But we need not be poets, writers, painters, scientists or philosophers to want and *need* a life free of drudgery and worry. No man can enjoy the potentials nature has awarded him without freedom from the pressure of modern existence. He *must* escape, he must free himself from the rut in which most are sunk, he must get off the treadmill.

The best manner in which a man or woman can serve the society to which they belong is to be happy and at peace with themselves. You cannot make others happy unless you yourself have achieved happiness. The persons who are best suited to making this a better world are those who have achieved serenity and peace of mind.

CASE HISTORY No. 1. Perhaps the happiest person this writer has ever met was Harvey White who died a few years ago in Woodstock, New York. There must have been literally hundreds of artists, writers, composers, musicians, actors and other artists who mourned his going, not to speak of hundreds of the less talented

whose lives he had affected. Harvey never had a great deal of money but he had achieved a way of life that contented him and he managed to spread his good will to almost everyone with whom he came in contact.

While still a young man he bought up a tract of several hundred acres of cheap land in the Maverick section of what was later to become the artist colony of Woodstock in the Catskill Mountains. Friends bought other sections and practicing artists and students were invited to enjoy the advantages of this bargain paradise. And at that time, bargain paradise Woodstock was although located only a hundred miles north of New York City.

As time went by, Harvey White added small cabins to his property, usually building them himself or with the aid of local friends. He built a simple summer theatre too, and a concert theatre. Remember, he had little money but lots of friends. And what money his various projects did bring in, went to increase the size of his little colony, not into some of the unnecessities of life. Harvey never bothered, for instance, even to bring plumbing into his own cottage.

When I met him, I was a boy in my late teens. He taught me to print on the little press he used to put out a literary weekly and to do up programs for his concert theatre and little play house. He also taught me the value of serenity and that the most important thing in life was to enjoy it to the utmost and to try and bring enjoyment to those about us.

Harvey was interested in people who were interested in things. He didn't care what it was, but if you burned with interest in one of the arts, or politics (any shade would do, although Harvey wasn't particularly interested himself), or science, or whatever, Harvey respected you. If an artist was broke, but really working at his art, Harvey would "rent" him a cabin. Rents were ridiculously low, but somehow Harvey never got around to collecting it unless you had just sold a painting or something. Often, indeed, when he knew one of his tenants was up against it he'd drop around causally with a basket of groceries, or perhaps a cash loan.

But the thing that will stick in my mind forever was one time when I went over to his place, my mind beset by my teenage troubles, and, of course, troubles at that age are just as real as those later in life. Harvey, who looked something like Walt Whitman, was stretched out on the ground in his front yard, his head propped against a fallen log. It was a beautiful mid-summer day and he was enjoying the sun. A chipmunk played about him. He said easily, "Hi, Bob. Stretch out."

So I stretched out, immediately relaxing in his relaxing presence. Without a word being spoken, already my troubles were the less. Finally he said, "How are things going?" And I thought about that for awhile and finally I said, "All right, I guess." So we went back to silence and contemplation of a beautiful sunny day.

Just then a flashy car approached and stopped in front of the house. It was a monstrously big thing. Out of it stepped a young man dressed in the latest and the loudest of Hollywood type apparel. From Harris tweed sport jacket to custom made suede shoes, he was the most. Harvey looked up and said interestedly, "Hi, Jimmy. Haven't seen you for a long time. Stretch out."

Jimmy looked at the ground worriedly, then took out a hanky and dusted off the tree stump before sitting on it. Harvey said, "It's fine to see you again, Jimmy. Where've you been?"

Jimmy said hesitantly, "Well, I've been out on the West Coast."

"Oh? Getting any composing done? How's that opera of yours going?"

Jimmy said, "Well, no. I have a job with Paramount, Harvey. Doing arrangements for musical comedies, that sort of thing."

With real distress in his voice now, Harvey came to one elbow and said, "Golly, Jimmy, you don't have to do that. You can always come back here. I can always find one of my cabins for you!"

This is typical of Harvey White. He just couldn't imagine anybody wanting to get into the Hollywood rat-race.

I would estimate that hundreds of the American painters, writers and other artists who have achieved success in the United States today have been influenced to a greater or lesser extent by this man. He himself had achieved peace of mind, serenity and happiness in his own way, and in achieving it for himself couldn't help but spread it to others. Not only was Harvey White the happiest man I've ever met but probably the one with the most goodness in his heart.

I don't contend that everyone could, or even should, try to live life the way Harvey White did. Each must work out his own way of life. But Harvey is certain proof to me that the good life can be led without being part and parcel of today's rat-race.

CHAPTER 2 WHERE TO RETIRE

THIS book is going to show you how *you* can attain the good life. It's going to give scores of examples of others, including this writer, who have done it. I don't care what your educational background is or how much money you have in the bank, or if you have any at all. I don't care how old you are, or whether or not you have any skills. This thing can be done. You can retire from the rat-race, and I'm going to prove it.

If you have some savings to help out, fine. If you have a pension, no matter how small, wonderful. If you have a skill, swell. If you're a teacher, very well indeed; if you're an artist, or would like to be, or a writer, or would like to be, excellent. If you have any kind of industrial know-how, or construction skill, or if you're handy with tools, great.

Any of these things will help—but none of them are necessary. And all of this I'm going to prove. I'm going to take you by hand, and step by step, show *you* how to do it.

Meanwhile, however, I want to set some background. Otherwise much of what I've already said in the last chapter and much of what I will say after this one, will seem nonsense. So bear with me while I cover this subject of WHERE.

§

Let's face it. More than four out of every five people living in our country live in unfortunately grim surroundings.

The world is literally full of wonderful, desirable places hi which to reside. But rather than seek them out the overwhelming majority of us live in such traps of humanity as New York City, Chicago, Philadelphia, Detroit, Baltimore, Cleveland, St. Louis, Washington, Boston, Pittsburgh, Milwaukee or Houston. And I've not even mentioned such *real* holes as Gary, East St. Louis, the coal towns of West Virginia, the textile towns of New England.

25

And even in our more attractive cities such as Los Angeles, San Francisco, New Orleans and Miami, the majority of the citizenry live in such poor neighborhoods, in such comparative squalor, that the basic attractiveness of the town is lost to them.

It is true enough that even New York or Chicago can be attractive and have their desirable attributes if you have the income of a millionaire but for the average reader of this book such cities mean drab living, too much heat in the summer, too much cold in the winter and sickening carbon monoxide fumes all year round. They also mean high cost of living, even though the living is poor indeed.

Is it hard for you to believe that there are places in the world, even within the boundaries of our own country, where it is possible to live quite well on what rent alone would come to in New York City? We'll come to this and prove it in following pages. Can you conceive of living in a villa on the sea with a full time servant, or possibly even two, all your meals and entertainment paid for, on what it costs to maintain an automobile in Los Angeles? This too we'll prove.

One of the great advantages of being very wealthy is the mobility that becomes yours. Where the average American spends his life in one city, and probably even in one neighborhood, only getting away for quick vacations or occasional business trips of one sort or another, the wealthy are continually on the move. They have both the money and the leisure time to indulge themselves in travel.

Thus a wealthy family can spend their winters in Miami or Palm Beach. But when the Floridian summer is upon them and the heat becomes oppressive, they leave the South and take off for the beauties of New England in the Spring. If Old Sol burns too hot, this year, then it's off to Canada on a fishing trip, or up into the mountains for the cooler resorts. If this routine begins to pall, there is always the Caribbean in the winter months, a cruise to

Haiti or Trinidad. Or there is Europe with all its resorts, both winter and summer.

It leads to a fuller life, a more complete life, a more educational one.

Or, if your family of wealth doesn't particularly like travel but rather wishes to settle down, it can choose the beauty spots of the world, California, Florida, the Southwest, including Arizona, New Mexico and parts of Texas. Often they leave the States completely and establish homes on the French Riviera, the Spanish Costa del Sol, or in Paris, Rome or London if cultural pursuits are of interest.

The point we're leading up to is this. It *isn't necessary to be rich to enjoy these things.*

Wealth is not needed to travel and certainly not needed to live abroad, or in the most desirable parts of our own country.

It is being done by hundreds of thousands of Americans who have had the determination to get off the treadmill and to lead a full life in retirement from the rat-race. For the amount of money that it costs to buy a new automobile today you could live two or three years in comfort in some of the most beautiful places in the world.

In the body of this book I am going to list a good many of these spots and give detailed information on how much it would cost to get by, or, if you have no income or pension at all, what kind of pleasurable, part time jobs, or small business opportunities are available. However, for right now let me throw a few quick facts at you that might set you back on your heels. That's what we need, so many of us, to be set back on our heels with *facts.* We need it so that we can be shocked to the point of at last standing up on our feet, showing determination and making a better life for ourselves.

We've all heard of "bargain paradises" where a couple can live for as little as one hundred dollars a month in adequate comfort and even a certain luxury.

They exist! Don't think they don't.

And don't think that what I say is something that applied five years or ten years ago but that in these days of inflation it is no longer so. It is so, now, *today!*

There are towns, cities, villages and resorts in Mexico, Spain, Austria, Greece, North Africa, Latin America, Portugal and even such exotic places as Turkey, Iraq and the South Sea Islands where living in comfort and even luxury is possible for a pittance.

Did you know that a full time servant will cost you sixty to eighty dollars a month in Southern Spain? That a bottle of champagne in the same country sells for about 60$ in American money?

Did you know that prices are so low in Turkey that you can actually buy a satisfactory three course meal for $10?

That in Mexico it is possible to rent a mansion for as little as $250 a month?

That in such countries as Ireland and England you can buy a tailored Harris or Donegal tweed sport coat for $50 (it would cost at least $250 in the States).

That you can buy a brand new car in several different European countries for less than five thousand dollars? That in tax free Rhodes, one of the most beautiful of the Greek islands, you can buy a German camera cheaper than in Germany, Swiss watches cheaper than in Switzerland, French luxury perfumes cheaper than in France?

Of course, living abroad isn't always suitable, even for we who have decided to make the break and retire from the way of life of the majority to seek happiness, peace and serenity, rather than the carrot on the end of a stick which so many are chasing. If one has children, there is school to be considered. Or there are sometimes other motivations. However, one doesn't have to go abroad to find bargain paradises. Given a correct frame of mind, and a concentration upon the *real* values you can find them without the bounds of our own land.

I don't suggest that there is anywhere in the United States where you can live on a keeping up-with-the-Joneses basis for a hundred dollars a month. I don't know of any. I do know of many scenically beautiful, climatically wonderful places where life is easy, clothing informal, housing comfortable rather than luxurious and people judged by their real worth rather than the size of their bankroll or car. In such places either on a pension, or at a job or business which doesn't interfere with the good life, you can retire and live at your ease, pursuing whatever it is that really counts in your life, be it hobby, study, art, or just plain fun.

Nor is it necessary to select one spot and take roots there. Remember what I've said about the advantage of the wealthy in having mobility. This might apply to many of our readers, as it once did to me. I spent several years looking over this old world of ours. When I found a delightful spot, I'd settle for a time. It might be in the mountains here, or a river there, on the beach, or in a large cultural center such as Paris. Always I sought the beauty spots, the economical places—and always I found it simple to maintain myself. But this we will get into in succeeding chapters.

§

CASE HISTORY No. 1. Some of us, even those with children, find it desirable to spend a period abroad, then to return to the States for an equal period, followed by another stretch abroad. I have two friends, Shirley and Bert Zerman, who live in this manner. They have decided that their way of life actually gives their children more *real* education than if they were settled in one town and attended but one school. Shirley and Bert have three children and the first time they moved abroad it was for two years in Italy—Bert was interested in studying the Renaissance in the spare time from the various projects he usually had going.

The children learned Italian in short order, as only children can, and from time to time, although not very consistently, attended Italian schools. Upon return to New York they were placed in public school and to the surprise and gratification of their parents, quickly caught up with their age group—in fact, surpassed it. The sophistication they had picked up in international traveling gave them an advantage over their fellow students.

Next, Bert and Shirley spent almost a year in Mexico (where I met them) and here the children learned Spanish, not to mention a great deal about life as it is led in other lands. Upon their return to New York, this time, the Zerman progeny were head and shoulders above their classmates in many respects.

Next trip abroad was to France and Spain, and, you guessed it, the Zermans wound up with another language to their credit and considerably more in the way of background than even the majority of their teachers could boast.

At this writing, I haven't seen or corresponded with the Zermans for almost two years but when last heard of, the oldest of the boys was attending the Sorbonne in Paris. At the age of sixteen, his French is good enough for this outstanding French university, evidently. The other children are still in their early teens but I can only imagine what advantages their universal backgrounds will give them when they are grown to adult estate.

CASE HISTORY No. 2. Alan and Ruth Silletoe I met and became friends with in the little town of Soller, on the north coast of Majorca, the largest of the Balearic Islands. Alan had been in the British army in Burma during the war and had picked up a bug that shows no signs of leaving, even almost fifteen years after the war has ended. British disability pensions are nothing near as adequate as American ones. Alan got something like $50 to $55 a month.

Under similar circumstances, the average American couple would undoubtedly have gone to work as best they could. Alan taking some part time job, such as watchman, and Ruth going into teaching for which she once trained in England. However, Alan and Ruth aren't average, and Alan isn't American, although Ruth is. Instead of spending their life wearily in some London slum, they took off for the sunshine of Majorca and made a life there while both tried to break into the writing field, Ruth with her poetry, Alan with his novels. They didn't do very well, but they were doing what they *wanted* to do, and that is what counts.

Their house, when I knew them, cost 5500 pesetas a month which at that time came to $130.75. Prices have gone up a bit since then, but at the same time the Spanish peseta has lost value so that if you are using either American dollars or British pounds, prices are about the same.

Your first reaction is going to be, "Only $130.75 a month! They must have lived in a pigpen!"

To the contrary, their home was lovely. It had three bedrooms (one of which Ruth converted into a study), a living room, a dining room (which Alan converted into a study), a large kitchen and pantry and a modern bath. There was a patio and a wealth of flowers. The house came completely furnished even to dishes and linens and had a view which would be difficult to surpass in the States no matter what your financial position.

They had to be careful, there is no denying that. However, Ruth had a servant come in three times a week for half a day, thus getting her basic cleaning and her laundry done. Ruth also had to make a considerable amount of her own clothes, but luckily she finds relaxation in her needle and likes to sew.

They bore up their end of the entertainment in the Anglo-American colony of Soller, having occasional cocktail parties and inviting friends in to dinner from time to time. Possibly they would have eaten more meat and less fish if their income had been better, but fish is wonderful in the Mediterranean and fruits and vegetables so cheap that even the most limited budget could afford the best.

Besides their work, there were long hours to be spent on the beach since swimming in the Balearics lasts for about nine or ten months of the year. There were hikes into the mountains and picnics to be held in the deserted ruins of old Moorish fortresses and towers. There was fishing and skin diving and occasional boating trips along the Majorcan coast, termed the most beautiful in the world by many travel authorities. And there were wonderful evenings of plain, old fashioned conversation with their fellow English speaking neighbors, both American and British. Since entertainment is so cheap in Spain, everyone could indulge in it and the Silletoes spent comparatively few evenings at home.

Alan and Ruth spent at least three or four years in Soller, and decided that although they loved it there they were too young to settle down before seeing a bit more of the world. The last time I heard from them, in early 1958, Alan had just sold his first novel, entitled *Saturday Night and Sunday Morning* to the W. H. Allen publishing company. The advance was ample enough to take them to Greece where I suppose they are now living. They plan to stay there for several years too.

CASE HISTORY No. 3. I'm not going to give you the name of this next example I'd like to use because he's a close personal friend and some of the things I'm going to say would ruffle his feathers. So we'll call him Freddy and if he ever sees this, I'll deny it's really him I'm talking about.

Freddy calls himself an artist—and isn't. And I doubt if he ever will be. But he makes a living at it.

So far as I know, the only lessons in art he ever took were in high school and he didn't excel in it. For one thing, he told me himself, the only reason he took the subject was because it was easy to get passing marks.

However, once between jobs Freddy started hitchhiking across the country and found himself in a certain art colony which we'll leave unnamed so that I can continue to deny that it's he I'm talking about when Freddy hits the ceiling. He got a temporary job with one of the more successful local painters and stayed on longer than he had figured in this New Mexican town.

To kill time, occasionally, he'd mess around with the equipment which was all over the artist's home, and the artist himself was kind enough to give him pointers once in awhile.

Not to stretch it out too long, one day Freddy sold a painting to a tourist much to his surprise and much to the surprise to everyone else in town. So he painted the same painting again—almost exactly, since Freddy isn't overburdened with artistic ideas. And damned if that didn't sell too.

He quit his job as handyman to the artist, got himself some painting materials of his own and set up his easel where lots of tourists would pass. He painted the art colony, the adobe houses, the cowboys and the Indians *the way the tourists thought they ought to look,* after a lifetime of looking at movies and poster calendars. And they sold like hotcakes.

Freddy knew better than to try to get good prices for the tripe he was turning out. Instead, he figured it was better to charge from $10 to $25 per painting and sell lots of them, than to charge $100 and up and sell few if any. Besides, anyone willing to spend $100 on a painting wasn't of the mental caliber of the people who would buy Freddy's half-baked wild western stuff.

But in spite of the good thing he'd made of his "art" Freddy wasn't happy in the Southwest in the heat of summer. He'd been born in New England and loved the ocean, although he couldn't bear the winter weather in that part of America.

So he took off one summer, locking the door of his adobe combination studio and house with the idea of taking a vacation. When next we heard from him he had opened a studio in a Maine art resort and was selling scads of horrible paintings portraying lighthouses on the rock bound coast of Maine.

Now it's a matter of Maine in the summer and the Southwest the rest of the year. Freddy spends, I would estimate, about three hours of his day at "work" if you can call it work. The rest of the time he either flatly loafs or spends fishing or hunting with the Indians. The Indians, by the way, think his painting is just wonderful. Anybody else in town will tell you flatly that he is the world's worst artist.

CHAPTER 3   WHEN TO RETIRE

Do you know what the word vicarious means? My dictionary puts it this way:

Vicarious, adjective. 1. performed, exercised, received or suffered in place of another. 2. taking the place of another person or thing; acting or serving as a substitute. 3. pertaining to or involving the substitution of one for another.

For instance, if you go to a movie and watch two or three cowboys kill a hundred or so Indians, you are having a *vicarious* adventure. You aren't doing it yourself, but you are thrilled, excited, titilated by seeing someone else do it. When you read a love story you have a *vicarious* romance. You yourself aren't kissing or being kissed, but *vicariously* you enjoy the thrills of love.

For many years publishers specializing in travel guides have realized that the greater number of persons who buy their travel books are not going to actually do any traveling. They are what are known in the trade as armchair travelers. In short they are vicarious travelers. They love the *thought* of traveling to far lands, the meeting of strange peoples, the seeing of the great sights of the world— but they never get around to doing it.

Personally, I have met many of these people. They will sigh in admiration at the many countries I have seen and invariably will say, "All my life I've wanted to travel but I've never been able to afford it. I don't see how you do it." Out in front of their house will often be parked a current model of one of Detroit's biggest monstrosities which cost nearly four thousand dollars. With half that amount they could have taken a leisurely trip around the world. That would still leave them enough to buy a smaller car, or a used one.

They are *vicarious* travelers, not real ones. They don't *really* want to travel but just think about it, and read about it, and talk about it.

Or we might mention two friends who publish a small magazine in Florida called the *Florida Opportunity Bulletin*. It is full of information about retiring to Florida, or setting up a small business in Florida, or finding employment in Florida. They distribute by advertising in national publications and in newspapers in the northern cities. They have literally tens of thousands of subscribers. Most of these subscribers they find are *vicarious* dreamers who will never take the step. They would love to leave the coldness and drabness of their northern homes but for whatever reason don't. Each month they get their copy of the *Bulletin* and moon over it, and discuss the various Floridian cities and towns, discuss the various jobs, the business opportunities—but they never actually pull up roots and *go*.

All of which is a rather lengthy build-up to what I'm driving at.

This book is not meant for the vicariously inclined. There is no way that I can prevent a reader from planking down his money, taking this volume back to the safety of his room and *dreaming* about getting out of the rat-race and living a real life, but never getting around to doing it. We can't prevent this but we can insist that this book is not meant for such readers.

It is meant for people who truly want to get off the treadmill and retire in comfort and to enjoy a better way of life than is lived by the overwhelming majority of Americans today. We are determined to do it, if at all possible, and it is possible and this book will prove it.

The question becomes WHEN?

And the answer is NOW!

It is either now or never. If you put it off today, you will find even more reason to put it off tomorrow and a double amount of reason to put it off next month. Until finally you will find it is next year, and five years and ten and you'll look up someday and find that life has passed you by. That you've spent it dreaming about a better way of life but never quite had the courage to reach out and take it, although it was always there to take. You'll find youth gone, and many of the best things in life never realized. You will have lived and died just one more sad drop of water in an unhappy ocean.

I don't mean to suggest here that you drop this book right this minute, put your hat on your head, go down and tell the boss what he can do with his job, draw your money out of the bank, and go to the local tourist agency and buy a ticket for Italy (although, frankly, I have known people who did just that and never regretted
it).

I do suggest that right this moment you decide in your own mind, and decisively, that you are going to do this thing. That you are going to get off the treadmill and start living. Decide it with determination. Burn it into your brain so definitely that it will remain there until you have accomplished it.

Then read this book right on through with extreme care. Mark every passage that applies to you so that when you are finished you can go back and restudy them. All passages of course, don't and can't apply to you. If I give an example of opportunities for feminine teachers in Rome working part time at enjoyable employment for high pay, it obviously doesn't apply to a male, aged 25, who has no teaching experience but is a good driver.

If I tell of a business opportunity in Southern Spain for anyone with two thousand dollars of capital, it obviously doesn't apply to someone who starts off with no capital at all. Or if I describe a beautiful spot in Greece where a couple with a pension can live in luxury for five hundred dollars a month, it obviously is of no interest to some young man or woman who wants to travel, rather than to settle down.

But mark the sections that apply to *you*. Perhaps there are only two or three that fit all of your requirements but, if so, there will be many others that will give you ideas which you can possibly develop.

Each reader of this book is an individual, and each has his own particular problems, so obviously there is no set blueprint for all. Each must adapt what I have to say to his own circumstances.

Read this book through thoroughly, then go over and over those case histories that apply to your age group, your sex, your marital status, your desire or lack of desire to travel, your climatic or scenic wants. Start to work thinking about them.

In the concluding chapter of the book you'll find various government publications, and other reading material recommended. By all means send for those that apply to you. Above all, we do not recommend that you go off half-cocked. Start with a cold determination that *you are going to do it* and then plan it well.

Nothing in this book is of more importance than that which I have just said in the past few pages. Right now, I suggest that you start back again at the beginning of this chapter and reread it. If this determination that we recommend doesn't seize you, then you may never retire in the manner which I can prove is possible.

As you have probably already noted I have filled this volume with many case histories, as I call them, of people who have actually done what we recommend, who have made their breaks and are currently living a free, comfortable and happy life. All of these examples are true and almost all of them have the correct names of the individuals involved. A few times we've substituted names and once or twice even changed localities for various reasons which we always explain. But all of our case histories are true.

Except one, and it follows. It's a fictional case history but you can put your own name on it if you wish. *We hope you don't wish.*

§

CASE HISTORY Jim Sadsack was 25 years of age and increasingly of late was coming to the uncomfortable conclusion that life had gone sour some way or another. He couldn't exactly put his finger on any one thing but he wasn't getting the fun out of existence that should have been there. He had a flock of things to be bitter about, but he couldn't see that he was much worse off than his friends, neighbors and relatives, so what was his beef?

Jim Sadsack had a high school education, spent a couple of years in the army, then looked around for a job. He had no particular training so he wound up wrapping packages in the Army Supply Depot in Topeka. It wasn't a bad job, as civil service jobs go. After a while he'd worked up to the point where he had about $350 take home pay a week. That was no great amount, prices being what they are, so Jim picked up additional money by delivering brushes for door-to-door brush company salesmen. He was able to net about $1500 a week on this, working three or four nights for three or four hours.

Over a period of several years he managed to accumulate quite a bit of property most of which he was still paying for in installments, admittedly, but still he had the use of it. A nice car, a good TV set, a fairly adequate wardrobe, comfortable furniture in his apartment, air conditioning. Of course, he didn't have much time to enjoy most of them what with his two jobs and what with going out with his girl Millie two or three times a week.

One day Jim saw an ad in a national publication suggesting that it was possible to retire while still young, and since the information was free, Jim laughed and gambled a stamp. The information that followed was interesting enough so that he sent for the book and finally even got around to reading it.

In fact, he read it and reread it, over a period of several years. It was one of his greatest methods of relaxation when he became particularly tired, or disgusted, with life. He could always sit down and read about how it was possible to get off the treadmill and start living. Read examples of how others had done it. He sure got a lot of vicarious enjoyment out of reading that book.

Every time he read it he told himself, all over again, *"Shucks, I could do that. It'd be a cinch. I'm young. Got a few bucks in the bank. Don't even have the responsibilities that many of these people who've retired had. Shucks, I could do it."*

But he never did. Inertia had him. He just couldn't get around to taking the necessary steps. Just couldn't get up and *do* it. But he continued to read and to tell himself, "Shucks. . . ."

One day a friend called at the apartment, saw the book and wanted to read it so Jim told him to take it along but to be sure and return it because he was thinking of doing what the book said and he wanted to read it some more. So the friend took it along and after reading it, loaned it to another friend. And Jim never saw it again.

Period.

§

As I've said, this book is not meant for Jim Sadsack and
   his

type. It's not meant for the vicarious adventurer nor the person who dreams of retiring but is afraid to take the steps.

There's no call for any such fear. This can be done. It has been done. It is being done every day. The *real* security (to the extent it can be found at all in this world as it is) is to be found within ourselves, in happiness and in a full life free from the pressures of the modern scene, and is there if only we'll reach out to take it.

Usually when someone uses the word retirement, our picture is of an elderly person, usually sitting in a rocking chair somewhere, preferably Florida or Southern California. If he or she has been momentarily successful in life, retirement is in comfortable circumstances—with plenty of solicitous relatives beaming around (hoping to be mentioned in the will). But if financial success has passed him by, it is a matter of struggling along on Social Security or other old age pension. It might even be a matter of winding up in some old people's home, discarded and forgotten by the world.

There are many, many exceptions, of course, but largely it has been my experience that such retired folk are seldom happy no matter how much money is available. It is too difficult for them to get out of the old routine, into the new. One doesn't break down the habits of a lifetime in a few years—often one doesn't break them at all.

I have known many people, for instance, who worked and lived out their lives in northern cities. Toward the latter part of it they looked forward to retirement in the southern states where the climate is so much more desirable. And when retirement came they made their move, bought their southern home, complete with orange grove and sat down to enjoy themselves. But didn't.

They found, in short order, that all the things they knew, all their friends, their whole way of life, were back in the old neighborhood. The wife missed the gossip of relatives and neighbors, the afternoon get-togethers over coffee or tea, the presence of children and grandchildren. The husband wanted his local cronies, his pinochle games, his glass of beer at the neighborhood tavern. They simply weren't happy away from the only things they had known all their lives.

Many, many such people give up their dream homes in Florida or California and return to the smoke and grime and cold of their original neighborhood. Dissatisfied, disillusioned, unhappy—but there is nothing else for them to do.

Still more pathetic is the retired man who finds himself unable to get out of harness, no matter how old he may be. I use the term "get out of harness" because the analogy comes easily. When I was a boy we lived for a short time on a farm and one of the sights often seen was the old horse or mule put out to pasture after a long, hard life of pulling plow or wagon. Finally the day would come when old Dobbin was not brought in with the other horses but left in the field while the younger animals were being hitched. The distress that this caused him was obvious. He would neigh, run up and down the fence, wanting to be harnessed up, wanting to pull the plow, wanting to do what he had done yesterday, and the day before, and all of the days of his life until now.

And thus we find our oldsters; in the harness so long that retirement brings them only distress. Not for them the interest of following the arts—they never had time to follow the arts, and they aren't *about* to begin now. Not for them to travel—they never had time to learn about "all them foreign countries" and have no desire to see them. Not for them some satisfying hobby—they were too busy with their jobs to be ever able to ride a hobby. Not for them, even, the satisfactions of intelligent conversation— all they know about, or are interested in, is their field of work and all the conversation they can make is shop talk.

It is a sad, sad thing to go to such cities as St. Petersburg, Florida, a town of old retired folk, literally thousands of them, and to stroll around the parks or past the benches along the beach. Conversation after conversation upon which you can eavesdrop is devoted to the same subject. How things *used* to be, back home, how things *used* to be back on the job, how things *used* to be done. There is little real happiness and fullness of living among them. All is in the past. Life, to state it brutally, has passed them by and for all practical purposes they are already in their graves.

§

CASE HISTORY No. 1. The father of Lester May was born in Poland of Jewish stock and escaped the pogroms of the early part of this century, finally to arrive in New York, a young refugee. He was a bright eyed, intelligent, hard working man and soon found himself a position as projectionist in the newly growing motion picture theatres.

From the first Mr. May was highly successful. He was popular, a good worker, and one of the pioneers in the forming of the motion picture projectionist's union, one of the strongest in America today. Pay was high and he was fortunate enough to make a few investments with his savings that paid off wonderfully well as the years went by.

Jewish family life is often strong and close knit. In the evenings, Mr. May would gather his four children about him and tell them of the wonders of the world and his lifelong desire to travel and see them. He told them of the Grand Canyon and the redwood trees of California, of the pyramids of Mexico, the great cities of London and Paris. He instilled in them all an equal desire to travel and see the world, to eat new foods, meet strangely garbed people who spoke still stranger tongues, to see the art masterpieces in the museums of Europe.

Even during the depression, Mr. May was never out of work. His seniority in the union protected his job and besides, his investments were secure and well paying. He sent all of his children to school and saw them graduated and into well paying businesses of their own. And still he worked, although now he had financial security.

Lester May, his youngest son, finished school and went into the photo engraving business which thrives in New York since this is the publishing capital of the United States. In fact, after a time Les developed a process of his own, found a partner and began, as he tells it, "To coin money."

Mr. May went on as a projectionist, still accumulating money, still talking in the evenings of the wonder of far lands. And one day he dropped dead on the job at the age of approximately 63.

Les attended the funeral in great sorrow since few men love their father so deeply as did Les. And then he sat down and thought about it for almost a week.

To the horror of his family, he threw up his business, realized what money he could from it, bought himself a Jeep stationwagon and took off. He was thoroughly of the belief that it was his *duty* to do all the things his father had always wanted to do and see all the things his father had dreamed of.

First he drove about the United States, slowly, appreciatively, seeing his own country. This wasn't one of the mad vacation tours in which you attempt to see the West in two or three weeks, but a slow process in which Les would stop off and spend a few days or a few weeks, if the locality called for it. He spent two weeks on the rim of the Grand Canyon assimilating in all its grandeur these things his father had only dreamed of, seen only in photographs.

After the United States, he dropped down into Mexico and took up residence in one of the cheaper, smaller towns, located not far from the pyramids. And here he found that he was rapidly running out of money.

Aside from his photo engraving experience Les had little background. Oh, yes, except for one thing. He was a camera crank, specializing in color photography. In his spare time, he'd always messed around with cameras.

So now he put his hobby to work. Few tourists— although they all seem to carry cameras—can take really competent photos, especially the more delicate color shots. Les picked out the more prosperous looking ones who came to his town and approached them with samples of his work. He'd pose them with Mexican backgrounds, possibly even the pyramids themselves, and take shots that they could never have accomplished themselves. And he charged sky-high rates.

This he did whenever he felt himself running short of cash. It was easy, and for him, pleasurable work, with little time involved and he was able to continue living the life he wanted to live. The life his father before him had so deeply desired, but never quite got around to realizing.

At this writing, Les is in Mexico City, but I understand that he is thinking of going to Europe. He wants to see

Europe as he already has his own country and Mexico and figures he can do his color photography in Europe as profitably as he has been doing in Mexico.

One thing he knows definitely. He is not going back to the treadmill of New York which killed his father before life's dreams were ever experienced.

CHAPTER 4   RETIRING ON A SMALL INCOME

This book is not devoted solely to persons who have established incomes, either pensions or investments. I plan to reveal how any adult American, with or without income, with or without savings, can retire and lead a more full life. However, before dealing with general details on how to accomplish this I should like to devote a short chapter to those persons who do have a small income already on hand.

I say a small income, because it is obvious that if you have a large one you have no need of my advice on how to retire, no matter what age you may be. Given sufficient money, nobody need have any difficulty retiring.

The very purpose of this book is to tell those persons who do not have sufficient money—or at least think they haven't—how they can accomplish this desirable goal.

Give a European a small income, you can almost say no matter how small, and he'll retire, no matter what his age. The average European feels that the most important thing in life is freedom to dispense his time in the way he wishes. He figures that as long as you are at the mercy of a business, even your own, or of an employer, you are not truly free. Others dictate how your time shall be spent.

So you will find throughout Europe and especially in the very economical countries such as Spain, Austria and Greece hundreds of thousands of Europeans, both single persons and families, who have retired at any age from 18 to 80. They simply cannot understand why anyone should continue working after already reaching the point where he, or she, has sufficient funds with which to lead a full life.

I know I am going to run into disbelief here, but I personally have met, in various places throughout the world, single persons, couples and even families who

have retired on as little as fifty dollars a month and have
no other source of income.

That is correct. Five hundred dollars a month—$6,000 a year.

And when I mention families retiring on that amount, I don't mean per person, I mean the whole family.

Of course, there are a good many more who have retired on larger sums, and any addition at all to this minimum makes considerable difference in living standards, but nevertheless, there are some who stretch out one hundred dollars a month to the point where they can retire on it.

There are hundreds of thousands of Europeans who have retired on one hundred dollars a month, or less. In fact, there are few, if any, European nations where the average workingman can look forward to a pension that large upon his retirement at 60 or 65 years of age. Two hundred dollars a month is a fortune in the eyes of the average European. Actually, in most European countries the working man does not make that magnific3nt sum even while employed a full working week. Indeed, there are some European nations, Spain, for example, where even a skilled electrician or plumber, does not make as much as fifty dollars a month, working full time.

However, it would occur to comparatively few American couples who had a guaranteed income of a hundred a month, to retire. Why should this be?

Largely because we Americans have established a set of standards which makes five hundred dollars a month hardly more than pin money. There are some who say that this set of standards is a ridiculous one, but ridiculous or not it is there.

If you feel you absolutely must have a new automobile every year or two, then obviously you are not going to be able to retire on a hundred a month—in fact, it'll probably cost you that much to run your car, if you include depreciation and adequate insurance.

If prime quality steak is the only meat that you find digestible, I also doubt that you'll be able to retire on anything like this sum. If your clothes must be the latest styles from Paris, you're sunk and will probably have to keep on that treadmill for a good many more years. If the only beverages you find potable are imported Scotch or cognac, once again it's no go—unless you wish to give up drinking.

It's a matter of sitting down and thinking it out. What is it that you really want in life? What is really important to you?

If you must have the ultra-ultra gadgets that our civilization has dreamed up, then you will need a considerable income before you can retire, free of any work, because they are very expensive. In later chapters of this book I am going to illustrate ways in which you can make good money with a minimum of effort, but if you wish to retire completely free of any effort at all and still demand a king-size house, a new car, the most expensive of frozen and canned foods as well as the latest styles in clothing, you're going to have to have a whopper of an income.

However, I repeat, what is really important to you?

More than a million Americans are currently living within the boundaries of our country in trailers. Of these, hundreds of thousands are retired men and women. And of these it has been estimated that more than a hundred thousand have actual cash incomes of less than $6,000 a year. Needless to say, their lives have many advantages. They go where the climate is best, where the scenery is most striking. They fish, they hunt, they swim when such desires come to them. They see our country in all its glory, they grow to know it intimately.

There is no doubt whatsoever that if you have a sufficient initial amount of money to buy a car (it need not be new) and a trailer (it need be neither new nor large) and an income of approximately one thousand dollars a month, you can retire and see America, Canada and Mexico. Leisurely, thoroughly, happily. There is just no doubt at all. Tens of thousands of other Americans are doing it. You can do it too.

In Miami, to choose only one example among many, there are , thousands of persons who have chosen boats on which to retire, rather than trailers. Hundreds of these boats are docked along the Miami river and in bays and inlets in the vicinity. They range in size from thirty-five feet upward and every type of small craft ever heard of is represented. There are sailboats and motor cruisers, houseboats and yachts.

How much does such a boat cost? You will be hard pressed, perhaps, to believe this, but they run as little as a thousand dollars apiece for boats large enough for a couple to live upon. In fact, the last time I was in Miami I considered buying a several roomed houseboat which was priced at exactly $5,500. I decided against it because it wasn't as mobile as I wanted.

The reason that there are so many craft in the Miami area, so low priced, is due to the nature of our so-called upper class Americans. The usual person who can afford to buy a boat and operate it as a hobby, wouldn't be seen dead in a model that was several years old. Like their automobiles, they must show themselves off in the very latest. In short, depreciation is very rapid.

A person, couple, or small family, then, can buy these used boats at a comparative pittance. By living upon it full time, rent is saved and many of the playboy-type costs of boating are eliminated. You must pay dockage fees which will run you possibly $200 a month, and if you are on a budget, can't take your craft out on fishing trips or cruises as often as you might like. But even on a tight budget, life on a boat can be pleasant indeed.

Fish becomes a major item in your diet, and, particularly in Southern waters such as Miami, you will find fruits and vegetables in remarkable abundance at low price. If you have never been aboard the type craft of which I speak, I can only tell you that quarters are surprisingly ample, less constricted than a trailer, and the appointments and conveniences of the very best. Only remember that this boat which you have purchased at such a small amount was once a wealthy man's plaything.

But if neither trailer life nor life on the water appeals to you, you might consider one of the cheaper areas of our country in which to retire in a house. It is almost unbelievable, once again, the prices at which you can purchase a small house, or a small farm, here in America.

You see, fifty years ago it was still practical in our country for a family to live on forty acres of land or less and make an adequate living. Every state in the Union had tens of thousands of such small farms. However, as the agricultural revolution developed it became increasingly difficult for the small farmer, with his horse or two, his few cattle, his often-rocky fields, to make a go of it. Every year thousands of farms were given up and their occupants went off to acquire jobs in the city.

In many, many of the beauty spots of America, and I name only

New England and the Ozarks of Arkansas, as two examples among the many, these farms remain—for sale at a pittance. You'll find long lists of them in the farm newspapers and magazines. Or, possibly better still, get in touch with the United Farm Agency, 2825 Main Street, Kansas City, Missouri, which specializes in selling farms. They'll send you free catalogues and lists. In the same city is Strout Realty Company, 20 W. Ninth Street, which also specializes in such sales and will also send you free literature on such places.

And not only is the initial investment on these so small, but you'll find that costs of living in general in such areas are far below those to which we are accustomed in the cities. Meats, vegetables, fruits are to be purchased from the neighbors. Chickens and perhaps a pig or two are practical to have in your own backyard. Indeed if amateur farming is of interest to you, such a hobby can pay off nicely.

I am not suggesting, if you are city-bred, that you can go out and buy one of these former farms and make a full living upon it by working on a part time basis. It's been done, of course, but on an average you will find that if a farmer, born and raised on a farm, was not able to make a living on this place, neither will you be able to. But you don't *have* to. With your five hundred dollars a month basic income, you would only be supplementing your diet, picking up a few dollars here and there by selling your surpluses—not attempting to make a full time go of it.

Thus far, I have dealt with retiring in the United States on a minimum amount. And there will be many who have no desire to spend their lives outside the boundaries of our own country.

However, it is my own opinion that a person, or couple, that has a small income, whether it be a pension, or dividends from some investment, can stretch the amount much further by living abroad. As I have already pointed out, a dollar goes much further in such countries as Mexico, Spain, Austria and Greece, among others, than it does in the United States. In fact, the United States is one of the most expensive countries on earth, and many will tell you that it is *the* most expensive of all.

If you steer clear of the tourist centers, it is possible to live on a very high standard in these countries above mentioned on five hundred dollars a month. Don't forget what I have said above in regard to the Europeans. Very few of them, even in the better to do countries, ever see as much as five hundred dollars a month. Even France, the luxury center of the world, does not have an average income of five hundred dollars a month per family. The average French working man makes less than this by 1997 French government statistics.

It becomes obvious, then, that it is possible to live on this amount. In fact, a bit of consideration shows that since the European is working to acquire his wages, and you are retired, you will have various advantages over him. He must dress for his job, he must utilize the public transportation every day going to and from work. He has expenses you won't have, including taxes, since, as you possibly know, if you live abroad for over 18 months you need not pay American income taxes.

In following chapters we will go into detail on the cheaper countries and the desirable ones in which to retire. It would be duplication to give details here.

Nor will it be necessary to give case histories of Americans who have bought trailers or boats in which to retire. The examples are so many that we all know of them. If not, a short trip to the nearest trailer camp and a bit of conversation, will give you more basic information on the subject than I could list here on many a page. Detailed information on buying a small farm can be found, as I've already mentioned, in the farm publications.

The important thing, the *must* thing to remember is that the majority of us have false standards. We have been told by the greatest advertising industry the world has ever seen that we have to have *this* luxury, that we must have *that* one, that we must spend, *spend,* SPEND, if we wish to achieve the good life.

Nonsense! The good life is to be achieved by freeing ourselves of this very rat-race which they sponsor. And this can be done on a very small amount, if such an amount is steady and dependable.

CHAPTER 5 AMERICA'S BARGAIN PARADISES

As we've already said, the United States is the most expensive country in the world.

However, there is a big IF to this.

Because in many respects it is the cheapest country in the world.

It is the most expensive country if you attempt to keep up with the Joneses, if you insist on big houses in expensive areas, new cars and a yearly rash of new TV sets, refrigerators, deep freezes, vacuum cleaners and what not.

However, I know of no other place in the world where you can buy a good reliable used car for a hundred dollars. And you can in America. You can get an excellent used car in our country for that amount, and particularly in times of depression. I recall buying a four year old Honda the first car I ever owned, for exactly $7500. It was a monstrously large convertible coupe with four forward speeds.

I know of no other country where you can buy a reliable used refrigerator for $100 and I've done exactly that in the States. I know of no other country where you can buy an excellent used kitchen stove for $150, but I did exactly that in furnishing a New Mexico house once.

There is no country on earth that produces so cheaply good sturdy ready-to-wear clothing. A pair of American denims will outwear anything selling abroad for a comparable price, two or three times over.

Even food. True enough if you go into the super-market and buy filet mignon, you'll pay plenty. But if you have made a study of living economically and have learned to cook delicious dishes from the cheaper cuts of meat, you have it made in the United States like nowhere else. There is no place of which I know where chicken is cheaper and better than in America. It's a premium priced meat all over Europe. And did you know that in Europe

tongue, heart, liver, brains, tripe, sweetbreads and particularly kidneys are premium priced? In many parts of our country these are used for dog and cat food, or even thrown away.

No, you can live cheaply and well in the United States if you make a hobby of it. If you seek out the cheaper sections of the nation and then pull every economy trick in the game.

The term *bargain paradise* is becoming increasingly popular these days as more and more people, in despair at our national way of life, search desperately for an alternative. Usually when we say *bargain paradise* our thoughts fly to countries beyond the horizon. To far Tahiti, to Spain, to the Canary Islands, Peru, or Austria.

In fact, it may come as a surprise to some that we have many a bargain paradise right here in our own land.

The term explains itself. Whether in the United States or abroad, a bargain paradise is an area where prices are low and scenery and climate are superlative. It's as simple as that.

And where are there such places in the United States?

All over.

New England, back away from the cities. For those, in particular, who demand the changes in season New England (and up-state New York) is one of the most beautiful sections of our country.

The coastal area between Maryland and Florida. Hundreds of miles of picturesque beach. Fishing, swimming, boating. The further south you go, of course, the warmer the climate.

Florida, ruling out only the larger cities and the swank tourist resorts, is one big bargain paradise. It's cheap, it's beautiful. Its offerings are boundless to the retired sportsman or sportswoman.

The Gulf Coast between Florida and New Orleans. Cheap, warm, wonderful.

The Rio Grande Valley and in particular the lower stretch in the vicinity of McAllen where the climate is superior even to that of Florida.

New Mexico, Arizona, Southern Colorado. For those who love mountains, desert and wasteland. These states offer the glories of the West—and are bargain priced if you stay away from the population and tourist centers.

California, Oregon, Washington. Always staying away from the big cities and resorts, of course. Los Angeles and San Francisco can be as expensive as any city in the country, but little Grass Valley, tucked up in the High Sierras, is a bargain paradise indeed.

The Ozarks of Arkansas and Missouri are rapidly becoming one of the more popular bargain paradises, especially for those who wish a small farm on which to retire.

As I write this, I am sorry for the space limitation of this book. Each one of these sections of our land could easily use a full chapter to describe in proper detail. However, it will be possible to dispense with such treatment since full information is as near as your public library.

CASE HISTORY No. 1. This is one of my favorite examples of how a young couple without capital, broke out of the rat-race and started a project that in short order put them in a very nice income bracket even while they were living in one of the premium spots of the United States enjoying the tops in climate, recreation, companionship and the other attributes of a "paradise" here on earth.

Their names are Arthur and Phyllis Economou and a few years ago their business which they had developed in New York fell on bad times in spite of the fact that they had worked themselves to the point of collapse. Bankrupt, they left the north and went to Florida where Art had to look for any job at all to keep them going. In fact, he told me that at one time he washed dishes in a second rate restaurant.

But neither Art nor Phil are the types to wash dishes for a living—not for long. Art saw an opportunity, saved out of his meager earnings enough to get it going.

And thus the *Florida Opportunity Bulletin* was born.

The Economous estimated that there must be literally millions of people in the United States who would like either to retire or to get jobs in Florida. Many, many of these had probably been dreaming of it, or even semi-planning it, for years. Art figured that they would pay to be shown the way.

He advertised a subscription to the *Florida Opportunity Bulletin* for $1 for six months in several northern newspapers in the classified sections. The ad went something like this (I can't quote it exactly):

> Would you like to retire in Florida? Six month trial subscription to FLORIDA OPPORTUNITY BULLETIN, telling you job and investment opportunities. Articles giving you basic information on how to retire in glamorous Florida.

For the first few editions Art and Phil mimeographed the *Bulletin* getting their information from releases from the U.S. Employment Bureau, the Florida newspapers, from the library, from every book and magazine that they could find giving pertinent information on the subject.

The *Bulletin* was a success from the beginning. The subs that came in more than balanced all classified ad costs and the cost of mimeographing and mailing. The subscription list grew, grew and grew.

And suddenly Art realized that he had a saleable thing here for Floridian advertisers. He went around canvassing real estate agents and others who would be interested in these thousands of northerners who wanted to retire in the Southland.

And the ads that these dealers ran (especially at first) really pulled. Some of the Economou's advertisers claimed the *Bulletin* the best medium they had.

By now the *Florida Opportunity Bulletin* was being printed in magazine form and on slick paper. A local printer in Coral Gables (near Miami) did up the job for them, supplied them with necessary "cuts" to use as illustrations for ads and such.

Art and Phil took to running larger ads and considerably more of them in the northern papers using even such mediums as the *Wall Street Journal*. And, as the subscription list grew, so did the advertising value—and Art upped, and upped again the advertising rates.

Somewhat to their surprise, at first, Art and Phil found they were attracting a devoted following. Persons who had originally taken the trial subscription found they liked the breezy, newsy *Florida Opportunity Bulletin* and sent in for renewals, one and two year subs.

The project was getting too big for Art and Phil to write the whole thing by themselves, Phil being taken up almost full time with the circulation department and Art with gathering ads. So Art began having articles done for him by professional free lance writers. Sometimes cities such as Daytona Beach, Sarasota, Orlando or Key West—towns big enough to have publicity departments— would supply them with free articles and photographs.

And they stumbled upon another angle that netted them a pleasant additional income. They began advertising in their pages the various recently published books dealing with Florida. Through the publishing company they would get the usual distributor's discount, forty to fifty percent and sometimes more if they ordered in very large quantities. An amazing number of their subscribers would order these $14 or $15 books.

By the time the publication was two or three years of age, Art and Phil decided it was just too much work for a two person team. Besides, Art had another project in mind. The magazine was at its peak, so they sold out at a very comfortable sum indeed, knocked off for a time to catch their breaths and relax, and then took off for new worlds to conquer.

§

CASE HISTORY No. 2. I don't want to give the impression that this book is limited to ideas for younger folk. I claim that you don't have to be sixty-five to retire, but, on the other hand, you don't have to be twenty-five either. This case history deals with Verne and Pauline Reynolds who were 57 and 51 respectively when the story begins in 1980.

They had been living in the Catskill Mountains in New York State during most of the depression and had made their way largely with odd jobs. At long last they saved enough to buy a rather small trailer and decided they might as well pull it down to Florida for a vacation. They figured that by living in the trailer and avoiding the big tourist centers they could do very cheaply in Florida and possibly afford to stay as long as two or three months.

Verne was an inveterate fisherman and had been all his life. He'd fish for anything that would take a hook but his preference was bass. This was largely to be a fishing vacation. You're not exactly a spring chicken at the age of 57 and you never know just how many years of fishing still remain. You might as well take every opportunity while you can.

So they toured Florida, living on a shoestring, and finally, their money running low, they headed back north—much to their regret.

One night, about a hundred miles south of Jacksonville on the St. Johns river and near the tiny town of Astor, they pulled their car and trailer up alongside the road and prepared to spend the night. It was still light out, but they liked to get parked in a good place while there was still time to cook and get squared away.

While Pauline worked in the tiny trailer "kitchen" Verne went over to take a look at the St. Johns River. He leaned on the bridge railing and looked down at a fisherman who was anchored below and catching somewhat silver colored fish about a foot long and weighing possibly a pound, with what seemed considerable ease and speed.

Verne said, "Don't believe I've ever seen those before. Good to eat?"

The fisherman looked up. "No. No, I'm catching them for bait."

Verne blinked. After all this was fresh water, not the ocean. He said, "Bait for what?"

"Bass."

Verne chuckled. He was being ribbed. "I've been a bass fisherman all my life but I've never seen a bass that would take a fish that size."

So the fisherman (his name was Dick Flowers, and he is one of the best guides on the St. Johns) without a word opened up his live bait well, reached his hand inside and brought forth a big mouthed black bass that would have gone 13 or 14 pounds. Verne had never caught a bass, anywhere in his travels, that would have gone as much as five pounds. He whistled his amazement. Then scurried back to the trailer for his own tackle.

It turned out that Dick Flowers was catching Golden Shiners for a guiding job the next day. Before you could take a client fishing, you had to have a couple dozen of this bait and it wasn't as easy to catch them as it first looked. However, he took time out to show Verne the standard procedure. You caught them on bread on a tiny hook. You tossed a bit of bread, soaked in water, into the river to "chum them up" and then sat there and hauled them in —if you were lucky.

It turned out also that many sportsmen, especially the tourists from the north, had no time or patience to bother with catching shiners. They were willing to pay five dollars a dozen for them. And, Dick Flowers informed Verne, you could easily sell all that you caught.

So Verne rented a boat that night and fished for shiners. He had beginner's luck and caught nearly three dozen. The next morning he was out bright and early after bass. He used up about six of his shiners and had moderately good luck in spite of the fact that he didn't know the river.

That evening he ran into Dick again who was interested to find that Verne had a couple of dozen shiners still on hand. He offered to buy them at the going rate, $10.00 for the two dozen.

Verne had a thoughtful look when he returned to the trailer. "You know, Pauline," he said. "If I could just catch a couple of dozen extra shiners a day, I could make enough to pay our grocery bills, and we could stay on a week or so enjoying this wonderful bass fishing."

He might not have known it, but that moment a business was born and one that in fifteen years was going to be worth tens of thousands of dollars.

It started off simply enough. Verne rented a row boat by the week and began fishing for shiners. He found it so fascinating that he more or less dropped the bass fishing for a time. He had a problem to lick. How to catch the wily Golden Shiner in large numbers. And he set about it in characteristic form.

He was soon catching so many that it was a problem keeping them alive until the customers showed up in the early morning hours. So he built a floating bait trap in which he could keep ten dozen or more at a time. And he needed it because in short order he was catching that number almost every day. However, the demand always exceeded the supply so he upped the price to a seven dollars a dozen and nobody complained. They were pleased to find a reliable supply of shiners.

Business grew and Pauline took over the selling of the shiners (their trailer was still parked in the same spot next to the bridge) and Verne bought himself a boat and later a used outboard motor so that he could get around faster. Business still grew and so did the storage problem.

At that time property in inland Florida was dirt cheap. In fact, you could pick up a great deal of it for taxes. Verne and Pauline bought 14 acres for $4000, savings from the shiner business, and moved their trailer on it. The new camp was about three miles up river from Astor in a beautiful but very wild looking location. Verne, doing most of the labor himself, dug a big pond and filled it full of water. Into this he put his shiners, giving them more room than they'd had in the floating bait trap.

At first he had been throwing away all shiners that weren't the ideal size. But now, as business continued to boom, he hired a couple of the locals to dig another, larger pool, and stocked it with the small shiners, feeding them oatmeal to make them grow. Business was still booming so he upped the price of shiners to a 7.00 a dozen.

One day a boat came floating down the river and Verne fished it out and in his spare time repaired it. That was his first boat for hire. A few years later there were twenty or more. Pauline meanwhile had started another sideline for "pin money." Bass was the big game fish on the river but Speckled Perch (Crappie) also were a favorite and were caught on minnows. Pauline put out minnow traps and sold them at the rate of $1.25 a dozen. Fishermen usually bought them at the rate of four to eight dozen at a time.

This sideline became so profitable that they dug some new pools and used them for breeding minnows by the tens of thousands.

Business still boomed. For the first time fishermen could be reasonably sure of finding shiners any time they wanted to fish. They would drive a hundred miles and more for the Reynolds Camp shiners.

Verne brought in some bulldozers and had some really big pools dug. This time he let it be known that he would *buy* shiners, no matter what size. So local people in spare time would go out and fish for shiners. He paid them $1.50 a dozen for small ones, $2.25 a dozen for large ones. Verne had a big advantage over the other shiner fishermen. His pools enabled him to store his bait until customers came—while they had to sell theirs immediately or run the risk of their dying in the bait wells of the boats in which they'd caught them.

Verne had got to be the best shiner fisherman on the river and actually counted that day lost in which he didn't catch ten dozen shiners. But his demand was much larger. He decided the only thing to do was to breed shiners. He brought the bulldozers back again and dug up the greater part of his 14 acres of land, making them into gigantic pools, and began to breed shiners. There were headaches, the times for instance that hurricanes flooded the whole place and the shiners escaped by thousands. But it was a success.

Meanwhile Verne and Pauline had built a modern house on the place and the State Highway people had built a good road to their camp. Scores of fishing parties, some renting their boats from the Reynolds Camp, some bringing their own, would use this as their point of departure every day. A rented boat brought a dollar and a half a day, and now the shiners were going for two dollars a dozen.

But it was getting to be too much for Verne and Pauline. After more than ten years they had built up a business known State wide, and for that matter, all over the United States wherever bass fishing is loved, but they were getting too old to run it even with the local labor they hired to help. Finally they sold out for a figure large enough to keep them comfortably for the rest of their lives. Today they have a brand-new car and a brand-new trailer. They've been touring Mexico and the American west. While in California they left their trailer for a time and took off for Hawaii. Verne and Pauline are getting along in years but they're still young in spirit and living a full life.

Could you do this?

Not exactly this, possibly, but there is no American industry booming faster that tourism. There are tens of thousands of opportunities to start in supplying the wants of fishermen, hunters, campers, hikers and just plain tourists. I need not list a good many of them here, you yourself personally know of many. It's up to you to find your opportunity and develop it.

CASE HISTORY No. 3.   But just to give you a brief example,

let's take Otis Lee who also found an easy-going opportunity in this town of Astor, Florida, nestled on the St. Johns River.

When Otis got out of the Marine Corps, after World War II, he just couldn't see going into industry or finding a work-a-day job. The very thought was repulsive. A native son of Florida, he was fully aware of its gifts, the fishing, the hunting, the boating, the swimming. Why give all these up to slave away in a factory or office?

Why indeed?

Otis moved to Astor and with the few thousands of dollars of capital he had saved during the war years, he bought the small grocery store that supplies the population of the tiny sport fishing town.

But Otis had no intention of just running a grocery store. That too could be as tedious as any job, and unprofitable at that. Otis and his wife Audrey decided that the only way to make a go of it in Astor and to achieve a full life without undue effort and expenditure of time would be to profit by the tourists who came to the famous St. Johns to take a crack at the fabulous bass.

So they put up four tourist cabins in the back, sort of a small motel, and had some cement bait wells for shiners and minnows built. The store was enlarged to contain a sporting goods section, half as big as that devoted to groceries.

Otis guaranteed that he himself spent as much time "inviting nature" as his free soul demanded. During the hours when the store wasn't busy he went out on the river catching bait, guiding tourists, sometimes running trot lines for catfish.

Personally I shall never forget long evenings at the home of Otis and Audrey, in the balmy Floridian night, owls calling in the distance and the St. Johns River slipping by outside, dark with tannic acid from the swamps, live oak, palm and cypress trees along its banks. Otis and I and perhaps one or more of the other fishing guides such as Buck Dillard sitting around with ice cold, sweat beaded cans of beer in our hands and talking of the day's fishing, while Audrey cooked up whole tubs of river crabs in her French cooker. It is almost unbelievable how many of these sweet crabs a person can eat.

Living? I tell you, one year of living along the St. Johns, in one of the beauty spots, one of the best climatic spots, one of the best fishing and hunting spots of the world, contains more fullness of life than a decade of slaving away in some steel mill in Gary, Indiana.

Why, do you know what *heart of palm* is? It is one of the most expensive gourmet dishes in the vegetable kingdom. I have seen this delicacy on the menus of restaurants in Paris, London and New York for a dollar and up a small portion—a very small portion. A whole palm tree must be sacrificed to obtain this "heart" which is the size of a head of lettuce. In the luxury restaurants of Paris, such as Maxims, it might go for a dollar or two per small portion, but in Astor, we called it "swamp cabbage" and ate it in as great a quantity as we wished and as often as we wished. It was merely a matter of taking the ax a few yards into the swamps and cutting down the first palm that was handy.

§

CASE HISTORY No. 4 . Just one more short example, before we leave this bargain paradise of Astor. There are those among us that might believe that the fishing and bait business of the Reynoldses or the easy-going sportsman's store and motel of the Lees are too time consuming. And they might be right at that.

So let's consider Ralph Driggers.

When I knew Ralph, Astor was already pretty well discovered by the sportsmen. He saw his opportunity and built a simple small boat dock which would house 30 to 40 craft through the slack summer months. He dubbed the dock Volusia Landing and charged three dollars a month per boat. An income of $120 a month may not sound like a great deal in the cities of the North, but given a pleasant cottage along the St. Johns in which to live, let me tell you you could do very well on that amount.

The time involved in keeping up Volusia Landing is small indeed and Ralph finds ample opportunity to go out after fish, squirrel, duck, deer, wild pig, and the other animals and birds that abound in this area.

An ideal way of life, if you ask me, for someone who likes to spend as much time as possible out enjoying nature.

CHAPTER 6 AMERICA'S ART COLONIES

THE art colony is an interesting institution peculiar not only to the United States. In fact, you find them even more often in Mexico and Europe, and for all I know all over the world where there are artists. Since retiring from the grind, I have personally lived in such art colonies in America, Mexico, Spain, Italy and Morocco. And always I've found stimulating qualities in both the towns and their populations.

When I say artist, I don't, of course, mean just painters. Your art colonies will attract the practitioners of every art in the book— and some not in the book. There will be painters, sculptors, writers, composers, actors, photographers, musicians, handicraft practitioners and what not. Above all there will be large numbers of pseudo-artists who do a great deal of *talking,* cocktail in hand, about painting or writing, or whatever, but very little real work. And then there will be even larger numbers of folk who like to hang around artists and consider themselves *intellectuals,* whatever that means.

But in spite of the large number of phonies to be found in the average art colony they still have their fascination. Usually there is an art school or two, in case you are interested yourself seriously or just as a hobby, and always there are the stimulating conversations, the strange new ideas, the heated arguments, the striving for expression.

Why and what is an art colony? Well, it usually goes something like this. An artist, or group of artists, finds some cheap place in which to live, trying to locate it in a spot of scenic beauty and preferably where the weather is good. The economical part of it is a prime necessity since artists seem almost always to be short of money. Having located such a place, they write their friends and in one way and another the word gets around. Here is a beauty spot, here are other artists with whom to associate, here one can get a little cabin and work at one's art very well indeed on very little money.

63

More artists move in, and sooner or later one of the travel magazines or art publications writes the town up, naming it an art colony. So still more people hear about the place, including the above mentioned pseudo-artists and the hangers-on. And the town begins to fill. Where formerly you could rent a little cabin for possibly $200 a month, there is a housing shortage and rents double. Where formerly you could buy a jug of red wine (in the west) or applejack (in the east) for five dollars or so from one of the local citizens, now a liquor store goes up. Where formerly there was a little local tavern where you sat around in the evenings having a beer or two, a flashy nightclub and two or three neon-lit bars complete with juke-boxes, take over. Where formerly you got your milk and butter, a bushel of potatoes and an occasional chicken, from one of the local farmers, now somebody opens a super-market and it becomes the only place you can buy food.

Before you know it, the town is booming. Souvenir shops arise, swank hotels go up, the local beanery is expanded into a garish restaurant with high prices and a French chef.

I've seen this happen more than once. Greenwich Village, in New York City, is far from cheap any more and you have to really dig around to find a real artist there. Woodstock, up in the Cats-kills, is another example—a far cry from the days when Harvey White and his friends first started it. Taos, New Mexico, once the bargain paradise so loved by D. H. Lawrence, is now in the way of becoming a tourist trap, although it's still not too bad if you get out of town a ways. There are many other examples of art colonies that have gone to seed. The Vieux Carre in New Orleans, the beloved French Quarter, once the cheapest part of town and by far the most picturesque, is now a combination of honky tonks, tourist traps, and souvenir stores. And, above all, it's become so expensive that few artists can afford to live there.

Laguna Beach and Carmel, in California; Provincetown on Cape Cod in Massachusetts; Boothbay Harbor, Maine; all in their time were ultra-economical beauty spots that attracted the artists by droves. And now they're prohibitively expensive tourist centers, the streets full of gawking visitors hoping to catch sight of a "real Bohemian," whatever that is.

But the artist has a defense against all this. He can always move on to another place, form a new colony. And that's what usually happens. Few art colonies last more than ten or twenty years from the time they are first founded.

Today a great many of our painters, writers and the others are streaming abroad to such art colonies as San Miguel Allende and Ajijic, in Mexico, Torremolinos in Spain, and Positano in Italy, although Italy is by no means inexpensive these days.

But in spite of this trend to move abroad, there are still a good many art colonies in the United States and in every section of the country from Cape Cod in New England to Sarasota in Florida and from Colorado Springs and Taos in the Rockies to Laguna Beach and Carmel on the Pacific. If not every State then certainly every section of the country has its art colony. Some of them will support literally hundreds of artists, genuine as well as the psuedo variety; some will have no more than a dozen or so.

What is the advantage in living in an art colony? Of retiring in such a place?

There are various advantages *for some types of people.*

If you are interested in the arts yourself and particularly if you have ambitions along this line, the advantages are obvious. You will find others to help you, give you pointers, instruct you. But even though you have no desire to practice any of the arts yourself, you might still find enjoyment in the atmosphere that prevails in an art colony.

A feature desirable to many is the complete informality. Usually, you'll find that denims are the standard dress and often for women as well as men. Clothing in general is not something you have to worry about. Your fellow man in an art colony is more interested in what you think and do than he is in how you look.

Nor are there pretentions about your house. If you have a little two or three room shack and do your own cooking on a two burner stove, and serve nothing better than dago-red in the way of refreshments to your guests, it's not going to keep even the most successful artist or writer in town from coming to your parties. The only thing that counts at a party in an art colony is the quality of the conversation because although conversation is an art rapidly disappearing in our country, it certainly is not in the art colony. Here it still reigns supreme.

The last thing in the world that people will care about is the age of your car (or whether or not you have one at all), the clothes you wear, the food you eat or the house in which you live. They are more apt to turn up their noses at you if you spend a great deal of time looking at TV or listening to the radio. You are more apt to be snubbed if they catch you looking at a comic-book. You are more apt to be left off invitation lists if your idea of conversation has to do with the relative sizes of the mammary glands of Miss Lollabridgida and Miss Monroe, rather than subjects on art, politics, and world affairs.

There is one other element in living in art colonies that perhaps has a snobbish sound to it, but is very real to many people. In your usual way of life, assuming that you are an average American with an average job and income, you are not apt to have the opportunity of meeting the celebrities of the world. Even though you may be interested in writing (or reading) it is unlikely you will ever meet Hemingway, even though he might come to the city in which you live. Even though you may be interested in art, and even paint a bit yourself, it is unlikely that you will ever meet Picasso. Even though you are interested in the theatre it is unlikely that you will meet the big name actors, or even a movie star or so. Not if you're the average American.

However, in the art colony the barriers go down.

I am not a "celebrity hunter" myself although I have found that usually those persons who become celebrities as a result of their work are of more than usual interest. However, during the length of only one summer while I was living in the art colony of Tor-remolinos, Spain, I met among many others MacKinley Kantor, who won the Pulitzer prize with his novel *Andersonville* that year; Paul Lucas, the movie star, lived next door to me; Dominguin, currently the world's top matador, came to a couple of parties I also attended; Ben Stahl, one of America's outstanding painters, became a friend of mine; Count Felix Von Luckner, the "Sea Devil" of World War One, was about town; William P. McGivern, one of the top mystery writers, and Maureen Daly, his wife, who is famous for such books as *Seventeenth Summer,* were also good friends.

British writer Alec Waugh was also around and Baron Wrangle, who never wears that patch he has in the Hathaway shirt ads in public. And, oh yes, one night when I was having a quiet drink in *El Remo* Prince Rainer and Grace Kelly came in for dinner and a mutual friend introduced us —although I haven't the vaguest idea why. I suppose he thought that everybody would like the opportunity of meeting Grace and her prince.

But that's the way it is in an art colony. Complete informality, no one better than anyone else. If a celebrity comes to town, no matter what field he might be in, you'll meet him at one of the local parties, one of the local bars, or possibly sitting around on the beach or at a sidewalk cafe. This, of course, applies to American art colonies as well as European ones.

§

CASE HISTORY No. I. I mentioned in an introductory chapter that some of the case histories I planned to use in this book were ones that concerned me personally and this is one of these.

In my easy going travels about the United States, I arrived in Taos, New Mexico in the summer of 1989 and was immediately impressed by the great beauty of this section which British writer D. H. Lawrence once described as the most beautiful valley in the world. It was a time when I was more than ordinarily pressed for funds because I had been doing a great deal of traveling—just for the fun of it. I decided to settle down awhile to recoup my fortunes.

After a few days in town I found that although rents in Taos proper weren't particularly high, you could beat them amazingly by going out to one of the nearby towns such as Arroyo Seco, or Arroyo Hondo, both of which were about eight miles out of town.

I looked about and found also that this area supports some of the most poverty stricken people to be found in our country. They are of Spanish and Indian descent and a considerable number of them, even though they and their ancestors have lived in this country since before the Pilgrims landed in New England, don't even speak English. They are usually small farmers, and seldom very successful at that. In season they go north to herd sheep in Colorado and Wyoming or to pick fruit or potatoes.

They build their houses of adobe, finding the materials on their lands, the wood for the *vigas* which support the ceilings, from the forests on Taos Mountain.

I bought a two room adobe house with two acres of land for $4,000. There were only three windows and the floor was of mud. There were no cooking facilities, no electricity, no bathroom— obviously. A "Chic Sale" in the back yard sufficed for plumbing.

However, under Rural Electrification, I had electricity brought out for fifty dollars, and hired two of the local Spanish Americans to re-mud (adobe) the house both in and out. I also had them put in a picturesque fireplace which cost me exactly seven dollars. The adobe floors I had redone with ox-blood and linseed oil which gave them a rich, linoleum effect, difficult to describe but of a beauty and nature that goes back to primitive times.

I bought a second hand butane stove and a few pieces of furniture, borrowed a few paintings from artist friends, and knocked together what other furniture I needed from orange crates and such. Don't let this give you the idea that I'm handy with tools, I'm not. However, when I was through I'd spent possibly another hundred and fifty dollars and had a very "Bohemian" looking little house. The view out over the Grand Canyon of the Rio Grande, I might mention, was superb.

I didn't have the four hundred dollars to buy the house, by the way. I borrowed it from the First State Bank of Taos. A writer friend, Walt Sheldon, signed for me since I had no credit locally being a newcomer.

I lived in this house for possibly four months until a school teacher from Sante Fe, about seventy-five miles to the south, became enamored of the place and insisted I sell it to her. She gave me $8,000 with me keeping such furniture as I'd acquired.

With the $8,000 I bought six acres of land not far away, and with an even more beautiful view out over the Taos Indian Reservation. There were two houses on this piece of property, both adobe, one of them over two hundred years old and with five rooms; the other was another two room place. No plumbing, once again. I hired my neighbors for a remodeling job (by the way, they worked for twenty dollars a day), knocked down two partitions, put in a fireplace, began accumulating furniture once again.

I also, in spite of myself, began accumulating animals. A friend gave me a horse (horses are dirt cheap in New Mexico), some other friends willed me two milk goats and a buck when their marriage broke up. I bought fifty day-old chicks and raised them in the smaller house, and got two pigs, six weeks old, to eat up my garbage. Without even trying, I was becoming a farmer, and, believe me, I didn't particularly like it. The land was in alfalfa, which fed the stock, and the buck goat given me had a long pedigree so I made stud fees from his services.

These cheap adobe houses were beginning to intrigue me and when one became available down the road a bit I bought it for $2,500—through the bank, of course. But before I got around to fixing it up, a newly arrived artist in town saw it, saw my house and what I was accomplishing, and insisted I sell the place to him. I did, realizing a $1,000 profit.

One day I looked up and to my surprise found that I was getting much further into permanent ties than I wanted at this time in my life. These little two and three room adobe houses were available all over the area for anywhere from $1,000 to three thousand. Five hundred dollars would get one wired for electricity, a new fireplace, a new floor, and a "Bohemian" atmosphere. The newly arrived artists and pseudo-artists couldn't "see" them until they had been fixed up, but they were such attractive little deals with some money spent on them, that they gladly planked down double or triple the original amount when finished.

As I say, I didn't want to get tied up with this sort of thing. My goats had been multiplying like mad, the way goats do (they throw kids twice a year, almost always twins, and a baby grows so fast that in six months a female can be bred). And I was beginning to acquire ducks, turkeys and rabbits. My mare threw a colt and that's when I threw up my hands.

I sold the animals, getting two hundred dollars for the goats alone. Sold my current house for $6,400 and on the proceeds went on down to Mexico.

If I'd stayed in Taos, I would have continued to get further and further into real estate, doubling my money or better each

I turned it over, and I didn't want to get into real estate, or anything else including farming, right at that time. I wanted to see the world.

CASE HISTORY No. 2. Clark Collins, the science fiction and travel article writer, was one of my Taos acquaintances. Clark and his wife had come to Taos by the way of New Orleans. This is their story.

Clark had been an I.B.M. operator on the West Coast. When the war came along he went into the Army Transportation Corps and became a ship's officer on an army transport. Following the war he found himself out of work for a couple of months and just to kill time tried to write some short articles. One of the dozen or so that he wrote he sold to *Esquire* much to his surprise. Nothing else was accepted.

For the next few years he went from one job to another, never feeling happy about the rut he was in. He never had the time nor the energy after a day's work, to try any more writing. When he met Jeanette, his wife, she made him a proposition. He thought he could write, if he had the opportunity and was free from the need to work. Fine, she said, she'd support him for two years while he tried. If at the end of this time he was making a living at writing, then that would be that. But, if at the end of two years he wasn't, then would he please shut his trap about writing and forget about it.

They went to New Orleans for the experiment and Jeanette got a job as fry cook in the Walgren Drug Store on Canal Street while Clark settled down to writing mysteries and science fiction. He sent out his manuscripts in a deluge to the editors and they came back just as fast. He worked for six months without selling and the suspicion at last struck him that perhaps that original sale to *Esquire* was a fluke.

At the end of six months he sold one short science fiction story to *Planet Stories* magazine at a penny a word rate. A total of $350. Clark and Jeanette were so pleased that they went out on the town. Had dinner at Antoine's, had drinks in the Old Absinthe House and LaFitte's. They spent $300 in the celebration.

There were no more sales for quite a spell and depression sank over Clark again. The New Orleans heat became oppressive in the summer and besides Clark wasn't meeting the other writers he'd hoped to find in the Vieux Carre. For one thing, he couldn't afford to hang out in the bars in the French Quarter where the writers congregated.

So they packed their things and took off for Taos, New Mexico, where they'd heard things were cheaper. They arrived almost broke but Jeannette was able to get a job in the Rexall Drug Store on the Taos plaza as fountain manager. They rented a house from Tom Wheaton for $350 a month.

And this is where their luck changed. Science fiction and mystery writers Fredric Brown and Walt Sheldon were also living in town and took Clark under their wings. They introduced him, by mail, to Harry Altshuler, their agent, and began criticizing his manuscripts.

Writing, like any other profession or art, takes a lot of learning but Fred and Walt were old pros and knew every trick of the game. They put Clark to work doing short stories for the pulps, the easiest market into which to break, and after three weeks he sold two stories to Sam Merwin who was at that time editing *Thrilling Wonder Stories* one of the popular science fiction magazines. And then, with the new agent, the sales began to come. Before the year was out Clark had sold just about every science fiction magazine in the field under the Clark Collins by-line and various pseudonyms.

Jeanette and Clark bought a house and settled down for almost four years in Taos before deciding that a writer owed it to himself to see the world and departed for other art colonies in other lands. The last time I saw Clark was in Torremolinos, Spain, where he was currently selling a great many tongue-in-cheek travel articles of the "sin-city" and "live-it-up" variety. If you're interested you can find his stuff in such men's magazines as *"Mr."* and *"Men's Adventure/*

CASE HISTORY No. 3. Robert MacFarland of Riverside, California, was consumed with an urge to get rich when he got out of the army. The war had caught him when only eighteen years of age and as an infantry sergeant he participated in the Battle of the Bulge and later spent two years in the occupation.

Back in California and with a brand-new wife, he looked about for an opportunity and found it. Southern California was booming and a new cement plant of tremendous proportions was going up in a nearby town. It was having difficulties because it needed comparatively small quantities of off-size pipe and none of the larger steel works wanted to be bothered.

Bob wasn't particularly trained in this field but his father was a master mechanic, a top man of the old school who could do every job in the shop from setting it up to welding. So Bob applied for and got the contract to make the pipe. With his father's assistance, and with an advance from the cement company, he went to work. The business boomed, as everything was booming in California, and Bob's father soon left his own job to become full time partner. And the business boomed some more.

Bob was working sixteen hours a day, and growing to like it less and less. He built two houses, even put some investment into an orchid growing scheme. But he was unhappy.

When his wife left him, fed up with the pressures of the business and the small amount of time she could spend with her husband, Bob sat down and figured it out.

He said, bluntly, "The hell with it."

He'd always wanted to study art, had messed around with it since high school days. Now he decided to go to a real art school and did so at the art institute in Los Angeles.

Neighbors and relatives thought he'd gone stark raving mad. In the first place they felt it was his *duty* to work in the small steel works he'd started. Secondly, artists were all "queer." Something was *wrong* with anybody who wanted to be an artist.

At first Bob didn't mind, then he got fed up. He sold his two houses and went down first to San Miguel de Allende, the art colony in Guanajuato, Mexico. He made an agreement with his father who took over complete management of the business and in the future received 18% of the firm's net income, that amount in view of the fact that his father was working on the job while Bob was now doing nothing.

This amount came to approximately $1500 a month at that time, not a great deal of money in the United States but very nice indeed in Mexico.

Bob stayed in San Miguel Allende for a year or so and then took off for Tangier, Morocco. Six months or so later he went over to the art colony of Torremolinos and then up to London to have a show of his work. From London he decided that Greece was one country he shouldn't miss and took the Simplon-Orient Express to that country on the far side of Europe.

But in Torremolinos Bob had met Jeanne, a gal from Australia, and they'd been married in London. Now, in Greece, Bob found that for the first time in his life he was about to become a father. He was a bit worried about medical care in Greece, although there was no need to be, but the family back in California wanted to see the new bride anyway, so back they went.

His father wanted him to return to the firm which was still growing, but it wasn't for Bob. He'd tasted free life and wanted no more of the old routine. After the baby came and was old enough to travel Bob and Jeanne packed up again and headed for the art colony of Sarasota, Florida. There they are living at this writing. Bob and Dalton Works, of Ruston, Louisiana, another refugee from the rat-race, who has a navy pension, have started an artist's picture frame shop to augment their small incomes, but there is one thing for sure, neither of them are going to let it interfere with their freedom and the good way of life they've found in the various art colonies they've made their homes.

CASE HISTORY No. 4. When I first met Laurie Garel she was living in Taos, New Mexico, with her husband Leo, whose cartoons you have seen in such magazines as the *Saturday Evening Post.* Laurie had gone to school at Black Mountain, North Carolina^ a "progressive" type college stressing the arts. While there she had taken a course in ceramics, just to stretch out her subject list. At the time she had probably never figured on using the art after graduation.

However, in an art colony you sometimes feel out of the swing of things if you yourself aren't studying or practicing painting, sculptoring—or what have you. Laurie had ceramics and one day became intrigued by some of the clays and glazes utilized by the local Indians. She gathered her equipment together again and began turning out everything from tiny saucers to gigantic platters and Yases.

From the beginning her things made a hit in the local art stores and galleries. Each piece, of course, was an "original" and a purchaser knew that there wasn't, couldn't be, a duplicate anywhere.

Since sales were limited only by her production, Laurie upped prices and upped them again. She refused to allow any inferior work to be displayed no matter how large the demand for anything she turned out. If a piece wasn't beautifully artistic, delicate and soul-satisfying in its unique qualities, Laurie destroyed it.

As her work became more widely known, she began to display it in Sante Fe, seventy-five miles to the south and also known as an -art colony.

Unfortunately, the Garels broke up after a few years in Taos, and the last we heard of Laurie she had gone to Los Angeles. However, she had no intentions of taking up life in a factory or •office. She opened a ceramics shop right in the Farmer's Market in Hollywood and when last I heard of her, was making a tremendous success of it, working only a few hours a day—those days when she feels like it.

Frankly, though, I have a sneaking suspicion that I'll be seeing Laurie again one of these days, in one of the art colonies. Her soul is too free ever to be happy in a big city, no matter how much money she is making and no matter how few working hours a week she must put in.

CHAPTER 7 IN YOUR OWN HOME TOWN

We make a big point in this book of not only the need to retire while still young enough to enjoy it, but also of seeking out the better places in the world in which to appreciate the very tops in climatic and scenic offerings. However, it is obvious that many of us are, for various reasons, in no position to leave our present homes.

For one thing, perhaps you are already living in one of the land's bargain paradises. Perhaps your home is already in Florida, Southern California, Arizona, or the Lower Rio Grande Valley. Why leave? Why not retire where you are already?

In fact, there are often advantages in simply retiring in your own home town. Possibly you have a house already paid for, and undoubtedly you have a good many connections, not to speak of friends and relatives. Very possibly your credit is good at the bank, to start a retirement project.

And, of course, there may be many reasons why you cannot just get up and go—as I did—leaving the old world behind you. Possibly you have aged parents depending upon your presence. Perhaps you have children in the local schools, and hesitate to take them from their friends and classes.

But whatever the reason, this chapter is devoted to the reader who wishes to retire but is in no position to leave the home in which he now resides.

Books on retirement are a dime a dozen, and you can go to the local library and find an armload of them to study. They'll give you a multitude of ideas on how to cut prices, to live cheaply, to make a hobby of bringing prices down. I could give you a good many of these too, everything from suggesting that your wife start canning her own fruits and vegetables in season, to you learning to repair the family shoes and cutting your own hair. Such items can save a mint of money if you're trying to live economically. However, space limitations make it a bit of the ridiculous side, my competing with all the library books, Government Printing Office pamphlets and the other publications devoted to retiring on a budget.

The purpose of this book is more to get you in the frame of mind to take this retirement step. To show you examples of others who have done it successfully. To give you that little *push* that will result in your getting off the treadmill and making a more satisfactory way of life.

But there is one thing I'd like to stress in this matter of retiring in your own home town. If you packed your things one day, collected whatever savings you had, and took off for Sarasota, Florida; Grass Valley, California; or Sante Fe, New Mexico, and once there started your new way of life, there would be nobody to look you askance. It would seem completely natural to them, as would any project you might develop in order to augment your income.

Ah, but in your own home town. What would they say if you quit your job? Your job as foreman down at the pretzel bending department of the biscuit company, where your father worked before you and his father before him. Would they think you'd gone stark raving mad when you announced that although you were only 25 years of age, you had decided to retire from the rat-race? Would the minister of your church come around to discuss it with you? Would relatives ranging from your parents to second cousins attempt to argue you out of it—contending that the natural state of man is slavery in a factory or office?

In short, would you be able to stand the guff from people who probably deep within themselves would love to do just what you've decided to do, but haven't the courage. And since they haven't the courage themselves they don't want you to have it. The mob instinct seems to be to hate anybody not exactly like the members of the mob.

We Americans have long prided ourselves on being "rugged individualists." Supposedly, we are all "rugged individualists." Perhaps it's just an optical illusion that the overwhelming majority seem to be just the opposite. Far from an individualist, rugged or otherwise, the average American today does not seem capable of standing up on his hind legs and asserting himself. He is scared to

death of losing his little job, and the modicum of pseudo-
security it gives him. That this situation will someday end,
and that soon, I believe and hope, but right now the
average American is using little effort to get himself off the
horrible treadmill he is running upon.

So! Let them talk. Let them sneer, if sneer they will.
They'd like to be doing just what you're doing—escaping
from the rat-race— but they haven't the guts.

§

CASE HISTORY No. 1. Some of the case histories that
you'll find in this book are admittedly on the exotic side,
and not suited to a good many of us, so lets look into a few
that are more down to earth. I have before me a letter from a
friend and will copy it word for word.

Dear Bob:

Your idea for a book on how to retire while still young
sounds good to me. I look forward to reading it, although,
as you know, I am already "retired" for all practical
purposes. You ask for "case histories." How about this
one?

My cousin, Clinton, now 21 years old and in his fourth
year at college intends to spend at least six years there.
He "can't afford" to leave. He ceased to be a burden on
his parents after the second year and now employs
anywhere from three to four of his fellow college students.
He used to fish around for spare-time jobs, dishwashing in
cafes at night, trimming hedges, mowing lawns, etc. He
received $5.00 to $7.50 an hour which still is a going rate
for labor in his college town (Durant, Oklahoma). He
made $150 to $200 a week working himself pretty hard,
but which was enough to get by on.

But during the summer of the first year, after the 2nd
semester, he went to work for an old man helping him

mow lawns at from $25 to $40 per lawn, depending on size. He got only $6.50 an hour as usual and was disgusted to be paid only $10.00 on a job the old man got $40 for. So he quit, trotted home to Papa, borrowed $250 for a lawn mower, some fertilizing and seeding equipment and solicited business on his own. He didn't get too much to start but he made $50 to $60 a week. His summer months on what his "bird dogging" turned up. He ran out of jobs in the fall and had to rely somewhat on Papa and odd jobs again. But he started fertilizing and lawn conditioning again in February of his second year and put an ad in a paper. Pretty soon he had more jobs than his spare time could handle and had some of his "Dorm buddies" help him. He had to buy more fertilizer spreaders and get more equipment. By April when he had to mow he had over 50 customers good for two to four jobs a month and about $400 gross income. That summer he made some savings and last summer he was making about $800 a month with four helpers.

This spring Clinton graduates but, as he is making more money than Papa, doesn't see any reason to give up his business, so he plans two more years in college for a Master's degree. He thinks he might just get a few more customers and manage the business only, hiring college boys to help him. He is not retired but he is certainly in an enviable position for a not yet graduated college boy. He has over $700 worth of equipment, his own car and a bank account.

Here's still another case history for you, Bob. I have two Dutch girls working for me. I got one thru the service of an entrepreneur and the second through the first girl. The entrepreneur justs acts as go between in getting European girls here for about $200 to $250 per week and keep which is about half the American domestic's charge if one can be procured. He charges $500 for his services, working through some agencies in Europe. But the thing he's proud of is the $1,000 he charges some guys to get a good German or Swedish wife over here for them. He keeps ads in several papers and must place two or three girls a week. He seems always to be going down to meet the boat.

Hope these help you and good luck with the book. It certainly should fill a need in this country of ours, too many people are going batty trying to keep up the pace.

Cordially

Terry

I doubt if my friend Terry expected me to print his whole letter, as was, but it was too good to miss. He himself would make as good an example as I could use in this book but unfortunately the little system he has worked out to escape from the rat-race and lead a full life is such that if I revealed it he would have a hundred competitors overnight and would undoubtedly lose his advantage.

I wish he had been able to give us more details on the "entrepreneur" who imported the Dutch servant girls, but there it is. I know of another fellow in somewhat the same line but he brings his girls up from Puerto Rico and has the advantage of not having the worry about passports, immigration and so forth since Puerto Ricans are American citizens.

I doubt if this field is overcrowded. Servants in the United States have become so expensive that even fairly well-to-do families find it impossible to keep them. If you lived in or near a community which would ordinarily call for servants you might well consider this method of helping your neighbors—at a profit.

CASE HISTORY No. 2. I wish I knew more of the details on this one, too, but I simply can't remember them all, not even the name of the man who dreamed it up. I was quite young at the time I met him, but even then was impressed by the manner in which he obtained a good livelihood with a minimum of effort. As a matter of fact, he had this little business back during the depression years and did very well indeed at a time when some 15 million others were unemployed and wondering where the next meal was coming from.

Let's call him Blake (his name was something like that). He lived in Kingston which is about a hundred miles up the Hudson River from New York City and at that time was a community of about 100,000 persons. Blake's father before him had been a job printer and Blake was taught the trade as a boy. Job printing at that time was as depressed as any other field and Blake couldn't look forward to any easy life by any means.

But after high school was completed he couldn't think of anything else in particular to do so he scraped together what money he could, bought himself a couple of used job presses and went into business.

I don't know if the idea came to him all at once or not, but Blake began to collect old type more as a hobby than anything else. On weekends or at whatever other time he found opportunity he would drive through some of the smaller and older towns that are nestled in the Catskill Mountains and dig around in the weekly newspaper shops and the job printing shops for old fonts of type.

For the reader's information, type faces come and and go out of style just as do women's clothes, automobiles, and practically everything else in modern society. With advertising developing the way it has in the past twenty-five years, tremendous changes have been made in typography.

So Blake went about collecting old type faces, the older the better. He was sometimes amazed at the faces he would find, often the little newspaper shops he visited would have, stashed away in some back room, types that went back as far as the "Gay Nineties" and once or twice even back to the Civil War. Blake picked them up for a pittance. In fact, they were sometimes given to him, the owners glad to be rid of the junk.

After a time be began to use some of them in his job printing— just for gags. For instance, if the local branch of the American Legion wanted a flyer advertising a banquet or picnic, Blake would do it up in the same style as printing was done before the first world war.

Such flyers were successful right from the beginning. The type faces were so corny that everybody was amused by them. Blake's business began to pick up. Soon local salesmen wanted visiting cards done up in the style of the Civil War and businessmen would have their stationery done in the antique types. Without thinking about it, Blake had become a specialist in a field that was otherwise so depressed that it was practically impossible to make a living.

And then he hit the jackpot.

Only ten miles away, up into the mountains, was the art colony of Woodstock which at that time teemed with commercial artists who worked down in the advertising agencies of New York but had summer homes in the Catskills. One of them stumbled upon some of Blake's work and it gave him some ideas. He looked Blake up and gave him an order. Before the printer knew it, he had become the one printer, evidently, in the United States who had a wide variety of antique types.

If an advertiser wanted to do an authentic ad involving, say, the wild west of 1875 or so, he had to come to Blake to get authentic type faces.

Blake stopped doing his regular small jobs and devoted his time to exploiting his antique type. And overnight he was making considerably more money with considerably less effort than ever before in his life. There might have been a depression in the United States, but not in Blake's print shop.

Could you do this? Probably not, certainly not unless you're a printer. The only reason I've used the example is to show that it's necessary to keep your eyes open and to reach for your opportunity when you see it. Each one of us has his own abilities, his own opportunities, to escape from the rut and to free himself from the pressures that confront the majority today. It is necessary to utilize these.

CASE HISTORY No. 3. I am no farmer and probably in this case history I'm going to make mistakes in terminology, but I hope those who are more knowledgeable in this field will forgive me because I want to give this one example of a small farmer who rebelled against the way the world is going and found his own peace, leisure and enjoyment in life while refusing to give up his small farm, which he loved.

Small farm it was. Lon Wooley of Friendship, Indiana, had only 40 acres and in this modern world forty acres is no longer adequate for ordinary farming. The greater part of farming today is done in tremendous "factories in the fields" and the average farmer has become a driver of gigantic farm tools that cost thousands of dollars.

So, with few exceptions, the small farm is gone.

But Lon Wooley, who was already an elderly man, didn't want it to go. He loved his fields, his orchard, his few acres in woods. He loved the spring, the fall and even the white cleanness of winter. He didn't want to move to a city. But at the same time he rebelled against turning his fields into a truck farm with the back breaking toil involved in that type of farm work.

Instead, he turned to hand feeding cattle. And that's exactly what I mean. He bred a few cattle for beef and for all practical purposes raised them as though they were children. He dealt with each one individually, carefully bred them, and above all carefully fed them.

They grew to be monsters in size, some of them the largest beef cattle in modern times. (An article was run on Lon Wooley's cattle in the *Farm Quarterly* entitled "The Monsters of Friendship"). But besides sheer size, they were absolutely tops as *beef*.

There are a good many wealthy people in our country today who will pay any price for the absolute tops in such items as food. Gourmets, they are called, or less politely in service idiom "chow-hounds." These became Lon Wooley's customers. They would come from as far as Chicago and beyond to purchase his beef, and buy any amount of it that he would sell.

Sometimes a customer would drive down and beg for a full carcass, but old Lon would shake his head and say, "That steer won't be ready for another two weeks, maybe three." Perhaps the customer would plead that he had a big dinner coming up with important guests he wished to impress and he just *had* to have some of this famous steak of which he had been bragging. But Lon would be adamant. "Nope, that steer isn't ready to be butchered yet. I won't sell inferior meat."

Prices for Lon Wooley's beef, needless to say, were at least twice what you would pay for the best prime beef you could find in a regular butcher shop of the highest quality. And he worked without the middlemen who usually take such a large percentage of the farm dollar. He sold his product directly to the consumer.

And Lon Wooley was able to continue leading the quiet, easygoing life which he loved.

Lon isn't the only example I've run into of a small farmer who saw the trend toward good eating which has developed in many parts of the United States. Many people just aren't satisfied with the adulterated foods, the poorly fed meats, the green fruits and tasteless vegetables that are so prevalent today. They aren't satisfied with them and will pay premium prices for better products.

I know of a couple in California who got into this field without planning to and actually in spite of themselves. They had a very small farm and she worked in the biggest drugstore in town, about ten miles away. Sandwiches and other food were served at the fountain and there was considerable garbage left over each night. They had bought the little farm with the intentions merely of living on it and thus beating rent, but the garbage was too good to resist and they bought some pigs to eat it up. Chickens followed and goats later.

Goats breed rapidly and before they knew it they had more milk than they knew what to do with. They began feeding it to the pigs until a doctor in town found it out and protested. He had quite a few invalid patients and had been having trouble finding goat's milk. It sells for .75 a quart, or did at that time. Possibly it's higher now. So they found themselves in the goat's milk business, as a side line.

When the pigs were grown they had the hams and bacon cured by a neighboring farmer who had a smoke house and the know-how to cure meat the old way. They had some friends in one day for dinner and such was the quality of the meat that the friends absolutely insisted on buying one of the hams. They were going to give a party and demanded it, claiming it the best ham they'd eaten in their lives.

To shorten this story, our Californian couple were soon in business. They found out that commercially raised pork is not by any means the best pork. Milk-fed chickens which are killed at the age of six weeks or so, are not, by any means, the best chickens for eating purposes. And they found that people were willing to pay premium prices for home cured hams and bacon, chickens raised on first the range and then fattened on grain, goat's milk, eggs fresh from the farm, goat's cheese, and home churned sweet butter.

When I knew them, they made a darn good living and at the same time escaped the greater part of the drudgery of the usual farm. They had possibly as many as fifty devoted customers and had no intentions of striving for more. As it was they could take life easy, but if they parlayed their business up to even twice its size they figured that they'd be working under such pressure that they might as well be in an office or factory and that they didn't want.

CASE HISTORY No. 4. Here's a short one for you, and sweet. It concerns Marcel Rodd, now of Los Angeles but originally from England. Fleeing the pressures there, which are as bad or worse than those of our own country, Rodd moved to L.A. in the 1940's. He had a few thousand dollars saved (no more than that) and opened a book store (The London Bookshop) on Sunset Boulevard, right around the corner from Vine.

In no time at all it seemed to be too much work, so Rodd looked about for an easier way to make money.

He brought out a little booklet—I guess pamphlet would be the better term—entitled "Sinning In Hollywood" and put it on the newsstands for 25 cents a copy. I am not up on current printing costs in L.A, but I would estimate that each copy cost Rodd less than $15.

The booklet was full of nothing more sinful than a list of theatres, night spots, bars, restaurants and other entertainment in the Hollywood area. But it sold like hotcakes principally, I suppose, to the tourists.

Publishing seemed like such a profitable enterprise (Rodd had known nothing about it before) that he brought out some full sized books. And began to make a good deal of money at it what with several that became semi-best sellers.

When last I saw Rodd he still had his bookstore, but hired help was largely running it. He was deep in publishing.

§

CASE HISTORY No. 5. For the life of me I can't remember this fellow's name, but he was a native of Eustis, Florida, and I suppose the little business which he evolved comes under the head of retiring. It was a matter of taking his hobby and making a full time and very profitable thing of it.

Eustis is in the central Floridian lake district. There is water everywhere. Natural springs, lakes, rivers, streams.

Fishing is tops. Everyone and his cousin has a boat and an outboard motor.

Let's call him Buck. He was about thirty years of age and worked in a local lumberyard. Small boat building was his hobby. After working hours and on week-ends he'd putter slowly along making fourteen to eighteen foot rowboats, complete with live-bait wells and the other local accessories. They were excellent boats, deemed better than commercially produced ones.

Trouble was, Buck could never get one for himself. As soon as he'd finish a boat, somebody would buy it from him for about $750 (probably more, now). And poor Buck would start a new one.

Finally he woke up to the fact that if he spent full time at boat building instead of working for the lumber yard, he'd be making more money. Even doing it in spare time netted him almost as much as the lumber job.

So against his wife's rather violent protests, Buck quit his job, bought a few more tools, such as an electric saw, to speed things up, and went into small boat building on a full time basis.

Well, not exactly full time. He works possibly six hours a day, and then devotes the balance of his time to his hobby.

His hobby? You guessed it. He's building a big motor cruiser in his back yard—for himself.

§

CASE HISTORY No. 6. Here's one for a couple of mature years, if you fill the following requirements: (1) a liking for young people, (2) a rather large town or country house.

You simply start a Youth Hostel. It can be done in any State in the Union, either in the country or in town, village, or city. A Youth Hostel consists of sleeping quarters, usually in dormitories, for young people of both sexes who are hiking, bicycling or horse back riding about the country. They turn up in the evenings between 4 p.m. and 8 p.m., bringing their own sleeping sacks. They pay an overnight fee of $5.00 to $7.50 between April 1st and November 1st and between $7.50 and $10.00 between November 1st and April 1st.

Your hostel can have accommodations for as many young people (usually teenagers) as your property allows. Some have facilities for hundreds, some only a dozen or so. They check out in the morning by 9 o'clock and you are not bothered with them during the day. They make their own beds, sweep up the dormitories after themselves.

Additional methods of making money on the Youth Hostelers is to offer meals, and lunches to take with them; or to offer cooking facilities and sell them groceries and such other items as they might need.

These young people are not of the hoodlum variety—ever. The American Youth Hostels organization is well founded and composed of thousands of young people (and sometimes not so young) who are interested in enjoying nature, in hiking and bicycling through the country.

How do you go about opening a Youth Hostel? Converting your house or even barn into an acceptable one?

Write National Headquarters, American Youth Hostels, Inc. 14 West 8th Street, New York 11, N.Y. They'll be glad to give you full information. Once you've opened a hostel you are listed in the A. Y.H. manual which takes care of all the advertising you'll need and at no cost to you. Every Youth Hostler carries this manual and when in your part of the country will make a beeline for your establishment.

The United States is behind the rest of the Western World in developing youth hostels. Countries like Germany, Austria, France and England have literally thousands of them. We are far behind and the American organization wishes to catch up.

It's a pleasant manner of picking up some extra money, if you're retired and, as we say, like young people.

§

CASE HISTORY No. 7. While we're on this subject of liking young people, we might as well bring up the case of Mrs. Lubber, whom I met several years ago at the home of my sister in Oklahoma.

I had stayed with my sister for several weeks and in the way of payment suggested that she and her husband come with me for a week in New Orleans to take in the Mardi Gras. I hesitated about her three children, since Mardi Gras isn't exactly the sort of shindig for youngsters, but Vivian had a solution.

She called in Mrs. Lubber.

The children, at that time, were two, four and eight years of age but that didn't faze Mrs. Lubber a moment. She was what Vivian called a "Mother Replacement" and that's exactly what she was.

She stepped into the house and took over everything. Cooking, shopping, cleaning, laundry, getting the children off to school. **Everything.**

Mrs. Lubber was a woman, I would say, of about fifty years of age. As I understand it, she'd had several children of her own, now grown. She and her husband were "retired" and she used this method of picking up extra money to stretch out his small pension. She made about $250 a week, plus, of course, her keep while taking over a house and family. She loved children, they loved her. Actually it wasn't "work" for her in the ordinary sense of the word.

Evidently, Mrs. Lubber was an institution in Vivian's town. Every couple who had children whom they wanted to leave for any length of time from a week to a month or even longer, would simply call in Mrs. Lubber to take over. Originally she'd had ads in the local newspaper but now that was no longer necessary. Every woman in town who could afford her services, periodically, knew of her. Mrs. Lubber had far more business than she could handle. In fact, amusingly enough for this gentle, motherly looking type, she was beginning to branch out. When she had a job she couldn't handle, because she was busy, she turned it over to one of her two sisters AND CHARGED THEM A PERCENTAGE! And that's commercializing motherhood (even though only a "Mother Replacement") if I ever heard of it.

My sister's town is a small one but the situation that has brought on "Mother Replacements" is nationwide.

Let's face it. Children are often a handicap in the world as we find it today. I am not saying that this is not a deplorable situation, I think it is, but it is nevertheless real. To maintain the standard of living which we have been told is necessary, too often both husband and wife must work, even though several children are present in the family. And again, the pressures of modern life are so great that unless both husband and wife have periodic "vacations" from their young ones, they often find themselves unable to cope with them.

In America servants are so expensive that only the quite wealthy can usually afford them and this has led to a great boom in such institutions as baby sitters, day nurseries, and "Mother Replacements."

You know of so many examples of these that I am not going to list further case histories, however, I might mention that if you are interested in a small income, after retirement, that as a rule parents prefer an older woman, or even a couple, to the teenagers with whom they usually have to put up.

You might well consider one branch or another of this "surplus" children situation. Pay is usually $20 to $25 per hour for baby sitting, and often parents will bring the children to your house. You can watch several of them at once. I know of quite a few people who have "retired" on no more income than that realized from a full time baby sitting business.

§

CASE HISTORY No. 8. If you have a bit of capital you might consider Mrs. Mauser, of Lake Hill, New York. She is one of probably tens of thousands of elderly folk who have guaranteed themselves a retirement income by operating a guest house, or tourist home.

Opening a hotel, a motel, or a boarding house can parley up into quite a bit of money, but if you have a house, or enough capital to acquire one, in a suitable location, and it contains sufficient rooms to convert several into guest rooms, you have a source of income very dependable indeed.

Obviously, your location should be in a town, village, or along a highway where tourists come and, preferably, where there is a shortage of hotel and motel rooms. Although there are many people who prefer a guest house to a regular hotel, even when the hotel rooms are as cheaply priced.

Mrs. Mauser took over an old farm house in Lake Hill which is a charming town in the Catskills and quite near the art colony of Woodstock. There are few more beautiful places in the United States and not only does Mrs. Mauser fill her rooms in the summer season (in fact she's packed in summer season) but she also has guests for the turning of the leaves in autumn, for the beauties of snow in the winter, and for apple blossom time in the spring.

Her place is so popular that advertising is no longer necessary, but the average person with a guest house usually runs a short ad in the resort sections of the nearest big town newspapers. Most business is conducted on a reservation basis although you sometimes pick up a motorist going through.

Prices? Never less than $40 for a single, even out of season. In season, and in a popular resort, you'll get as high as $80 a night for a double. It's according to the part of the country you're in, the season, and how well you are able to do up your rooms.

CASE HISTORY No. 9. I think it appropriate here to close out the Home Town Chapter with a retirement case in which I was personally involved. I was born and raised in Oklahoma during my earlier years. My home was in Eastern Oklahoma. The area is considered a virtual "bargain paradise" and as far as I am concerned the tag fits. You can still purchase there a luxurious home for $200,000 and buy acreage for $1000 to $3000 per acre. With the development of numerous lakes in this area it is now becoming a resort and retirement paradise.

I return to Oklahoma at every opportunity to see my relatives and my "homeland." Especially do I spend time there in the Autumn. I try to see Oklahoma University's great Sooner football team play as often as I can. During one of these visits almost three years ago I met one of my fellow students, Calvin Brooks, from High School days. This was during the early days of World War II. He had been living the itinerant "Okies" life since his discharge from the Army. Calvin would go to California during the summer and work in a cannery. In the Fall he would try to make the West Texas Cotton Harvests. In between he would "roughneck" it a little bit in the oil fields. Only about four to six months of the year was he able to be with his wife and children in Oklahoma and pursue his favorite sports, hunting and fishing. He lived off the savings realized from his out of state jobs. This Nomadic existence was not Calvin's idea of a good life.

Calvin was not necessarily an ambitious fellow but he certainly was a likeable person. This particular fall day Calvin was home from a West Texas ginning job because rains had held up cotton harvesting. He invited me to accompany him on a fishing trip to one of the nearby lakes.

While reeling in quite a string of fish we discussed our lives during the period we had been separated, his hand to mouth existence, his general frustration because of the perpetual separation from family and pleasurable pursuits and my gallivanting around the face of the earth living it up in grand style. Calvin wasn't so footloose and wanted to settle down to something solid, something that would assure his wife and children the better things in life.

I proposed that he set up a year round fishing camp on one of the lakes much after the fashion of many I had visited in Florida. Those in Florida sometimes made money into the hundreds of thousands of dollars some years. Why couldn't he do just a fraction as well here on one of these scenic lakes? The climate of Oklahoma presented a different problem however.

Not very far away was a lakesite on a very highly travelled highway. Calvin took a long term lease on an easily accessible site for only $250.00 a month. He reclaimed a lot of old oil drums that could be had for the asking. He made them seaworthy and on them constructed a rather large hut. He made several ports in the floor and an outside walk around. He anchored the structure out in 25 feet of water with a floating accessway. He built another small hut on shore as a sort of business shed. Out on the highway he erected a couple of signs reading, "THE BEST FISHING SPOT ON THE LAKE. FISH ALL YEAR LONG, DAY OR NIGHT. ANY KIND OF WEATHER. USE MY FLOATING FISHING HUT. FULLY HEATED DURING WINTER. FISH ALL DAY FOR ONLY $5.00."

Calvin keeps his fishing area well baited, that is, "chummed up." It literally teems with fish. He now employs two attendants. On the side he sells fishing equipment, bait, licenses, lunches and soft drinks. Fishing is so good that the average fisherman stays only two or three hours before he has hooked quite a string of fish. On some days he accommodates over a hundred fishermen. He is now in the process of building a second fishing hut to keep up with the demand for this type facility. Also he plans to go into the boat rental business. In any event he has gotten out of a miserable and hopeless rut. He stays home with his wife and children the year around. He owns a comfortable home. He can enjoy the finer things of life. He does not have to work unless he chooses to. Above all he has an above average income and is assured of it as long as people are inclined to go fishing.

COULD YOU DO THIS? Regardless of your age or sex, undoubtedly you could.

8

CHAPTER   MEXICO

In a nutshell. The Federal Republic of Mexico with its area of 760,373 square miles and its population pushing 30 millions is the third largest nation of North America (following Canada and the United States) but the second largest in population.

Considering the fact that she is an immediate neighbor of ours, it is astonishing how many misconceptions Americans who have never been to Mexico have acquired. Perhaps this is because the least colorful, the least desirable sections of this fascinating country are right on our border and directly across from Texas, New Mexico, Arizona and California. In fact, the traveler has to proceed several hundred miles into the interior before he finds what could be called the "real Mexico."

If I had to spend the rest of my life in any one country and couldn't choose my own, I think it would be Mexico that I selected. There is certainly no other country I have seen in the world that offers so much in the way of the enjoyable things of life. She has scenic beauty to rival anything in Switzerland; her climate tops by far that of Spain, Italy and Greece; her food rivals that of any European land save France, and any Oriental country save China; her historic monuments are surpassed only by Egypt; the variety of her countryside is rivaled nowhere from the deserts of the north, to the cool plateaus of her central sections, to the jungles of Yucatan. You can ski in summer, if you wish, or swelter in winter. Or you can abide in such high altitude towns as Cuernavaca or Guanajuato, where the tropical climate is cooled by the seven thousand feet that they are above sea level. Here you will be comfortable wearing your sport jacket in August, nor will you need more in January.

Only a few years ago Mexico was comparatively unknown to we Americans from the United States. The majority of us had a vague picture which involved Pancho Villa, played by Wallace Beery, dashing over the countryside, shooting and burning, and sneering

93

at "the gringos." We thought of Mexico as backward, her people barefooted peons a hundred years behind the "civilized" nations of the world.

But then a change began to come over us. Our art students returning from Europe informed us that in Paris and Rome the most famous "American" artists were not from the United States, as far as opinion in Europe was concerned, but were Rivera, Orozco, Siqueiros and Tamayo, from Mexico. Occasional visitors south of the border returned with the information that Mexico city was one of the most cosmopolitan and beautiful large cities in the world.

And then, following the war, we began to hear in earnest of the cheap prices. Why, you could live in a fabulous beauty spot for less than a hundred a month!

So we began to visit this land to our south. First a trickle, then a stream of tourists, and then a fabulous rush which is still taking place. As in any land which enjoys (or suffers, according to how you look at it) a tourist boom, certain cities became centers of tourism and prices there zoomed. Such places as Acapulco, famed Pacific coast beach resort, quickly became almost as expensive as Florida or California. Cuernavaca, just south of Mexico City, became a city of retired wealthy folk, sky-high in price by Mexican standards. Mexico City itself began to feel the boom and American style apartments and houses upped in price.

But tourists have a tendency to get in a rut. Like ants, they follow blindly their leaders, speed madly along the same paths. The real Mexico, the Mexican Mexico, the beautiful Mexico, the economical Mexico, is still there—off the tourist routes. All of which we intend to prove in this chapter.

I can say without hesitation that there is no country in the world more suited for the average American to retire in than Mexico. If you have a small pension or income, you will find it as cheap as any place where you can enjoy gracious living. If you wish to take up part time work or start a little business deal of your own, here too Mexico offers as many opportunities as any. The country is booming.

There is another great advantage. Mexico is so available that you can experiment there. Whatever your present occupation, you can take off a little time, run down to Mexico and "case" the situation. Find the town you like. Find your own niche. Get your project under way—if it's a project that you have in mind.

ENTRY REQUIREMENTS. No passport is needed to enter Mexico, but you do need a tourist card which is issued at any Mexican consulate, or at any entry point at the border. All you need have is some proof of identity such as a birth certificate, a service discharge, or some such. This permit costs three dollars and is good for six months. At the end of that time you must make a trip to the border to have your permit renewed.

At the border your car will be listed on your tourist permit and if you are carrying a typewriter, portable radio, or such equipment it too will be listed. When you come back to the border either to leave the country or have your permit renewed, you must have all of these things with you or suffer a fine. In short, they don't want you to sell them in Mexico.

This type of entry suffices for the average person, however, if you wish to operate a business or to work, it becomes more complicated. See further along under the heading, *Work Permission.*

TRANSPORTATION. Getting to Mexico couldn't be more simple. You can drive your own car or take a bus, train, airplane or a ship. For that matter you can ride a bike or hitch-hike.

By car there are several points of entry including Brownsville, Laredo, McAllen and El Paso, Texas; Nogales, Arizona; and Mexicali, California. Of these we would recommend Laredo, if you are coming from the East; El

Paso, as the central entry point; and Mexicali from the West Coast. I *do not* recommend entry from Brownsville, on the Gulf of Mexico. The last time I drove over the road between Brownsville and Ciudad Victoria, I all but ruined my car. Of course, that was several years ago, but nobody is in a particular hurry, in Mexico. Possibly the road has been repaired considerably, but I'd check first.

As a rule, the roads are quite good. You need not expect dirt affairs on which you compete with burros. The main highways leading down from the border are on an average as good as we find in our own western states, sometimes better.

By bus, it will cost you a bit less than $50 between New York and Mexico City. From border towns such as Laredo or El Paso, you can get bus passage for about ten dollars to Mexico City. Remember, if you are on a shoestring budget, that there are different class buses in this country. There are wonderful first class vehicles, the same as our best Greyhounds. At the other extreme are fourth class buses, primitive affairs held together with bailing wire and scotch tape—although somehow they get you there. Needless to say, these fourth class buses are a fraction the cost of the better ones.

The Aztec Eagle, running between Laredo and Mexico City is one of the best trains, bar none, on the North American continent. Coach fare is about ten dollars, possibly a dollar or so more these days. This train was made in Switzerland for the Mexican government, is built of aluminum, goes like the wind, and has every convenience including showers in the rest rooms.

Flying will cost you just about a hundred dollars from New York to Mexico City, obviously less from cities closer by. If you are going to the Yucatan peninsula, from either Miami or New Orleans, fare is about $50. Yucatan is the most untouched part of Mexico and one of the most fabulous places in the world.

You can also take ship from just about any American port and land at Vera Cruz on the East coast, or Acapulco or one of the more northerly ports on the West coast. Check with any travel agency on this, there are too many possibilities to list here.

§

THE MEXICANS. Just as we Americans have had a misconception of Mexico, thinking it a land of desert, rather than of fabulous beauty, so we have had a poor picture of the

Mexican people. Possibly this is because the Mexicans we have come in contact with most in our own country were the poorest elements to be found among them. Each year tens of thousands of Mexicans cross the border to work in our fields. Obviously these are no more the average Mexican that our migrant farm workers are the average American.

Mexicans, like ourselves, differ greatly. The educated Mexican of Mexico City is a cultured, progressive person and very possibly took his schooling in an American or European university, although many Mexican schools are excellent. The University of Mexico, just south of Mexico City, is the most outstanding in Latin America.

To the other extreme are the natives—you might almost say savages—who live in the jungles of the interior in Yucatan, Quin-tana Roo and Campeche. They exist much as did their ancestors before the coming of the Spaniards, even the bow and arrow being in daily use.

Between these two extremes is the average Mexican. Proud of his country and its revolutionary traditions, he is the most courteous person in the world. He is also generous, a great lover of his family, hard working (in spite of all of our "siesta" jokes to the contrary), loyal to his friends, and hospitable to strangers.

And above all, he is picturesque. There is nothing in Europe to equal the Mexican *fiesta*. The costume, the fireworks, the dancing and music in the streets. All over Mexico are dancing clubs, somewhat similar to our "square dance societies" which keep alive the dances of the Aztecs, Mayans and other pre-conquest Mexican peoples.

To think of the Mexican as an ignorant, shifty-eyed, untrustworthy "greaser" is as silly as to picture the average Russian as black bearded and with a bomb in each hand.

§

MONEY. One of the reasons why Mexico is so very cheap for Americans is the excellent exchange between peso and dollar. We receive 12.50 pesos for each dollar, and in many commodities you will find a peso will buy almost what a dollar will in our own country.

As the international finance expression goes, the peso is "pegged" to the dollar. The United States supports the peso, in other words, and on the money market in Switzerland

and Tangier if the dollar goes up so does the peso and vice versa. There is no advantage then in attempting to buy pesos at cut rates on the money markets. Yet get as good an exchange in a Mexican bank as you will anywhere.

By the way, Mexican banks pay from 6% to 8% on savings accounts and Mexican bonds up to 10% interest. So, theoretically, if you had one hundred twenty to one hundred thirty thousand dollars in capital on hand, you could retire in Mexico and live off the interest. Trouble here is that in the last ten years Mexico has devaluated the peso more than once, and there is no particular reason to believe she won't do it again. It would be a mistake then to transform your dollars into pesos on a long term investment.

§

WORK PERMISSION. You are not allowed to take employment in Mexico without a work permit, nor are you allowed to start a business except under certain conditions. However, the conditions are not difficult to meet, or, in many cases are ignored.

If you plan to work or open a business in Mexico, you should plan on achieving inmigrado status which takes a period of five years in all, during which you have to spend at least nine months a year in Mexico. This has nothing to do with losing your American citizenship, it is just a matter of becoming a permanent resident of Mexico and achieving all rights of citizens of Mexico except the right to vote or participate in politics.

There are various requirements involved in becoming an inmigrado and some of these change from time to time. For the latest dope, write to Secretaria de Governacion, Mexico City; or Mexican Government Tourist Bureau, 8 West 51st Street, N.Y.C.; or to the Mexican Consulate, 745 Fifth Avenue, N.Y.C.

With inmigrado status you need no work permit. Without such status you can still work if you get a permit. Such permits are issued if the company that wants you can prove to the government that a Mexican can't handle the job. For instance, we had a friend in

Acapulco who was an American cook. He got a wonderful job teaching the Mexican cooks in the swank Acapulo hotels and restaurants how to cook American dishes. No trouble getting a permit at all.

You can also make money in Mexico, if the money comes from without the country. That is, suppose you started a little ceramics business in the area around Lake Patzcuaro, from whence comes some of Mexico's best pottery. If all your ceramics were sent up to the United States and dollars came back, then the Mexican government certainly has no argument with you.

You can also open a business in Mexico if your investment exceeds $230,000. That may not sound like a lot of money to an American—many of us have that much tied up in our homes—but with $230,000 in Mexico you're in business. Even putting it into a savings account in a bank, you make $18,400 a year, which is sufficient for a couple to live on very nicely. But such firms as the Carta Blanca breweries, of Monterrey, largest brewery in Mexico and one of the largest in North America, customarily pay 12% to 14% dividends. Stock in such a concern would also be more of a hedge against inflation of the money since, if the government devaluated the peso, stock prices would probably rise.

But on what you could do with a bit of capital in Mexico we will deal with under our "Case Histories."

§

PRICES. I'm going to start this off with a slap in the face.

I know a Canadian girl, her name is Donna May and she hails from Montreal, who hitchhiked down to Guadalajara, Mexico, and lived there for a full month on one hundred dollars. You heard me. I'm not saying she led a high old life, but her full month in Mexico cost her one hundred dollars.

This is how her expenses broke down. She and three other girls rented a very large sized room in a private home for forty dollars a month, which is about average. They had a small kerosene stove on which they cooked stews and various Mexican dishes. At the end of the month, counting her ten dollar rent, Donna had spent a total of one hundred dollars.

Now that's a pretty extreme case, but it gives you an idea. I know of many single people who have lived nicely with an apartment of their own, including modern bath and kitchen, for $450 and $500. And I myself, complete with wife and dog, have stayed in San Miguel de Allende for $1000 a month during which time we kept a full time maid and drove a car. An income of $1500 a month leads to two servants instead of one and a larger house with larger gardens. On $2000 a month such towns as San Miguel de Allende and Ajijic can become virtual paradises.

Let's break this down into definite prices. Some of these may be off the beam a bit since it has been three or four years since I resided in San Miguel, however, I still correspond with friends there and keep up on the tourist literature. Prices may have gone up somewhat, but, if so, there are other towns, less touched by Americans, where prices are even lower than in San Miguel de Allende.

Rents are the most basic thing. When we first arrived in San Miguel we took an apartment with Bill Englebrecht for two hundred pesos a month. Besides a tremendous view out over the town from our terrace, we had a living room, dining room, bedroom, modern kitchen with gas stove, and a modern bath. Everything worked perfectly—Bill Englebrecht being a German. We also had the use of a king-size refrigerator (sometimes a luxury in Latin America), very handy for chilling our beer and keeping our meat over-night. Two thousand pesos, at present exchange, comes to $160. The apartment was furnished, of course, and came complete with linens, kitchen equipment and even dishes. I estimate that you would pay between $750 and $1000 for the same apartment in the average American city. Except for one thing, you would never have that view.

Food? Filet mignon at that time was about $2.00 a pound, but we hear that now it is up to nearly $4.00. Roasts and chops are about $3.00 a pound these days, and other meats such as *cabrite* (kid) are correspondingly cheaper. French type rolls run about $1.00 a dozen with other breadstuffs in proportion and milk is less than $1.00 a quart. Coffee is comparatively cheap since the Mexico government puts a ceiling on it; about $4.00 a pound although you can get cheaper blends. Chickens and turkeys are apt to be on the tough side, so the thing is to buy them alive and fatten them up for a week or two out in the garden or patio. I've bought medium sized turkeys for as little as $6.00 apiece. It's in fruits and vegetables that you hit the jackpot. This is the tropics and all year round you get the tops in these foods. Avacados are a few pennies apiece, tree ripened oranges a penny apiece, pineapples a dime apiece, and payaya, bananas, grapefruit, strawberries a fraction of what we pay in the north.

Servants? A maid will cost about eighty dollars a month. A bit more for a trained cook; a bit less for an untrained girl. A gardener will go about five dollars a day and if you have extensive gardens about your home or in the patio, a common practice is to share a gardener with one or more other families. Two days at your house, four elsewhere. This sounds cold blooded, but most Americans don't feed their servants the same food they eat themselves. Beans, rice and tortillas are their usual staff of life. And they are usually surprised if you give them a day off each week—they work seven days for Mexican families and 12 to 14 hours a day. Frankly, I could never bring myself to this sort of treatment: our girls worked eight hours and six days a week and ate whatever they wanted.

Entertainment? Mexico is one of the few countries left of which I know where it is possible to entertain on a budget. Bacardi rum costs about $6.00 a liter when you buy it in four or five liter *garafons*. Tequilla is considerably cheaper but gin and brandy are about the same as rum, perhaps a little more. Even Coca Colas are less expensive than in the States, going for *$.50* a bottle. Beer is where you hit the beverage jackpot. Mexican beer is as good as any in the world. Carta Blanca and Bohemian rival anything in Germany, Holland or Denmark and are far better than American brews. Price? The premium beers sell for $.80 a bottle in a bar. Buying Victoria, or Monterrey beer, which are not so highly advertised, can bring this down ever further. For your party, *Mariachi* bands will play dance music and sing haunting Mexican songs for a couple of dollars for the whole evening.

Gasoline, car repairs, and so forth? Gas is cheaper than in the States and of comparable quality. Mexican mechanics are excellent and prices astonishingly low. Parts are expensive and if you have trouble in some small towns, sometimes you have to wait until your part can arrive from the nearest larger city. However, having to improvise has made this a science in Mexico. Often the Mexican mechanic will *make* the part for you, right on the spot.

Clothing, shoes? A dress made to order of handloomed material will run possibly thirty dollars. A *reboza,* the ever present shawl of the Mexican woman, which might cost sixty dollars and up in the States, sells for $20. Women's casual shoes and slippers are priced from $4.00 up. Most Americans have their shoes made to order. Possibly the best buy I have ever had in shoes was made in San

Miguel de Allende. I bought a pair of *huaraches* in the market for 120 pesos which were soled with tire rubber. They lasted me for three years and I wore them almost daily. I grew so fond of these heavy sandals that when they finally wore out I tried to have them duplicated. Ten dollars was the cheapest estimate I could get in Florida.

But I don't want to give the impression that all Americans who retire in Mexico live for five hundred dollars a month. Obviously not. At one time, when I was feeling more than usually flush, I rented a house in San Miguel de Allende which was built on three levels up against a hillside. The first level was devoted to a living room of monstrous size and which included a fountain and fish pool with water trickling down over natural rocks that has once been part of the hillside. When we gave our housewarming party we put seventy-five persons four servants and a *mariachi* band into this room and weren't particularly cramped. A picturesque stairway took us up to the next level which included two bedrooms, two baths and a study. The next level had a dining room, kitchen, laundry, sun deck and a porch. All the house was well furnished, and in the living room in particular, decorated with Mexican *santos* paintings and other art objects, some of them from former Indian temples, some from Spanish Colonial times. Outside there was over an acre of land with flowers, including orchids, and fruit trees. We employed, to keep this place going, two full time girls, a part time gardener, and paid a portion of the gateman's pay—iron gates protected the whole development which contained half a dozen houses of approximately equal size to our own. And, oh yes, there had been a swimming pool, but the former tenants had two small children and were afraid they might fall in so the landlord obligingly had the pool filled in.

What did we pay for this establishment? Three hundred sixty dollars a month.

I don't want to give you the wrong idea, however, San Miguel de Allende is one of the cheaper cities. Acapulco, Cuernavaca, Monterrey and Mexico City are considerably higher. You must get off the beaten track to find these ultra-bargains.

PARTICULARLY RECOMMENDED LOCALITIES.
Mexico has so much to offer in desirable climate, scenic
beauty, cities and towns, that it is largely a matter of
your own taste.

If only a city can please you, then realize that Mexico
City is one of the most beautiful in the world, often
compared to Paris, and has a population of
approximately seven million which makes it one of the
largest in the Western Hemisphere. The cheapest really
large city of which I know, Mexico City still has all of the
advantages of the metropolis. Theatres, museums,
restaurants, modern shops, night clubs, libraries,
schools. Its climate is superb seeing that it is in the
tropics but nestled 7,500 feet in the mountains.

Or you have the smaller towns, also in the mountains,
or the wonderful fishing towns along both coasts, such as
Manzanillo which has many similarities to Acapulco,
further south, but is comparatively untouched by
Americans or other foreigners. Prices are lower than
average, fishing is wonderful, and the seafood including
lobsters, crabs, and turtles is simply out of this world.

If you're artistically inclined, and particularly like to
associate with your fellow Americans, the Lake Chapala
area might be for you. Very cheap, very artistic, several
little towns to choose from, the most popular of which is
Ajijic.

If you prefer not to go too far from the States, but are
still inclined to the "away from it all" dream, you might
consider Alamos, a former silver center with mansions
and palaces galore from the days when Mexican silver
supplied the world. For a time almost a ghost city,
Alamos is making a comeback through Americans who
have drifted down. It's located only a couple of hundred
miles or so south of Nogales, Arizona.

But my personal favorites are San Miguel de Allende, where I lived off and on for eighteen months, and Merida, Yucatan, for me one of the most charming cities in the world and one of the more remote.

San Miguel, which I've already described to some extent above, is an old Spanish Colonial town and so attractive that the Mexican government has made it a national monument. The streets are cobbled, no signs, neon or otherwise, are allowed and no changes can be made in a building without government permission. No new houses can go up until approved as not conflicting with the town architecture.

Some years ago an art school was begun in San Miguel and for a time was extremely successful. However a scandal arose and the school lapsed to be followed not long afterward by the present *Instituto Allende* which teaches just about every art and handicraft ever thought of and at cut rate prices. There are a good many artists of all types in San Miguel besides those at the school. In fact, it is estimated that approximately 1000 Americans either practicing the arts or interested in them are present at San Miguel at any one time.

The presence of so many Americans has led to the establishment of an English book store, the presence of American canned foods and American drugs, and to the coming of English speaking doctors and dentists. American movies can be seen at the local theatres.

Although 7,000 feet high in the mountains of Guanajuato, you have year around swimming since there is a hot springs a short ways out of town. There are two pools, one extremely hot, one pleasantly warm.

Mexico City is approximately two hundred miles to the south over good roads. In fact, some of the local bullfight fans drive down in the morning every Sunday and then, after the fight, drive back home that night.

But as pleasant as I found San Miguel de Allende and as much as I loved living there, I believe that if I were to return to Mexico I would wish to live this time in Merida, or Progresso, in Yucatan.

Although Merida, Yucatan's capital, is one of Mexico's larger cities with its population of more than 1,660,000 it is practically unknown to the average Mexican—not to speak of the average tourist. This is because although Yucatan is a Mexican state, it is cut off from the balance of the country by all but inpenetrable jungle. It is *possible* to get to Merida by land by using a combination of train and road, but it is a difficult expedition taking the better part of a week. Instead, for years the usual method of reaching Merida was by boat from Vera Cruz to Progresso and thence by road to Merida. Now, the airlines use Merida as a stopping point winging their way south, and this is the most popular tourist method of arriving in the country.

Cut off like this Merida gets few tourists and as a consequence has built up a culture of its own in many ways dissimilar to the Mexican way of life further north. Then too, the Mayan Indians are considerably different in appearance than those nearer Mexico City.

Prices are so nearly the same as elsewhere in Mexico that I shall not comment upon them, but I must point out that here fishing and hunting are supreme. The jungles are so thick that it would be impossible to hunt them out and consequently game is available at all times. Venison is on the menu every meal of the day, in every restaurant, and the Mayans have developed some venison dishes I've never seen elsewhere.

Food in general is all but free, so lavishly does the tropical climate supply it. And as generous as is the land, so is the sea. Sea food such as is to be found in the markets of Merida is unrivaled elsewhere in quantity and in quality.

For the student, the fabulous ruins left by the Mayan civilizations are everywhere and awesome in their beauty. Some architects are of the opinion that the House of the Governors, in Uxmal, is as beautiful a building as man ever erected, not excepting even the Parthenon of Athens.

I might mention that since Yucatan is so seldom visited by foreigners, Americans or otherwise, the people are even more hospitable than usual. An American in Merida, or Progresso, thinking in terms of a permanent or semi-permanent stay, and looking about for a business opportunity or an easy going job, should have few difficulties in supplying his wants. He would find fewer Americans about, with whom to associate, than he would in Ajijic or San Miguel de Allende, but, on the other hand he would find fewer competitors in his attempts to make a good living the easy way. In fact, he might very well start up one or more of the projects that are already in full swing in these more northern towns.

it comes to excellent income with little expenditure of time or effort. Possibly you have seen his ads which he runs in the American magazines. These will differ slightly according to the magazine but here is a typical one:

RETIRE IN MEXICO
ON $150 A MONTH

or less in a resort area, 365 days of sun a year; dry temperature. 68-80 degrees. Or maintain lux. villa; servants; ALL expenses $200-250 a mo. Am.-Eng. colony on lake 60 mi. long. 30 min. to city of 1/2 million, medical center. Schools, arts, sports. Few hours by air. Train, bus; PAVED roads all the way. Full time servants, maids, cooks, $7 to $15 a mo., filet mignon .45 lb., coffee .40, gas .17 gal. Gin, rum, brandy, .75-.90 fth. whiskey $2.50 qt. Houses $10 mo. up. No fog, smog, confusion, jitters. Serene living among world's most considerate people. For EXACTLY how Americans are living on $50-$90-$150-$250 a mo. Airmail $2.00 for COMPLETE current information, photos, prices, roads, hotels, hunting, fishing, vacationing and living conditions from A. viewpoint. (Pers. Chk. OK) to Bob Thayer, Ajijic, Lake Chapala, Jal. Mexico. (Allow 2 weeks for delivery—Money back Guarantee.)

There is no gyp about this. Bob's information is accurate and complete. For the $2 sent him he *delivers*!

And makes a beautiful profit!

I would estimate, knowing Mexican printing costs, that the material Bob sends out costs him possibly .12 per mailing. His postage and his advertising increases this, of course. The advertising, the "promotion" in other words, is the big expense. But, adding all of his costs together, I would be surprised if Bob doesn't net $1.50 on each response he gets.

Nobody is being cheated. Bob Thayer collected his material thoroughly and well. He had it printed up, and now is marketing a commodity that people really want. There are some 40,000 Americans already living in retirement in Mexico, and there are hundreds of thousands who are thinking about retiring there, or dreaming about it. These are all customers, or potential customers of Bob's.

Could you do this?

There is not a reason in the world why not. And not only in Mexico, but in just about any other "bargain paradise" in the world where Americans might be interested in retiring.

Of course, it would be ridiculous to duplicate Bob Thayer's work in the vicinity of Lake Chapala—he's already covered that area. But just about any other American retirement spot would be practical. Yucatan would be a natural. So should San Miguel de Allende. So should Southern Spain, Greece, Austria, Morocco, Tahiti, Guatemala, Costa Rica, the Azores Islands, the Canary Islands, Madeira, Corsica, Elba, the French Riviera, Sardinia, Sicily, Haiti, the Virgin Islands, the Fiji Islands, Ireland, Tasmania, the Vale of Kashmir. Every bargain paradise in the world is a natural for this type of mail order sale.

CASE HISTORY No. 2. One of our favorite people in Mexico is old Bill Englebrecht. On two occasions I've rented an apartment in his large house and I've never been happier with a landlord than with old Bill.

His story is on the fabulous side. In the German army during the first World War, Bill was wounded on the Russian front and sent back to Germany for specialized schooling since his physical condition ruled the infantry out. He was trained as a spy and later landed in Canada from a submarine. He made his way down into the United States and was put to work sabotaging our war plants.

And they caught him.

Happily for Bill, the war ended just before he was scheduled to be shot and he was eventually pardoned. He made his way to Mexico during the revolutions and went through a series of inadequate jobs, mostly as a tailor in Mexico City.

Finally Bill had accumulated a very small amount of money and decided to "retire." He came to San Miguel de Allende and bought a wreck of a house—a semi-ruin. He fixed it up so that he and his new Mexican wife could live in it and then, slowly began to build it larger. Today Bill has a house that comfortably shelters he and his family below and has a large terrace on the second floor from which issues off six small but very efficient apartments.

When I was there last these apartments rented for 2000 pesos each and were *always* full. In fact, there was always a waiting list. San Miguel has grown since then and I have a sneaking suspicion that Bill's rents have gone up, but then it was a matter of $160 a month, per apartment, or a total of $960 net income.

This may sound like a small income property to an American living in the States but on it Bill drives a car, is educating his two daughters, keeps a cook, a general maid and a handy-man to take care of maintenance. And above all, Bill enjoys life. The people he allows to rent his apartments are young, enthusiastic and often one type or another of artist. There are few weeks that go by without two or three parties out on the community terrace. Entertainment being as cheap as it is, there will be a *mariachi* band of three or four pieces, dancing, rum cokes in profusion and food galore. It's always fun at Bill Englebrecht's.

Could you do this? You certainly could if you had a few thousand dollars in capital and wanted to settle down in Mexico. Labor is unbelievably cheap; even top masons, bricklayers, plumbers and electricians get only $15.00 a day. Either buying an older house or building one from scratch can be done for comparative peanuts.

However, you must remember that as a foreigner you cannot own property unless you are an *immigrado*. There are a few ways of beating this. If you have a child born in Mexico, he has dual citizenship and can have property in his name. Or you can buy a place and have it put in the name of a Mexican friend. Best of all, however, is to become a student. As a student you are able to buy property if you live nine months of the year in Mexico. Fine. You can become a student at the *Institute* * *Allende* for ten dollars a month studying any of a multitude of subjects from the Spanish language to oil paintings. For further details on this write Stirling Dickinson, Instituto Allende, San Miguel de Allende, Guanajuato, Mexico.

CASE HISTORY No. 5. Which brings to mind Stirling Dickinson himself. He came to San Miguel some years ago before the town became famed as an art colony, and, having a very small income, bought himself the ruins of an old mill on the stream that wanders down from the hills.

Spending money very slowly, over the years Stirling has built himself what in my estimation is one of the most attractive houses in Mexico. Possibly estate would be the better term, since the place rambles out over several acres. There are literally scores of gardens, and Stirling has even a special orchid hot house containing hundreds of these exotic flowers. The ruins of the mill look more like those of a European castle and Stirling has so fitted them that speakers from his hi-fi set are here and there, and a concert can be enjoyed anywhere on the place. The school periodically holds parties at the Dickinson home and a hundred or more guests are easily swallowed up at a time, wandering through the endless gardens, enjoying the fabulous things he has done with his time and vivid imagination.

But you must keep in mind that Stirling started with a very small monthly income. Consequently, when the opportunity arose to work out at the new *Institute* Allende* he welcomed it. Now his job as director there pays him sufficiently to enjoy his home to the limit while working a minimum time at a position he finds desirable since it deals in the arts which are close to the heart of Stirling Dickinson.

§

CASE HISTORY No. 4. I ran into this case history back before I had even considered the compiling of a book of this type so I failed to note down as much information as I should have liked. However, it's an excellent example and I'll pass it on.

His name was Herman Smith, or Smythe, or something like that, and he drove a jeep delivery truck. He drove it all about Mexico and here, there and the other place he picked up silver jewelry, handwoven textiles, beaten copper pots, trays, pans, pottery, *huaraches* (sandals), *rebozas* (shawls), antiques, Indian relics from Aztec times both fake and real, and handicrafts of all descriptions.

He would bargain hard for these, usually buying them in large quantities and thus getting a discount. He wasn't out for the usual tourist souvenir sort of gimmicks but real art work, real handicrafts, outstanding antiques. He bought no junk.

When he'd acquired a load he took it back to the United States and resold it largely in the border states such as Texas, New Mexico, Arizona and California. If I remember correctly, he sometimes took a load up to New York but as a rule he figured that the time and distance involved didn't usually cover the somewhat better prices he got there.

He had one special angle too that netted him, so he told me, an extra two or three thousand dollars a year. Herman was a gun crank, specializing in Colt revolvers. Some of the earlier Colts are so prized by collectors that they will pay hundreds and sometimes even thousands of dollars for certain models. At any rate, Herman in his travels to some of the more remote places in Mexico always had his eye peeled for old Colts. Since there were many thousands of these sold in Mexico in the old days and particularly during the revolutionary periods, they are still to be found in every hamlet, every town, every village, no matter how poor or out of the way. He'd buy broken old Colts, for a few pesos (the owners must have thought him mad to buy such worthless junk) take them back to the States, have them repaired and cleaned up, and resell them for hundreds of times what he'd paid.

I have no further information on Herman Smith and his easy going way of making a good living. Actually, I think his home was in Texas and that he kept his family there, spending only four or five months each year in Mexico. The problems involved in getting an importer's license to bring his things into the States, and possibly an exporter's license to take them out of Mexico, I am not familiar with. However, if Herman did it, obviously it can be done by anyone else.

You'd need enough capital to buy such licenses and to finance your trip through Mexico, not to speak of several hundred dollars with which to pick up your handicrafts, art objects and such. You'd also need outlets for your things and obviously it would be desirable to arrange for these before you undertook even the first expedition. You'd also need some background information on just what to buy, otherwise you might wind up with a truck load of unsaleable junk, rather than the objects that the art shops, department stores, and tourist souvenir shops would really want.

CASE HISTORY No. 5. When I began working on this book, I realized that I hadn't been in Mexico for a time and that to bring myself up to date I'd better write one of my "retired" friends down there for some fresh examples. The following case histories came from him and although some of them aren't as complete in detail as we might wish, the basic ideas are there. He writes:

"I know of several interesting cases of retirement at an early age, if that is what you can call it. In fact, I found some who beat the 21 year deadline that you set.

"For example, in Tampico a young boy who had accompanied his father on the Tarpon Tournaments held in March and April remained when he was only twenty to start a business of his own, a retirement business, it turns out. He bought for less than $500 two old boats and two used outboard motors. He bought fishing equipment and some guns. He started organizing fishing and hunting parties in that area. He charges $15 minimum and $5 per head if the party is over three. He hires Spanish Guides who speak passable English to take the parties to hunting and fishing grounds and direct them to the "hot" spots. He pays each guide only 5 pesos (.40) a day but the guide usually comes up with about 20 pesos worth of fish and a tip amounting to from 5 to 10 pesos. The gas and equipment costs, etc. do not run more than $2 to $4 per party. He clears more than $10 per party and he has up to five or six parties out on some days. He spends about two hours daily organizing, etc. He has little signs in the tourist hotels and motels in Tampico and a phone number to call. It works out well for him, earning him in excess of $10,000 a year with a very minimum of work. He is now 29 years old and still in Tampico plying his trade.

"In Lake Chapala I know an American whose only claim to fame is his ability to speak Spanish. He would rent for $10 to $12 a small Mexican home, fix it up, rent it out for $50 for one month or about $450 for one year. He would also act as go-between for house buyers and while the poor Mexicano was hollering 'best price is $3,000,' he was telling the buyers '$5,000 is the best the feller will do.' To make it brief, he is already rich at an age of less than 35 years.

"A girl in Ajijic sells Mexican handicrafts, ceramics, hand-woven textiles, copperwork, and that sort of thing to tourists, from right on her patio. She has the Mexicans bring the things and doesn't even pay them until she has sold the items. She charges ridiculously high prices to the tourists, pays ridiculously low ones to the poor Mexicans. Needless to say, she too is cleaning up.

"In Victoria I met a fellow who, with a Mexican partner, buys and sells. He puts up American money as collateral with a Mexican bank, borrows on it 100% (but so that he can always get the same amount of dollars back for the same number of pesos) takes the money and speculates in undeveloped farm properties, orange groves, etc. The inflation factor alone assures him a profit aside from his astute business dealings in buying and selling, and he can always get his dollars back for the same number of pesos he borrowed. He gets a low interest rate, only 8 % (which is very low in Mexico). He deals with only half his money, keeping the rest in the U.S. He makes over $5,000 a year clear with $10,000 of operating capital, that is, after interest, etc.

"Hope you can use some of these for your book. Actually there are many many more. I would estimate that there must be at least ten thousand Americans in this country making an easy and good living and doing precious little in the way of expending effort.

Cordially,
(signed) Harry"

§

CASE HISTORY No. 6. This young lady whom I shall call "Trixie" is active in the Lake Chapala, Guadalajara area. She is retired on Lake Chapala along with her middle-aged parents. As of now she is only 23. When I met her she was about the snootiest young thing around, yet SHE HAD IT MADE!

She went to an Art Colony in San Miguel de Allende. She tried peddling some of her art to tourist shops and had her father and mother sell some back home. Back home was Philadelphia, Pa. Her artwork sold only so so, then only to close family friends. On one occasion her parents sent her some color snapshots of themselves in the beautiful Pocono mountains of Eastern Pennsylvania. As a surprise she painted one of the scenes for Mom and mailed it off to her. When Mom received it she was so proud she showed it to anyone and everyone. It was so impressive some of the friends wanted a painting of some of their favorite color scenes too. Of course our sweet young thing obliged—at a price! She began getting quite a few orders from her Mom. In fact, she had so many in one mail that she had some of her fellow students help her out. And she was making some money. This sort of painting was selling better than her regular stuff. She got an idea to promote this kind of painting and proceeded to offer it to several Tourist shops. She took some samples of "before" and "after" color chromes and paintings down and arranged neat little displays. Tourists who wanted these paintings could order them, pay for them, have the finished painting mailed to them at home in the States. If they didn't have the scene they wanted painted with them they were furnished with a little brochure imprinted with the address of the shop they had visited. They could mail in their favorite color chrome along with a $25.00 remittance. The shop kept 30%, forwarded orders to Trixie along with her share. She had the scenes painted and mailed them to her customers. Things got busy and Trixie hired her fellow students to help out—at $5 per scene painted. $5 is a fortune in Mexico so she had many obliging helpers.

By and by she put little ads in selected U.S. publications offering to "paint your favorite scene from your color chrome." This went over big and soon she had a booming business. $25.00 checks and money orders were pouring in from all over the U.S. and even from some foreign countries. She branched out a little more in the Tourist shops. By the time she was twenty she painted "only when she felt like it." She invited Pop and Mom down for a prolonged stay. It was an amazed Pop and Mom that met their daughter in San Miguel, well along the world in wealth. She was living like Pop and Mom had never dreamed of living back in Philadelphia.

When I last heard of Trixie she and her parents had moved to Lake Chapala. She was still plying her trade among the tourists and with occasional ads in selected U.S. publications.

ARE YOU CAPABLE OF DOING THIS? If you have the least inclination to art I have no doubt that you can. In Trixie's case her success was not necessarily based on her ability as an artist but her enterprising ability in marketing the artistic talents of others. It is my opinion that this particular field is practically untouched.

CHAPTER 9
SPAIN

IN A NUTSHELL. For some reason most of we Americans who have never visited Spain think of this country as a small one and it comes as a shock to find that of all of our States only Texas and Alaska is larger than she. And her population is pushing 50 million which makes her one of the more populous countries of Europe.

Possibly our ignorance of Spain is due to the fact that few members of this generation have visited Spain. Her civil war broke out in 1936 and didn't end until 1939. Hardly was it over but the Second World War began and for nearly seven years Europe was wrapped in conflict and tourism was a forgotten luxury. Both Spanish and American officials are trying to ignore the fact now but Spain was, and is, a fascist country and during the war she supported the Axis Powers. This undoubtedly helped, when the war was over, to keep American tourists from the country. For years Spain was virtually ignored.

Tourists were coming to Europe as never before, but the main points of interest were further north, England, France, Switzerland, Italy. In 1947 only 3,700 of our countrymen entered Spain and the figure only slightly more than doubled in 1948.

But finances have been chaotic since the war and everywhere prices have literally zoomed. France, once a bargain paradise, became as expensive as the United States, or nearly so. And Switzerland and Italy trailed not far behind. Rumors began to drift up from the south that Spain was still operating at pre-war prices. That you could travel in Spain at a fraction the price in the more popular tourist countries, or could retire on a pittance.

And nothing spreads so fast in the traveling set, and those who live permanently, or semi-permanently abroad as such rumors. Thousands began to drift into Spain, and then tens of thousands, until at this writing at least a million Americans visit

115

Spain each year, and thousands have become permanent residents.

Of course, just because a country is cheap is no reason to retire there. Possibly the cheapest place I have ever been is the interior of Turkey. I would estimate that given the current black market rate of exchange, you could live there *like a pasha* for $500 a month for a couple. But what would you do? What would you see? Who would you talk to? You might live in a palace and have a swarm of servants on $1000 a month in one of the smaller towns of inland Turkey—but you'd probably go stark raving mad after a couple of months or so.

But Spain offers a good deal more than economy. Her scenery is varied, her climate probably the best in Europe, with the possible exception of the Greek islands, there is a wide Anglo-American population which guarantees companionship if you cannot find it among the Spaniards, and the luxuries as well as the necessities of life are available.

§

ENTRY REQUIREMENTS. All you need to enter Spain is your American passport. If you decide to stay for more than six months you'll need a resident's permit but this is no more complicated to acquire than expending a few minutes at the local police station. In fact, as soon as you leave your hotel or pension and take up residence in a house or apartment, you are supposed to register the new address with the police. However, these things are usually handled in a rather lax way.

When I first entered Spain I didn't know of this requirement until I'd been living in my own house for nearly four months. So one day I went around to the police and told them I wished to register. They asked me why I had taken so long and I shrugged and told them I didn't know there was such a requirement. So they looked at me for a minute, as though they didn't know what the hell to do, and then shrugged too and listed my name and new address in their books.

If you are thinking in terms of retiring permanently in Spain, or even living in the country for several years you might well consider bringing with you a *used* refrigerator and/or a *used* butane-gas type stove. These are ultra-expensive in Spain but you are allowed to enter with used ones, tax free, if it is for your own use and not for sale. Other household equipment comes under the same regulations.

TRANSPORTATION. Spain is almost as easy and as economical to reach as are England and France, but not quite. All of the great airlines have services between New York and Madrid: TWA, Pan American, BOA, KLM, SABENA and Swissair. At this writing 1st class is $3,500 one way, tourist class, $620.30.

In the past couple of years there has been a great increase in the number of travelers who sail directly to Spain when coming to Europe, rather than landing in England or France. In fact, the facilities in Gibralter and Algeciras are currently being strained to accommodate the visitors landing from Italian Line, American Export Lines, Home Lines and a score of other shipping lines ships. The Italian Line ships start at $400 tourist class, New York to Gibralter, in off season. American Export, at $510. You can also get passage by liner or freighter to Malaga, Barcelona, San-tander, Bilbao and Cadiz.

Transportation within the country has its grim side. There are some swank trains, particularly those running to Madrid from the French border, and the 2nd class diesel trains whose tickets are premium priced aren't too bad, but as a rule Spanish trains are not the best and schedules are poorly kept. They are apt to be crowded in all but first class and except for the special trains mentioned above, very dirty. The government is currently spending a good deal of money revamping the railroads but how long this will take is a question. However, rates are very cheap and this is one country in which we recommend that you travel first class, particularly if you want a seat.

Roads are no better than railroads. There are a few passable highways, once again mostly stemming from Madrid which is, of course, centrally located and dominates Spain as Mexico City does Mexico.

If you planned to buy a car in Spain upon arrival I strongly advise against it. At this writing it would cost you from two to three times as much to buy a car in Spain as it would in the United States or one of the other European countries. Taxes on cars are sky-high. Usually, Americans residing in Spain buy their car in Gibralter, Tangier, France or England and then drive it into Spain as a tourist. Under this arrangement you are at present only allowed to have it for two and a half years, then it must be taken from the country, and you are not allowed to return with it for another six months. Happily there are rumors, at this writing, of the law being changed. I suggest that you check with the A.A.A. if this is one of your problems.

Mechanics in Spain are good and repair prices low unless new parts are involved. The gas is expensive and of very poor quality and the oil is horrible.

§

THE SPANIARDS. It is possible to type a people such as the Swiss or the Danes with a certain amount of accuracy but when you take a country as large as Spain it becomes as difficult as it would be to type the American. Obviously all Americans aren't the same—neither are all 60 million Spaniards.

In Andulusia in the south, for instance, live the gypsies and although I have no prejudices in matters of race, nationality, or color I think I can truly state that the Spanish gypsy is the dirtiest, most poverty stricken, most dishonest, most untrustworthy people I have met in Europe, certainly they are the most lazy and shiftless. To the other extreme you have the residents of Madrid and also the Catalans of Barcelona who are modern, aggressive, hard working, honest folk who differ comparatively little from the average American.

Personally, I like the average Spaniard. I find him honest; clean, to the extent his poverty allows him to be; hospitable far beyond the extent he can afford; in love with his country, but with an amazing lack of knowledge about the rest of the world; a lover of his family, but also of good wine and good food, not to speak of good folk music. He is also, in spite of all misinformation to the contrary a hard worker (except for the gypsies).

§

MONEY. Spain has one of the softest currencies in Europe, and all indications are that it will become softer, especially if Uncle Sam discontinues plowing large sums of dollars into the shaky economy. At this writing, officially the peseta sells at a tourist rate of 45 to the dollar but in Tangier you get 53.50 to the dollar. I have seen it as low as 62 to the dollar in Tangier which is an indication of how greatly it can fluctuate.

No laws are broken by bringing pesetas into Spain. You are allowed to bring 10,000 of them for each member of your group. And you are also allowed to have your bank send you 3,000 pesetas a day. Before coming to Spain, however, I'd check this again with either the travel agent, your bank, or your money exchange house since laws can change quickly in this field.

§

WORK PERMISSION. You are allowed to work in Spain only if you have a work permit and if the job is of a type that a Spaniard could not fill. Actually this doesn't really affect you since Spanish pay is so inadequate that you would not be interested. As in all economical countries, labor prices are appallingly low. If you're interested in working, you'll have to swing some deal that involves a job other than an ordinary one for a Spanish concern. If you have some angle that will help tourism or in some other way attract dollars or other foreign currency, the authorities couldn't be happier.

If you work for dollars either for some American concern with a branch in Spain or for the American Armed Forces, no permission is necessary for such jobs. As far as I know they're the only jobs worth having in Spain.

Usually in opening a business, the American will take on a Spanish partner in whose name the business will operate. It is possible otherwise, but more difficult.

If you are the exception that proves the rule and do wish a work permit so that you can take a Spanish job, paid in pesetas, you apply first to the Ministerio de Informacion y Turismo and eventually are put in the hands of the Ministerio de Trabejo (Ministry of Labor). Address in both cases is simply, Madrid.

PRICES. As we've stated above, Spain is currently the cheapest country in Europe. It is still quite possible to live comfortably on five hundred dollars a month—for a couple. A single man or woman can make out on about $300. We know of various people who are doing it on much less. Adding to this amount, even just a little bit sends your standard of living up very rapidly. Doubling it puts you in a living standard group probably considerably higher than the average American's what with a really large home and two or more servants. An income of $1,200 a month in Spain is real wealth; you would live like a Spanish Don and his Senorita. Let's break this down into definite prices.

Rent, as always, is the largest single item on your budget. When this writer lived on Majorca in 1985 he rented a rather large villa in the town of Soller during the summer season when rents are highest, for 750 pesetas a month which today would be somewhat less than $15 but at that time was about $17.50 due to the weakening of

Spanish money. For this I had a three bedroom house, one room of which I converted to a study. I had a large living room, complete with fireplace, a dining room, a kitchen with gigantic pantry, a balcony which overlooked the town of Soller and the Mediterranean sea, a patio, a sundeck and two gardens.

The gardens contained more than twenty rose bushes as well as other flowers and also almond and fruit trees. A gardener's assistance came free with the house. The house was completely furnished including linens, dishes and kitchenware.

But this was in 1985 and prices have gone up since then although little faster than the Spanish peseta has fallen in the money markets of the world. Consequently, if your money is in dollars, you find prices little higher than they were then.

More recently we took a villa in the art colony of Torremolinos, just eight miles south of Malaga on the Costa del Sol, the southern coast of Spain. This area is booming currently and is by no means the cheapest section of Spain. For another three room villa we paid 2,200 pesetas a month which comes to $210.80 at the current exchange. That's rather high rent for Spain but not bad for Torremolinos. Our view was superb, we were in a pleasant, quiet, and "good" section of town.

But one thing must be understood in regard to Spanish villas. You must have servants. The modern American home comparatively runs itself, the Spanish villa doesn't. The floors are usually of tile and must be washed every day. There are few washing machines and laundry must be done by hand. Little canned food and no frozen food is used in the average home so cleaning and washing of vegetables becomes a daily chore.

In a small villa, if you wish to do your own cooking, one servant will be ample. If you want a cook, and you probably do since Spanish stoves and other kitchen equipment are primitive by our standards, that will make it two servants. If you go in for gardens, and most folk do in Spain, you can have a gardener come in once or twice a week. Cost? Sixty to eighty dollars a month for a good all around girl. Eight or ten for a good cook. The gardener will run you about 10 a day.

If you have your servants live in (most houses come equipped with servant quarters) you'll have the cost of their food added to the above, of course. If your house is quite small, one way to save is to have the girl come in the morning at about eight and work through until two o'clock which is lunch time in Spain. Then let her go home for the day. Cost? About sixty dollars a month, but you have no expenses feeding her, except breakfast which is merely coffee and bread in Spain.

Food prices? Almost everything is purchased fresh or in bulk in the town markets. Practically no canned or bottled foods are used. Those that are in the shops are usually quite high, prohibitively so to the Spanish themselves. In season vegetables and fruits are almost unbelievably cheap. Following are some typical food prices:

Bread, pound loaf $.50	Milk, quart $1.0
Rolls, apiece $.45	Cheese, pound $1.20
Oranges, apiece $.35	Butter, pound $3.00
Prawns, $6.50 a lb.	Steak, pound $5.00
Lettuce, head $1.00	Stewing beef, pound $2.50
Swordfish, pound $3.50	Leg of lamb, pound $2.99
Clams, pound $6.50	Pork chops, pound $4.50
Live lobster, pound $7.50	Eggs, apiece $.25

Spain is one of the few countries in the world where drinking is not prohibitively expensive even for the very poor. Foreigners usually soon get used to having an aperitif before lunch or dinner and either red or white wine, or both, with the meal. Red wine costs $3.00 a liter (slightly more than a quart) and white wine $2.50 a liter. Vermouth, popular as an aperitif, or dry sherry will go higher at $3.50 and up a liter. Really fine wines, the best sherries, which would cost you three or four dollars in the States, and even more, will go for about $15.00. Even spirits are not high. Cognac starts at about $18.00 a liter and the really fine brands are about $30.00 a bottle. Good gin is $8.00.or $9.00 a bottle and rum about the same. The only good whiskey is imported and prohibitively expensive. Spanish champagne starts at about $18.00 a bottle and very good bubble water will run about a dollar a bottle.

Even drinking in cafes and bars is not at all expensive. At a sidewalk cafe in Soller we used to pay one peseta ($3.00) for a vermouth and soda. In Torremolinos, the cheapest bar in town has a one peseta cognac, or you can sit at Manolo's on the square and have a large glass of white wine for two pesetas. At Manolo's this price includes a *tapa* which is Spain's equivalent of free lunch and is apt to be some shrimp, some bread and cheese, or a dish of French fried fresh sardines.

Clothing? Spanish labor being as cheap as it is, the usual thing is to have your clothing tailored, your shoes made to order. A suit of good quality will cost about $35 tailored in Malaga or Palma—a bit more in Madrid or Barcelona, a bit less in some of the smaller cities. It is customary in southern Spain for Americans and British to buy their textiles in Gibralter where the high British taxes that plague you in England do not apply. They are then taken into Spain and done up by a Spanish tailor. Thus you get the finest tweeds or gabardines plus the excellent Spanish tailoring. A pair of custom made men's shoes will run eight dollars in Torremolinos, but the price can be beaten in Malaga, only eight miles away.

Other costs of living are in proportion. A movie will go $7.50 to $10.00 admission. Doctors charge fifty cents to a dollar for a home visit. English speaking doctors, by the way, are usually graduates of the Barcelona medical school which boasts a world wide reputation. Transportation by either bus, rail or air is probably the cheapest in Europe—but not the best by any means.

§

PARTICULARLY RECOMMENDED LOCALITIES.
Spain has a score or more cities and towns that would be suitable for an American living abroad. Among the best of these are: Marbella, Torremolinos and Malaga, on the Southern Coast and Tossa de Mar, Cadaques, San Feliu de Guixols, Rosas, Tamariu, Playa de Aro and Ampurias, on the Costa Brava, north of Barcelona. On the Atlantic in the south both Cadiz and Huelva (from whence Columbus sailed) are attractive but have comparatively small Anglo-American colonies. As a contrast, American military bases have recently been built in the Seville and Jerez (from

whence comes Sherry) area and there are swarms of Americans. This ups your chances for employment or for starting a small business, but it also ups prices. On Majorca, the particularly recommended towns are Palma itself, the capital, and Deya, Soller, Formentor and Pollensa.

Of all these—and there are many more in Spain—I will choose two as examples, Torremolinos and Soller.

Torremolinos, just a short time ago was an unknown fishing

village nestled up against a cliff. It had scenic beauty, miles of beaches in both directions, and had a quaint Spanish charm which brought its first foreigners—artists. Art colonies, as I've pointed out in the chapter devoted to them, grow slow at first, then at a rapidly accelerating speed. One artist tells another. Here is a beautiful, inexpensive, untouched, unsophisticated paradise. Soon writers, musicians, sculptors drift into town and following them, would-be artists and writers. As the colony grows retired folk with an interest in the arts begin finding homes, buying them, improving them. An American bar springs up, an American store, an American restaurant. And then, overnight, there are thousands of foreigners in town.

And thus it was with Torremolinos. Today she still retains her beauty, her climate, and most of her economy of living, but the untouched, unsophisticated qualities are gone. A paradise she remains, and probably one of the best spots in Spain in which to retire at any age.

Soller is in contrast to Torremolinos. Not nearly as overrun with tourists and short time sojourners, she is quieter, and cheaper than the southern city. About ten miles from Palma as the crow flies, Soller is on the north coast of Majorca often described as the most beautiful coastline in the world. Actually, there are two towns, Soller proper and Puerta de Soller, the town's port which is about three miles away and nestled about a bay which has been used as a port since Phoenecian times. (In fact, skin divers are continually bringing up old wine and olive oil vases from Greek and Phoenecian times). A small trolley connects the two towns.

Swimming in Soller is superb with some of the clearest blue water this writer has ever seen this side of the South Pacific atolls. Such sports as skin diving reach their heights and boating is popular. Water sports are practical about nine months of the year, sometimes as many as eleven. Although on the water, Soller lays claim also to unrivaled mountain scenery since she is located in a small valley from which the tallest mountains on the island are seen to loom in all directions.

For the American on the lookout for a job, an investment, or interested in opening a business Torremolinos would be the better of these two cities, but a person primarily interested in retiring in a beautiful location and rock bottom prices would find Soller preferable. The number of Anglo-Americans is much smaller in Soller but those that do reside in this bargain paradise are more apt to be permanent. The "case histories" described below could in many cases be applied to either town. In fact, most of them could be applied to any of the dozen or more towns and villages enumerated above.

§

CASE IIISTORY No. 1. I doubt very much that Robert L. Trimmell was the originator of the little system he uses to make an excellent living in Palma, capital of the island of Majorca (also spelled Mallorca), and the Spanish province of the Balearic Islands. We doubt it because we've seen the same plan used elsewhere and assume that it will be used again and again because it is a natural, needs very little capital to start and makes everyone involved happy including the Spanish authorities who sometimes take a dim view of foreigners making good money in Spain.

Trim, as everybody calls him for short, puts out a papercovered book entitled *Trim's Majorca Guide* which is to be found on every newstand and in every magazine shop in Palma, and, for that matter, in hotels, restaurants, tourist shops and everywhere else he can think of as an outlet for distribution. The copy I have before me as I write this, cost about fifty cents in American money as I recall. I would estimate that, Spanish labor being as low as it is, it cost Trim approximately .05 per book to print; certainly not more. But his book sales are only a part of his revenue since *Trim's Majorca Guide* is crammed with advertising and his ad rates are high and justifiably so because advertising with Trim pays off.

What it amounts to is that any American or British tourist, or anyone else who can read English, who comes to

Majorca and fails to buy a copy of Trim's guide is being foolish. The book consists of some 75 pages of information on night life, beaches, shopping, maps, photos, timetables, history, geography, churches, museums and special tips on seeing the islands. Your fifty cents investment pays off in saved time and greater enjoyment a dozen times over.

English speaking tourists literally swarm to Palma and everywhere they turn on disembarking they are confronted with the opportunity of purchasing one of Trim's guides. Thousands of them do so every year. The shops, hotels, restaurants and real estate agents who take ads in the guide can feel the pull of his advertisements. Each year he brings out a new edition, keeping it up to date—and collecting for new ads.

Such a guide is not difficult to compile. Everybody in town wants to cooperate with you—obviously. The tourist officials will deluge you with material both printed and verbal. The police and other officials, realizing that you are performing a service that a Spaniard cannot, and that you are helping tourism in the vicinity, cooperate in every possible way. The maps and photographs in Trim's guide were provided free of charge by the tourist bureau.

It was a matter of Trim collecting his material, going around to potential advertisers and securing ads, locating a printer and then going about the book shops, magazine and newspaper stands and elsewhere to line up his distribution. Once the first edition was out, it was a matter of coasting. Changes made in new editions are not considerable ones. Prices might fluctuate a little, one restaurant close and another open, a new hotel might be erected, but basically Trim's Major can Guide remains about the same. Year in and year out this wonderful little source of revenue pays off while Trim enjoys the climate and scenic beauty of one of the most desirable islands in the world.

Just to give you a more complete picture of Trim's baby, here are the chapters into which his Table of Contents breaks down: Introduction; Majorca's Geography; the Majorcans and their Language; Palma; Rope-Sole Beach; How Much To Tip; Lotteries; History; How to Read the Map Without a Dictionary; Souvenirs; How Not to Spend a Fortune at the Bullfights; Airlines Serving Majorca; Passenger Ships; Train Timetables; Bus Lines; Excursions; Beaches; Where to Go by Night; A Place too Beautiful To Live In; Shopping Areas; Money Changing; Our Advertisers; Hotels.

Among his advertisers are: real estate agents, jewelers, bars, restaurants, night clubs, tailors, snack bars, hairdressers, a lending library, grocery stores and delicatessens, antique shops, garages, hotels and photo shops.

As I've said before, Trim isn't the only American abroad cashing in on this scheme and we'll investigate variations of it under different chapter headings. However, not even a dent had been made in this field in the great tourist cities of Europe. Every city that is deluged with tourists is a natural for such an English speaking guide. In the very large cities, of course, there are or could be more than one. But in the smaller cities and resort towns there are usually none at all and a crying need for such a publication.

What would I estimate it would cost to get such a guide going? In a cheap country like Spain, where printing costs are astonishingly low, less than one hundred dollars.

How much writing know-how would you need to produce such a guide? Very little. Practically none. If you've had a high school education, and didn't flunk too badly in English, you'd be able to do it. Most of the material you use is copied from tourist office literature. But if you are incapable of doing the little writing involved, you'll almost always find in such towns as these an American or British newspaperman or free lance writer who would do up for you that part of the booklet calling for writing. What would this cost you? Peanuts. There would be little time and effort involved on his part.

If you'd like a copy of Trim's Majorca Guide to give you a more complete picture of just what he publishes, a dollar to the following address would pay for the book and postage: Trim, 649 Calvo Sotelo, Palma, Majorca, Baleares Islands, Spain.

CASE HISTORY No. 2. Miss Valerie Wilson is a British subject but her method of making a comfortable living in Torremolinos, in Southern Spain, is one gaining popularity in a score of cities where there are large Anglo-American colonies.

There are literally hundreds of thousands of Americans living abroad and even larger numbers of Britons who prefer not to live in what is sometimes described as the worst climate in the world— that of England. Invariably the larger number of these expatriates gather into resorts and world beauty spots where they can enjoy not only the gracious living but also each other's company. Many of these Americans and British never learn the language of the country in which they reside. They stick to their own groups and live, to the extent possible, the same type of life they would at home.

Valerie Wilson, a quiet, cultivated girl of less than thirty years, rented a large house and converted the first floor to an "Anglo-American Club." She had built a small bar, bought half a dozen bridge tables and some chairs, decorated the place nicely but inexpensively with local art and handicrafts, and opened for business.

At any one time Valerie would have at least a hundred members of her club. They liked to have a gathering place, a meeting place, a place where you could always find sufficient friends for a game of cards. They paid a monthly membership fee of 500 hundred pesetas (about $20) which is almost meaningless in the States but added up to a comfortable $200 a month for Valerie.

But that was just the beginning. Valerie also put in a circulating library of papercovered American and British popular fiction and charged one peseta a day for rental. This item alone more than paid for her rent in book hungry Spain.

She also served tea, an absolute must in British diet. "My *dear,* don't you know, Valerie's club is the only place this side of Gibral-ter where you can get a decent cup of tea."

For American tastes there was coffee, small sandwiches and cakes.

The bar was another profitable source of income. Valerie's members were not the town's drinking set, but a glass or two of sherry in the afternoon, or a highball or so in the evening, were the usual thing. Liquor is cheap in Spain, but, as everywhere else, mark-up when you sell it over the bar is high—more than one hundred percent. Valerie hired an attractive young Spanish boy for a few hundred pesetas a month as a bartender and taught him the little he had to learn about the ins and out of polite drinking. She also hired two pretty Spanish girls to wait on table and to keep the house clean.

However, Valerie still had two floors to her large house that were not as yet in use, so she fixed up three of the rooms for permanent residents and charged them rates for occupancy that were slightly higher than those of local hotels. Her guests were willing to pay the premium for the sake of living in a completely English speaking atmosphere.

The large room of her second floor she rented in the mornings, when club members were seldom present, to a teacher of *flamenco* dancing.

On the third floor she made her own quarters, and very comfortable they were.

What were her costs? The house rented for exactly two thousand five hundred pesetas a month which is less than fifty dollars at the present free market rate of exchange. Her tables, chairs, the bar and decorations would have come to possibly another seventy-five dollars in all. Servants in Spain cost from six to ten dollars a month.

This case history even has a story book ending because Valerie no longer runs her Anglo-American Club in Torremolinos. Into the club, one day, came a young Briton who was on his vacation from his job in Kenya, Africa, where he was manager of a large cattle ranch. When he returned to Kenya, Valerie went with him as his bride.

What chance is there of an American woman opening a similar establishment? The chances are excellent—but not in Torremolinos. Someone else took up where Valerie left off and there just isn't room in town for a competitor. However, there are cities all over Spain (Marbella, Sevilla, Alicante, to name just a few) where there are openings. It would be a matter of traveling about a bit, asking questions of the local residents in each town touched, and settling down when a spot was located. Nor is Spain the only country where the plan is feasible. True, both rents and servants are cheap in Spain but the same applies to Austria, Greece, Morocco and other nations. For that matter, American and British residents in such expensive countries as France and Italy fully expect to pay more for their entertainment and would hardly object to double and triple the prices that prevail in Spain.

§

CASE HISTORY No. 3. The following is the story of an American boy of about twenty-five whom we shall call Friendly Ed which isn't his name—but on the other hand the compiler of this book has no intentions of being sued for libel, so a little discretion is in order. This case history may sound amusing to you, but it's true. The name of the town we'll call Huesca, an Anglo-American art

colony in Southern Spain and this is the way Friendly Ed
tells it as accurately as I can recapture his free-wheeling
method of talking: "I was working in this slaughter house
in Brooklyn, see. Geez you never seen such a job in your
life. Holy hell, that was work, see. Knee deep in guts. The
pay, it wasn't so bad. I took home maybe eighty bucks or
so, not bad. But, Holy hell, every week-end I'd blow it
around the bars, see, and on the dames. How about that?
Well, anyway, I got fed up with all that jazz. I woulda
been a old man by time I was forty. So I cut out the beer
and all and I started saving my dough. You'll never
believe this but I saved a thousand bucks in half a year,
maybe seven months, then me and a friend we took off
for Spain. We didn't even have enough dough to get back,
but we didn't give a Holy hell. First off where'd we hit?
Huesca. We went on a tear, see. Started spending what
little dough we had in the bars but, Holy hell, that doesn't
cost anything in Spain, we coulda stayed drunk for six
months. But the end of a couple of weeks or so, I was
standing around talking to this Spaniard who owns the
Cafe Continental. He's moaning about needing some
money to expand. Well, me and Dick we looked around
the place. It was jammed. Huesca was growing like Holy
hell. Tourists was just beginning to dig Spain. Geez, we
sobered up and got to thinking about it. What this town
needed was a real American bar. You know, a place where
you could get martinis, stuff like that. A place where they
got cold beer, like that. Well, we wrote back to the States
and we put the bite on everybody we could think of, my
old man and everybody. I had them sell some crap I had
back home, like this old beat up Hudson, I had, and when
I got it all together I bought into the Cafe Continental for
two thousand bucks. Two thousand lousy bucks for one
third. How about that? Well, then the funny thing is
neither me or Dick, he bought in too, could work there.
We could tell them what to do, and we could have the

place fixed up American style, we had this artist do up the walls, but the government wouldn't let us work behind the bar. Holy hell, all we could do was sit around and be our own best customers. Anyway, like me and Dick knew, it got to be the hangout for all the Americans and the foreigners. We had money coming in all over the place. So what'd we do? Huesca was growing like crazy so we opened up a nightclub, just a couple of doors down.

A swanky place, see. Holy hell, you'd think you was in Miami Beach. We had to borrow dough to get it decorated and all, but we wanted to open up before somebody else got the bright idea there was room for a night club in Huesca. So we opened El Simpatico and it boomed too so we added a orchestra and a floor show and boosted prices and it still boomed. So we borrowed some more money and enlarged again, see. If it wasn't for all this here enlarging and all we'd be rolling in dough, but just about time me and Dick figure we're going to start really living it up, Holy hell, some other chance comes along and we have to get into it. How about that? I don't know if we'll ever see any real dough. Anyway, it's a good place to live, Huesca, and we're still our best customers."

I repeat, the real name isn't Friendly Ed, the name of the town isn't Huesca and we've even changed the name of the bar and nightclub but otherwise the story is straight and that's approximately how Friendly Ed reports it. On a two thousand dollar investment he's parlayed up an enterprise now worth many tens of thousands of dollars.

This is a good example of having a small amount of capital, American dollars are always preferable, and stumbling onto an opportunity. Every country in Europe, Africa, Asia and South America, on our side of the Iron Curtain, is short of investment capital and particularly dollars. Opportunities are everywhere. Business opportunities, real estate, putting out money on loan at rates that would shock an American loan shark.

Could you duplicate this case history? No, of course not. The opportunity Friendly Ed ran into was unique. But there are hundreds, thousands, of similar opportunities, all of them unique in their own way. You have to be on the spot, have a little capital and recognize a break when one comes along.

§

CASE HISTORY No. 4. Possibly one of the best examples of Americans making a go in Torremolinos shouldn't be in this book because far from retiring, Mrs. Stevens and her son Paul have probably never worked so hard in their lives. It happened like this:

Mrs. Stevens, a still-young, attractive woman decided some years ago that the humdrum life wasn't for her. At one time or another she lived in such attractive cities as San Miguel de Allende, Mexico, and other art colonies. Unfortunately, she hadn't sufficient money to live without work and finding a job was in order.

The Stevenses arrived in Torremolinos even before Valerie Wilson. The town, a former sleepy fishing village, was already showing signs, however, of growing into the Anglo-American art colony it has now become. Mrs. Stevens, who had seen the success of the Book Shop in San Miguel de AUende, decided a similar shop would go in Torremolinos and on a shoestring rented a small place right on the plaza. American magazines, stationery, tourist postcards, some souvenirs, that sort of thing. In one of the back rooms, Paul, a boy in his early twenties, started a circulating library using mostly paperbacks.

Right from the first things went fairly well. As the Stevenses perfected their Spanish, they went better. *La Galeria,* handily located there on the plaza became somewhat of an information bureau and center of the Anglo-American tourists and permanent residents. Time after time tourists would come in and ask if there was a local photo shop where they could have film developed. Paul had to explain that there wasn't, that the film had to go into Malaga eight miles to the north. Finally he got tired of this and since he was an amateur photographer himself, altered another of the rear rooms into a dark room. He has a couple of Spanish boys now who do almost all of the printing and developing of the extensive Torremolinos area. A neat little business in itself.

Above all, American, English—and Germans, French and Scandinavians, for that matter—would come in and ask about house rentals. Not being able to speak the language themselves, they had difficulty in finding apartments and villas. So, without even trying, the Stevenses got into the real estate business along with everything else. And Torremolinos real estate was booming.

Meanwhile, business in *La Galeria* was growing. The more Torremolinos grew as a tourist and art colony center, the more the shop became the town center. Mrs. Stevens' taste is excellent and she began adding expensive art objects, antiques and Spanish clothing to her stock. Without doubt, *La Galeria* is today the best

establishment within many miles in which to pick up
Spanish art objects and handicrafts.

So today La Galena is the photoshop, one of the largest
real estate agencies, the largest circulating library, the
largest English language magazine shop, the smartest
souvenir shop in the booming town of Torremolinos. But
have the Stevenses, mother and son, retired? Afraid not.
They're working just as hard as they would in a similar
establishment in Southern California. There are several big
differences, of course. They hire half a dozen or so Spanish
to take the drudgery off their shoulders, and their income is
sufficient to allow them a way of life far beyond the average
American one. At the rate they are going it's not difficult to
imagine them selling out one of these days and really
retiring. It wouldn't be difficult, the business is worth a
mint.

Could you do what Mrs. Stevens and Paul accomplished?
Certainly, given a small amount of capital. Spain is currently
booming. The cheapest country in Western Europe, the
tourists are descending upon her like swarms of locusts. A
dozen towns, unknown a few years ago, are becoming
internationally famous centers. All along the Costa del Sol
age-old fishing villages are waking up to find themselves
deluged with money-heavy tourists. Literally tens of
thousands of pensioners from the United States, England
and all the European nations are retiring along this most
pleasant beach area of Southern Europe.

The thing you possess which is priceless in Spain is your
knowledge of the English language and of the things that
Americans and other tourists want. Not one out of a
thousand Americans who come to Spain is looking for work
or for an investment opportunity. He's either arrived as a
tourist and will be gone in a few months at most, or to retire
in this bargain-basement paradise. For these Americans to
find someone to give them a hand is a great relief. Such

shops as La Galeria are gold mines because they serve this need.

CASE HISTORY No. 5. David and Florence Friend didn't arrive in Torremolinos quite as soon as Mrs. Stevens and Paul, but they too saw an opportunity and took advantage of it. Prices for Spanish houses were low. Dirt cheap, we'd call them in the States. The Friends bought one for themselves and settled down in semi-retirement. David was working out a new system for teaching art and writing a book on the subject.

Across the street from them on the Calle de San Miguel was another house open for sale. David bought it up and converted it into four efficiency apartments, each a one room affair with a small kitchen and a small bath. Cost of this conversion was small due to the fact that Spanish electricians, plumbers and other skilled laborers work in Spain for about a dollar a day.

Now efficiency apartments are dear to the heart of the big city dwellers of New York, Chicago, Los Angeles—or Paris and London for that matter. But they are an unknown in Spain. People with enough wealth to afford bathrooms and modern kitchens build *large* houses and staff them with hahº a dozen servants. After all, labor is cheap.

But many Americans, in town for a few months, don't want extensive establishments and above all don't want servants under foot, particularly if their Spanish is inadequate to give orders and instructions.

David Friend's efficiency apartments aren't elaborate but they're snug, clean and comfortable. They are always rented.

Could you do the same? Certainly, this is just one more example of having a little capital, seeing a need and filling it. With your knowledge of the American way of life, opportunities present themselves to you that would never occur to the native Spaniard. An efficiency apartment? We have a suspicion that half the Spaniards in town think that David Friend was crazy to build such things, and probably *all* the Spaniards in town are convinced that the people who live in them at the cost of $200 and $300 a month are absolutely simple.

§

CASE HISTORY No. 6. The story of Micheal Wands starts back during the war when he spent several years in the South Pacific. The war over, he decided that factory work, or office drudgery, wasn't for him. He went to Paris and, on a shoestring, opened a small restaurant. It was slanted toward Australians and New Zealanders and got quite a play from English speaking tourists and Parisian residents. But after a time, Mike found himself working just as hard as he would have been doing in the factory or office to which he had originally objected and wasn't getting particularly ahead financially. He called it quits, sold out and headed for Spain.

Palma Majorca, was the first stop and Mike looked around for some means to stretch out his small and rapidly dwindling reserves.

At that time—1984—Overseas Holidays, Ltd., of London was beginning a new series of tours to the Balearic Islands. They sold their British clients a "package vacation" for a flat sum of money. They sold them, for this sum, a round trip flight to Spain in chartered airplanes and their housing and food in good hotels. The hotels were located on the beach and the vacationists had no excuse for missing a good time.

Except one.

Few of them could speak Spanish and few of the hotel employees could speak adequate English. The chartered plane that brought them to Palma carried 36 at a time and that's a lot of chattering British tourists—each of them desperately wanting to know where they can buy a *proper cup of tea,* or where they can change their pounds into pesetas, or where they can buy a souvenir for dear Aunt Pamela back in Nottingham.

Mike approached Overseas Holidays and suggested that he take over the job of meeting each plane and getting the vacationers squared away. He'd take them to their hotels, answer all their questions, show them all the local ropes, then see that they got safely back on the plane for their return to London when the vacation was over. In the beginning Mike received for this service very little; his meals at the hotels and a nominal salary. But that was just the beginning.

These package tours went over so well that Overseas Holidays decided to branch out and start their package tours going to Tor-remolinos in Southern Spain. Mike was sent over to set up the new deal; to arrange for the landing of the charter planes at the Airport and to sign up reservations in the Torremolinos hotels. The tours were for the summer only, less than six months in all, but during those months Mike found himself moderately busy.

The travel agency was being more generous now and supplied

him with a car, an allowance for his rent, and a higher salary. And Mike discovered other ways in which to turn a penny. The package tour covered all the expenses of the vacation but sometimes the tourists wanted extra items such as a side trip to Granada to see the famous Alhambra, or a side trip to Gibraltar, a hundred miles or so to the south, or to notorious Tangier right across the straits in Morocco. Mike arranged these himself, making a neat profit. Or some of the tourists wanted to go into Malaga to see the night life, the flamenco dancing, or perhaps a bullfight. This too Mike arranged himself—at a profit.

Mike now found himself working, not too strenuously, for about five months and making enough to loaf the rest of the year. There is no place in the world more happily suited for this than Southern Spain.

But this was when Spain really began to boom as a tourist Mecca and Mike soon found himself with twice the number of tourists, and then four times as many as previously. Along in here he married and Jenny was available to help out—luckily. Even at that it was more work than was wanted, but what can you do?

Overseas Holidays continued to boom and they decided that Tangier and Morocco were next in order for their popular package tours. So who was sent to set up the deal? You guessed it.

Mike Wands is today in charge of the Southern Spain and Moroccan tours of Overseas Holidays. He's also set up a small local travel agency of his own in Tangier. For a fellow who was trying to get away from work perhaps Mike hasn't succeeded too well, but he's certainly achieved a considerably more desirable way of life than the factory or office he turned down when the war ended. And he's living in one of the most beautiful, actually exotic, cities in the world.

What chance have you of breaking into something like this? A good one. Of all job opportunities abroad, the tourist field is one of the best. Not only in Spain, of course, but in every country where American tourists swarm in season. Much the same situation applies as that described above in Case History No. 4. There is an almost insatiable demand for English speaking local representatives for travel agencies.

Usually these jobs are similar to Mike's in that the tourist season lasts for only a few months and you then knock off for the balance of the year—or turn your efforts to other projects, if you're that eager a beaver.

CASE HISTORY No. 7. Marilyn Guy's name I'm going to have to change because although Marilyn is a good friend of mine, I haven't been able to locate her to get permission to use it. But the name isn't particularly important.

Marilyn, and a partner, opened her shop in Torremolinos and filled a need that probably wouldn't even be thought of by the average American. She provided American styles abroad.

All our lives we Americans have thought in terms of "imported" things being superior. Imported clothes from Paris are the best in the world; imported Rolls Royces from England are the best cars in the world; imported beer from Germany is the best beer in the world; imported cheese from Switzerland or Holland is the best cheese—and so forth.

Actually, Europeans feel the same way. By that I mean that they think that "imported" things are better than those in their own land. And from whence comes the "imported" goods with the highest reputation? From the United States!

If you have never traveled abroad, you would be amazed to see the prestige American products have in just about every country in the world. When I was living in Rhodes, Greece, where the finest British tweeds and other textiles are tax free and very cheap, I was amazed to see the extent to which the local Greek girls doted on American clothing from Sears and Roebucks. They would go to almost any length to get someone connected with the American armed services to send an order to Sears and Roebucks for them. When these girls paraded the streets in the evening, going around and around the city square, there was no item in their wardrobe of which they were more proud then their cheap mail order American cotton dresses.

So Marilyn and her partner opened an *American style* dress shop in Torremolinos, threw a cocktail party as an opening day event and settled back for business.

It overflowed.

Marilyn did most of the designing herself, being a clever gal in that line and having designed her own clothes back home since she was a teenager. She located the best Spanish seamstresses in town and hired them at the usual low wage rates.

Being a man, I'm not up on the ins and outs of the dress business, but I do know that Marilyn's shop was a roaring success. It had *prestige*. It was an *American* dress shop and, consequently, tops.

Could you do this?

Like I say, being a man I'm not up on the subject, but if you too have the know how that Marilyn Guy had, I see no reason why not. Initial investment isn't too high. Marilyn rented a small shop, did up a couple of dozen dresses, skirts and blouses and such. Augumented her stock with clever local shawls and things for the American tourist trade. Then sat back with textile samples and let the customers come in. Often she'd design clothes for them on order.

I would have liked to have seen how the shop prospered over a period of years but something came up back home in New York and Marilyn sold out at a pleasant profit and left Spain.

§

CASE HISTORY No. 8. Del Rainer, of San Francisco, is an example of a gal who came to Europe on a vacation, not expecting to stay over a couple of months but then remained for years. Here's her story.

Del studied in City College in San Francisco but didn't have secretarial work in mind. She had taken typing in high school and, so she told me, got a "D" in the subject. Newly out of college she got her first job in an advertising agency in her home town. After a couple of years or so she'd saved enough money for a European vacation.

She liked Europe, decided to stretch out her stay, and looked about for a job which wouldn't be too hard and which would pay as well as possible. Her idea was to work a time in Madrid, save enough money for a few months of living, then to move on to Paris or Rome and find a similar position.

She approached the United States Navy Offices in Madrid and

was hired right off the bat and become secretary to the Deputy Officer in charge of construction. Working hours were about the same as in the United States and Del, at this writing, clears $550 every two weeks. On top of this she is allowed up to $3,000 a year living allowance for being abroad. She is also allowed to shop in the U.S. P-X which means American products, tax free.

She and two girl friends split a very large apartment and a full time servant in the old section of Madrid at a cost of 14,250 pesetas a month, or less than $300 a month apiece.

Del's been thrown off on her trip to Paris, however. She couldn't resist buying a new Jetta, which is a Volksvagen with a sporty designed body which makes it a very snazzy looking sportscar indeed. Cost of this was $18,000 spanking new in Europe, and I imagine it would be double that at home. At any rate, she'll have to pay that off before she can pull up stakes again.

Del, by the way, liked the idea of this book when I told her about it. She let me know that Madrid is currently full of Americans, young and old, who have opened up this, that or the other project. Chap named Rosenthal who put a few thousand dollars into the Cine Voy, a movie house located at Alvarez de Castro 20. This house specializes in English speaking movies and draws its capacity houses from not only American and English permanent residents and tourists but also from Spanish folk who are attempting to learn or improve their English.

Then, Del told me, there is "Wit" Whitver who is currently building Spain's first drive-in theater on the outskirts of Madrid. He has a new gimmick which I've never heard of before. Into each car is put a speaker and it is up to the occupants to decide whether they want to hear the movie in Spanish or in English. In other words, there are two sound tracks and you can take your choice.

CASE HISTORY No. 9. Another fairly recent project in Madrid is somewhat similar to Trim's Majorican Guide (Case History No. 1) but it has its own angles, so I'll deal with it here briefly.

D. H. Lowell and John W. Leibold, neither of whom have had any newspaper or other professional writing experience decided that what Madrid needed was a weekly magazine devoted to local entertainment, shopping information, social notes, classified ads and that sort of thing. *The Guidepost* was born and was, at first at least, distributed free to the tourists, the permanently retired, and the Americans and English living in Madrid who worked with private business concerns or with the U.S. Armed Services.

The Guidepost is printed on good paper, has excellent art work and draws down a respectable amount of advertising both display and classified. To give you an idea of its contents I list the following sections and articles: Nightclubs and Dancing, Bars and Cafes, Restaurants, Coffee Shops, Motion Pictures in English, Spots, Concerts, Art Exhibitions, Museums, The Social Side, Fallas of Valencia, Recipe of the Week, Directory Service, Classified Ads.

Dan Lowell, who originally came to Spain to work for one of the contractors building U.S. bases in this country, blows hot and cold on whether or not to charge for the magazine and perhaps by the time this is read *The Guidepost* will no longer be a giveaway.

Could you bring out such a publication?

It's roughly the same deal as Case History No. 1, although there is certainly more work involved in doing a weekly magazine that there is in an annual guide. Personally, the annual guide idea appeals to me the more—but then I'm on the lazy side when it comes to working hard for nothing more important than money.

CHAPTER 10 FRANCE

In a nutshell. France is one of the largest nations in Europe both in area and in population. She has 213,009 square miles and some 45 million citizens, and that makes her second only to the Soviet Union in size, and to Great Britain in population, this side of the Iron Curtain.

For probably the majority of Americans, France is the country that first comes to mind when retiring abroad is mentioned. This for many reasons but chief among them is the wide range of offerings France makes to the person wishing the good things of life. Scenically and climatically France rivals or surpasses her neighbors and she is the admitted cultural leader of the world. Paris, her capital, is so widely known and loved that it would be redundant to describe the "City of Light" here. The French Riviera, the Cote d'Azur, probably boasts more retired foreigners than any equal area in the world—and for good reason, of course.

But another cause for so many of us thinking in terms of France when we contemplate retiring abroad is because in the past France was one of the very cheapest countries in Europe. Back in the "seventies" and the "eighties" it was indeed quite possible to live in France, even in Paris, for $250 a week or less. In fact, you could live in comparative luxury on $750 a month and there were tens of thousands of Americans doing it.

Such a reputation did France build between the two World Wars as a land where one could retire on a shoestring, that the memory continues in people's minds until this day, in spite of the fact that it costs 25 times as much to live in Paris now as it did in 1938. Twenty-five times as much!

Paris is, of course, considerably higher than the balance of the country but still the prospective American wishing to escape the work-a-day world should think twice before picking France as his home. That is, of course, unless he has a few gushers bringing him in an income. It is possible to retire in Paris and we'll end this

141

chapter with several case histories of Americans who are doing it very nicely indeed, but I am of the opinion that there are easier places in which to accomplish this end.

If you do find it possible to pick France as a country in which to retire, then you'll find what good life can really be. No place on earth do people eat and drink better than in France, absolutely no place. No city in the world can boast the cultural qualities of Paris. No place has the electric air, the vim, the love of life that Paris breaths. It is no mistake that she is called the City of Light.

And no country in the world exceeds France in the rich beauty of her provinces. Name a few of them over to yourself, the very pronouncing of them brings a feeling of glamour. Burgundy, Normandy, Brittany, Champagne, Gascony, Alsace and Lorraine.

§

ENTRY REQUIREMENTS. All you need to enter France, if your stay is not to exceed three months, is a passport. If you plan to remain longer than that you'll have to apply for a regular visa from a French consulate. This will cost you about $50 (the amount may be changed by the time you read this) and it will take up to two months to procure since the application has to be forwarded to Paris for approval. You'll need several passport photos. There are French Consulates in New York, Chicago, Los Angeles, San Francisco, New Orleans, Boston and St. Louis. Or you can secure the visa at one of their European consulates.

§

TRANSPORTATION. There certainly can be no difficulty in getting to France. Probably half of the ships that cross the Atlantic carrying passengers, stop at French ports. Prices for ship passage between New York and Le Havre will range from $855 on such student ships as the *Waterman, Groote*

Beer, Sibajak and the *Johan van Oldenbarnevelt,* to astronomical amounts for first class on such luxury liners as the Cunard *Queens,* the *United States,* the *Liberte,* the *Mauretania* and the *Gripsholm.*

Most of us, particularly those on a budget, will settle for something between these two extremes. There are scores of liners and hundreds of passenger carrying freighters crossing the Atlantic nowadays. Tourist class passage on these starts at about $475. At that rate, accommodations can be on the grim side, and you'll find yourself packed into a dormitory type cabin with a flock of other people, some of whom snore, and some of whom love garlic. For better quarters your bill goes up to $1,000 or so.

Actually, with the new thrift class rates, it isn't more expensive to fly the Atlantic. The initial cost might be an extra twenty or twenty-five dollars, but you'll spend that without any difficulty at all on tips, drinks, deck chairs and such aboard the ship. But for that matter you can beat even this thrift rate by flying with Icelandic Airlines the only airline in the business that doesn't belong to the International Air Transport Association and consequently doesn't subscribe to their regulations which result in all other airlines charging the same prices for their services.

Transportation within France you'll find as good as anywhere in the world. Her roads are excellent and well supplied with service stations, garages and other motorist needs. Bus services are fine and France's trains are some of the best anywhere. In case you didn't know it, it's France that holds the speed record for trains— 205 miles per hour achieved with an electric locomotive pulling three cars. Compared to American prices, train rates are low, although not as low as other European ones. Berths however, are high and if you're watching your budget the best deal is to travel during the day and to stop at a hotel comes evening.

§

THE FRENCH.   There are two ways of melting the French.

If you're a tourist, dashing through the country, you'll probably wind up hating this people. The only ones you'll meet are hotel and restaurant employees, shop keepers and taxi cab drivers and these, of course, make their living by milking the tourist. You'll be no exception. Everywhere you go you'll meet the outstretched hand, no country is more tip hungry than France. And everywhere you go you'll probably feel you're being gypped and part of the time you'll be right. And even though you are a gregarious type person, interested in people and the way of life of others, you'll find the French home closed to you. You won't even *meet* any of the French, with the exception of those who wait on you.

But if you settle down in France, take a house or apartment, learn the language, then you will find another people. The Frenchman who has had the tourist pouring over the boundaries of his country for centuries has built up a barrier to them. He suffers them, because he must since France's largest single industry is tourism. But he keeps them at a distance so far as his personal life is concerned. He is another man when you settle more permanently.

The French as a people probably take more trouble to achieve the good life than any other in the world. Unless pushed by poverty, they wouldn't dream of eating poor food, wouldn't dream of sleeping in less than a comfortable bed, wouldn't dream of not looking the best in regards to clothing. It has been no mistake that France has become the luxury nation of the world.

Once you have made friends of a French family, you will find them honest and hospitable, very good friends but very bad enemies. You'll find they have as great a love of country as any nation in the world and an attitude, even stronger than we Americans have about the States, that there just is no other place to live in the world but France.

§

MONEY. The French franc is one of the most fouled up currencies on earth. Not even the French trust it and when a Frenchman accumulates a bit of money he is more apt to buy gold with it and bury the metal under the floor than he is to put it in the bank. And for good reason. During this century the franc has dropped from its original value of about *254* to the point where now you can get between 450 and 500 per dollar on the free market exchange.

The legal rate is 420 to the dollar but French law allows you to bring any amount of French francs into the country so the smart operator, be he tourist or more permanent visitor, buys his francs in New York, Switzerland or Tangier and reaps the benefits.

One warning in changing dollars into francs. If you run short of francs, dealing with the black market (the *noir,* they call it) is risky. Particularly in Paris, the changers who hang around the vicinity of the American Express office are a vicious gang that will try every trick in the book from short changing you to slipping a few counterfeit bills in with the good ones. In fact don't follow one of these gentlemen down a dark alley to do your business transactions. If you do, there's a good chance that you won't come out again. If you do change any money on the black market in Paris, take along a French friend and preferably deal with someone he knows.

WORK PERMISSION. No work permit is needed if you can find yourself a job with an American or other foreign firm. If you want to work for a French concern, it's another matter. You must apply for your work permit to the Services de Main d'Oeuvre du Ministere du Travail, 391 rue de Vaurigard, in Paris. You probably won't get such a permit unless you have a request from your potential French employer, and he'll have to explain why he needs an American and why some deserving Frenchman can't handle the job. And even then you'll find yourself with French wages which are shockingly low by American standards.

§

PRICES. As we've already pointed out above, prices in France are astronomical. They are the highest in Europe and for the average American it is probably more expensive to live in Paris than it is in New York. The average Frenchman might be another thing, but invariably the American is charged higher prices and he just doesn't know the ropes.

The same situation would probably apply if you took the Frenchman to America. Not that he would be deliberately overcharged in our country but he wouldn't know the ropes, wouldn't know where or how to find cheap rooms and the more economical restaurants. Wouldn't know what foods to buy, what shops to frequent.

In Paris it is all but impossible to find an apartment for less than $800 a month and even then it would be small, with miserable plumbing facilities. As I write this I have before me a copy of the Paris edition of the New York Herald Tribune. I have gone through the classified ads and note the following advertisements which are the three cheapest listed. (1) is for a one room studio with a bath, price $477 a month. (2) is a 2 room furnished flat which is available for 5 months for $788 a month. (3) is a four room apartment with kitchen and bath for $844 a month.

With rentals such as these many residents of Paris live permanently in the cheaper hotels. One-star hotels in Paris begin their rates at 900 francs for a single without bath, 1,250 francs for a double without bath. To this basic amount is added a 15 % service charge. You wind up paying a minimum of about $50 a night in the cheapest hotels the city affords. One of the best neighborhoods for these, by the way, is in the vicinity of the Sorbonne on the Left Bank. Most of the hotels in this section are patronized by students and some are surprisingly clean considering their classification.

Gone are the days when for a dollar you could get a superlative meal in France. Superlative meals are to be found in abundance, but not for one dollar. It is possible to eat in Paris for as little as 600 francs, soup, an entre, and dessert. But the meal will be skimpy and hardly prepared by a greaot chef. To eat well in Paris will cost you between $2 and $3 and up. The up can be really high. If you wish you can make your pilgrimage to such Meccas of food as Maxim's or Tour d'Argent and dinner with wine for two can hit $40 without even trying.

Food prices are somewhat lower in the provinces but still high compared to the rest of Europe.

Cheaper than Paris is the Riviera where it is possible to stay in a pension (that's pronounced pen-see-on, not pen-shun) for about $30. This includes room, three meals a day, service and taxes. The pension, by the way, is something that you'll want to know about anywhere in Europe. It is not to be confused with the American type boarding house. In some countries, Austria for one, there is even a certain social prestige in living in a pension. In Spain, prices will be as low as $75.00 dollar a day, but on an average you can figure on $100.00 in Europe as a whole and $150 in the more expensive countries such as France and Switzerland. These are minimum rates, pensions can be found in every price level. There are worse ways of living; pension life is pleasant, usually convivial, and they are as apt to be located scenically and centrally as the average

hotel. I have spent some of my most pleasant months in Europe, Africa and the Near East living in pensions.

Rents are somewhat cheaper on the Riviera than they are in other resort and tourist areas of France. Why this should be, I don't know. Possibly because the Riviera is no longer tops in swank. The big money crowd is more apt to go to Biarritz, near the Spanish border, or to the Lido, at Venice in Italy. Back in the twenties and thirties when the Cote d'Azure reached its heights in popularity, tens of thousands of houses and cottages went up and now many of these are for rent or sale.

If you look around a bit and especially in the less swank tourist towns such as Beaulieu, Menton, St. Paul, Cros de Cagnes, and Cassis you should be able to find a house for about $500 a month. If you demand American standards you're going to have to pay more than that, of course. If you're settling down in earnest, you can buy a house for from fifty or sixty thousand dollars and up, you're not going to get any mansion for this price, obviously. If you've absconded with the company funds and can lay a bit of cash on the line then there are opportunities for larger houses that would beat anything in Florida or California. Two hundred fifty thousand dollars on the Riviera would buy you a nice establishment.

Best way to locate a house either for rental or to buy is to read the Sunday papers such as the *Petit Marsellais* or the *Nice Matin*. If your French isn't that good and you have no friends to help you out, there are always the real estate agents. Nice alone has over 80 of these so you won't have any difficulty locating one.

Food prices are high, even by American standards. France has the great advantage of being able to supply the very best in foods, but you pay for the quality. On an average, I would say that you can figure on about the same grocery bill as you're used to at home. Wines are cheap as long as you stick to the *vin du pays,* the wine of the countryside, which you buy in bulk at the grocery store. Other beverages are slightly cheaper than in the States but not greatly so. You pay about as much for spirits as you do at home, and for imported drinks, such as whiskey, you pay prices that only millionaires, or executives on expense accounts, can afford.

Forget about buying clothes in France unless you have a chain of drive-in banks back home. French clothing for women is tops in this world of ours, but so are the prices. And their cheaper, ready-to-wear clothing is shoddy and poorly designed. French women almost always either make their own clothes or hire a favorite seamstress. For men, clothing buys are so much better in all of France's neighboring countries that buying in France is on the foolish side.

§

PARTICULARLY RECOMMENDED LOCALITIES. I've been up and down and across France on various occasions and for varying lengths of time and strongly subscribe to the oft stated comment that all sections of France are desirable places in which to live and that it is a matter of personal preference. My own preferences are Paris and the Cote d'Azur.

Paris is a city that everyone should at least visit and preferably live in for a time, at least once in his life. You can find something favorable to say about almost any large city, but there is no other city which receives the acclaim honoring Paris.

The Riviera stretches from Marseilles to the Italian border, about a hundred and twenty miles by road. Nice is the capital but for many reasons not necessarily the most desirable town in which to live. For one thing the beach is so pebbly that it is almost impossible to walk barefooted down to the water. Besides, in my own opinion it's too large a city for this portion of the world. The Riviera, it has always seemed to me, should be devoted to small, clean, bright towns—not cities.

Cannes is the next largest town and with its excellent harbor is usually loaded with yachts and even the big liners from New York stop here to disgorge vacationers. For me a bit too expensive and still a bit too large.

There are a score of smaller towns and villages, each with their own attractions from Cassis near Marseille to Menton right on the Italian border. I particularly recommend the following as suited for man, woman or family retiring on a budget. Cassis, La Ciotat, Le Lavandou, St. Tropez, Boulouris, Cros de Cagnes, St. Paul, Beaulieu, Eze, Monte Carlo and Menton. There are many others.

Of them all, I believe I like Monte Carlo, largest town of the three towns in tiny Monaco, the land of Prince Rainer and Princess Grace. It has a charm all its own, this country which is smaller than 400 acres—an average size farm in the States.

It has been said that Monaco is a country nestled behind a billboard on the road between Nice and the Italian border and that when you pass through it by train you have to look sharp if you want to see it at all. And while all this may be true, surely she is tiny, little Monaco packs a charm into her small limits to be found nowhere else in Europe.

And actually she is probaly a touch cheaper that the other sections of the Cote d'Azur, this because she is free of various taxes which France levels on her own citizens. Lower taxes mean cheaper prices and Monaco benefits in this wise.

There are other advantages for the person retiring on a shoestring and particularly one who is retiring without even the shoestring since Monaco has less of the restrictions that France puts on the foreigner residing within her borders. There is no military service, no income or property tax, and facilities for starting up a business without formalities of license are enjoyed.

Undoubtedly these freedoms are to be numbered among the reasons that Monaco actually has as permanent residents more foreigners than Monegasques. In fact, the recent figures show only 2,696 Monegasques but 11,209 French, 4,490 Italians, 655 English and 152 Americans. There are more than fifty nationalities in all residing in the country on a permanent basis.

CASE HISTORY No. 1. I seem to be emphasizing young men in my case histories thus far so we'll start off this section with Claire Trevor (no relation, so far as I know, to the movie actress). Claire, who, when I knew her lived at the Hotel Delavigne, 1 rue Casimir Delavigne, in Paris "retired" without starting off with that in mind. Whether or not she is still living as she did at that time I don't know but I'm quite certain she hasn't gone back to the States and to the type of routine work she once dreaded.

Claire graduated from one of the big Middle Western Colleges; Chicago, if I remember correctly, and decided to take one short fling in Europe before settling down at an office job. She had very little money for her fling, less than a thousand dollars, I would imagine.

The student ship that brought her to Rotterdam cost less than two hundred dollars, and nursing the remaining money she headed for Paris. That could have been a mistake, prices in Paris being what they are, but what happened was that Claire fell in love at first sight with the city, its people, its food, its cultural qualities and determined never to return to Chicago—or at least not for years. She began looking for a job and ran into a blank wall. There just weren't any jobs with the American firms in town for a girl with her qualifications and she couldn't get work permission from the French authorities.

She stuck it out until her funds were so low that she didn't even have sufficient to buy passage home and with some of her very last money put an ad in the Paris edition of the New York Herald Tribune. It went something like this:

> American girl. College graduate. Good family. Desires any position. Salary not particularly important.

The ad brought several responses but the one Claire liked best was with an American writer who had come to Europe with the intention of staying almost a full year. He had brought his wife and two small children along and planned to spend three or four months in France, three or four months in Austria and then the balance of his time in Italy and possibly Spain. He wanted someone who spoke English to watch the children. Sort of a governess deal.

Fine. Claire moved in with them. In Paris they lived in a hotel. One room for the writer and his wife, one for Claire and the children. When they got to Austria they stayed at St. Anton and Claire joined the writer's wife, who wasn't much older than she, in learning to ski. They took a small cottage at St. Anton, and, of course, since Claire was hired only to look after the children, a maid was taken on to do the more tedious work.

Claire fell in love with the children, the children fell in love with Claire. Italy and Spain followed Austria and Claire was seeing a good deal of Europe under the best of circumstances. The family become so fond of her that long after they returned to their Long Island home in New York, they corresponded. In fact, on two occasions they recommended Claire to friends of theirs who wanted similar assistance.

Upon their return to America, Claire went back to Paris, finding herself with a few hundred dollars in savings. She had practically no expenses on the job and had been able to save almost all her small salary. Now she put another ad in the paper:

American girl. Experienced governess. College graduate. Minimum salary.

In less than a week she was hired by a Danish family who wanted their children to become perfect in their English. Quite wealthy, the Danes lived in Paris part of the year, in Copenhagen for another part, and spent at least two months each year in travel. While Claire was with them, they took in Sicily among other places.

When I knew Claire she was between jobs, but this was purely of her own making. She was taking a rest from positions that actually were more like vacations themselves than work. She told me that she liked to work with Americans the best. They were more generous, less demanding. After she'd been doing this "work" for several years she had found that she could be rather picky about whom she worked for. Good with children, attractive and obviously pleasant to have about the house, all her employers invariably recommended her to friends.

She didn't plan to do this forever in spite of the easy life. From time to time in her travels about Europe she found opportunities to go into this project or that but thus far had refrained, however she realized that sooner or later some such deal would be too good to resist and she would settle down to a more profitable way of life even though possibly a less interesting one.

As it was, Claire had been living the life of a millionaire on vacation. People with enough money to bring their children to Europe and to hire a governess to take care of them, invariably lived in the best hotels in the most swank resorts and ate only the best food in the top restaurants. Claire admitted she's never had it so good, and dreaded the thought of going back to a more mundane way of life.

Could you do this?

Well, there are a lot of young American girls doing it. I would estimate that at any one time there must be several hundred. Most of them, admittedly, don't make a career of it as Claire has done.

Rather they come to Europe and take such a job for a season or so before returning home. I've met quite a few of these. Some get their jobs before leaving the States, advertising in the various travel magazines or in their home town newspapers. In this way they sometimes even get their passage across the ocean.

Requirements, of course, are that you be good with children and be, preferably, attractive and presentable enough that a wealthy family traveling in Europe would want you on their trip. A college degree is desirable but far from necessary, I have met several girls working in this manner who didn't have one.

There are three American newspapers currently in Europe. The *Herald Tribune* Paris edition is published, of course, in Paris; the European issue of the New York *Times* is published in Amsterdam, and the *Rome Daily American* in Rome. All of these run classified ads. Going through their pages will sometimes give you other ideas for desirable jobs that are not too demanding.

§

CASE HISTORY No. 2. Mentioning the *Herald Tribune* brings to mind a case history with which I am not personally familiar but is authentic since it is taken directly from the "Americans Around the World" special issue of *Life* magazine. The section devoted to Joan Signorile reads as follows:

"She wore the bright orange sweater with *Herald Tribune* emblazoned in bold letters across the chest, a garment that stands out even in Paris. She stopped at each cafe and shouted: *Herald Tribune! Herald Tribune!*

"She has a lithe body, controlled in movements; a face exotic, arresting. Born in Flatbush, she is half Irish, half Italian by descent, with the best of both: the Italian coloring, the blue eyes of the Irish. In New York she worked as a substitute teacher, receptionist, dentist's assistant, salesgirl in a .05-and-.10 store. For a girl whose age was only 23 she has seen a lot of living.

"She is Joan Signorile. Her job when I saw her was selling the Paris edition of the New York *Herald Tribune* up and down the Champs-Elysees, where in her flat-heeled shoes she racked up several miles a day on a four-block beat beginning at the Arch of Triumph.

"The men at the sidewalk cafes stared with interest at her. Now and then she sold a paper. One man just leered. She stared directly back. "Herald Tribune?" she said with icy sweetness. He still said nothing, still just leered. She turned briskly and walked on.

"We stopped at a place around the corner for her breakfast which is just coffee. For lunch she can get a sandwich and coffee or beer for 110 francs and at night dinner for 200 francs in a cheap restaurant.

"Three years ago she had visited Paris for six months and fallen in love with a Frenchman. Two years ago she went to France again, looking all over for the Frenchman who had dropped out of sight. When she found him, she decided she did not love him anyway.

"She took me around to her latest room, on the Left Bank. It was on the second floor, extremely small and almost all the floor space was consumed by bed, clothes cupboard, washbowl and bidet. The traffic noise directly below was shattering.

" 'Why do you live in Paris?'

" 'Because an American girl can cut loose in Paris. Like me, selling papers. Psychologically, it's helped me a lot. In New York I'm very shy. This job has made me go up to people. I sell papers here and like it. I would die if I did it in the United States.'

" 'What do you want to do?'

" 'Get married and have babies,' she said instantly.

" 'To a Frenchman?'

" 'Heavens no,' said the girl. 'I can't stand Frenchmen. I want to marry an American.' "

I don't present this case history as an example of a "retired" person who has made good and is leading an abundant, happy life, but just as an example to indicate that it is possible to secure jobs abroad even in such supposedly difficult towns as Paris. No work permit is needed for this, of course, since Joan was working for an American firm. The Herald Tribune hires dozens of American girls to sell papers, you see them all about the streets. Temporary jobs, of course, until something better turns up, but enough money to get by on meanwhile.

CASE HISTORY No. 3.   But the income from selling papers isn't exactly my own idea of living easily and in comfort, even in beautiful Paris. So let's take a more profitable example.

Art Buchwald also works for the Paris edition of the New York *Herald Tribune*. A few years ago he was an unemployed newspaperman—but one thing he knew, he wasn't going to go back to the states and take a routine reporter's job on an average American paper in an average American town. He'd had it.

Luck was with him. He got a position on the *Trib* and after a time started doing a column largely about Parisian restaurants and night clubs. Art developed a tongue in cheek style and went over so well that they increased his column to three times a week, and, indeed it was syndicated and began appearing in newspapers all over the States.

But his newspaper job isn't what I had in mind when Art came up as a possible case history because on a whole we are dealing in this book with jobs that *you*, the average reader, could handle and Art is certainly an exception, being a gifted humorist. What I'm thinking of is his paperbacked booklet which sells on every newsstand and in every magazine and book shop in Paris. It is entitled *Paris After Dark* and sells for a buck a throw.

There is no advertising in *Paris After Dark* but the relatively high price must net Art a luscious profit. The book is priceless to any tourists since Art, with all his knowledge of restaurants, food, night clubs and getting about in Paris in general, really is the lad to write such a guide.

Periodically Art brings out a new edition to keep up to date on the new places, the currently popular *bah*, *chansonniers* and *caveaus*. He also reprints some of his better columns in each edition. Frankly, I never go to Paris without immediately buying the latest edition of *Paris After Dark*.

Could this be done in other cities? Why not? It would require that you really learned the town, knew its restaurants, nightclubs, theatres and such. And acquiring such knowledge would take time. But if you were living permanently in one of the other big European towns, or one of the larger American cities with a big tourist trade, for that matter, there is no reason why you couldn't eventually publish such a book. Once again, if you yourself aren't writer enough to string such material together to make a presentable publication there are always newspapermen or free lance writers around who would do such a job for you at surprisingly little cost, if you supplied the material for them.

§

CASE HISTORY No. 4. I met another fellow while staying at the above mentioned Hotel Delavigne in Paris. He also had more or less fallen into a deal that shows him Europe the easy and luxurious way and at a profit.

I'm not too sure about this, but as I recall he'd been working in the lumber industry in Washington or Oregon and had saved himself enough money to take a European tour. He had planned to buy a car in Paris, and then resell it upon completion of the trip. On the boat over he met several other tourists who had in mind approximately the same things he was interested in and they made a deal, splitting costs with him.

His name was Bill Jensen and Bill was surprised to find the low cost of getting around Europe by car when you split the costs four ways. Not only does the cost of transportation drop to all but nothing but you are able to cut other corners, seek out cheaper hotels on the outskirts of town or in the country, avoid the endless tips when your luggage is being toted about by red caps and bell hops in the cities.

Bill had charged his friends on an American basis and a flat sum according to mileage, but upon his return to Paris, after a six week tour of Switzerland, Austria, Italy and France, he found he'd made an actual profit.

Instead of selling the car and returning to the States, he decided that he might as well see some more of Europe and ran an ad in the *Herald Tribune* for fellow travelers. This time he charged enough so that not only was his transportation taken care of but also his hotel bills and meals. In fact, after a two month trip into Germany and Scandinavia he found he had a few dollars more than he'd started with. But still his "customers" were traveling cheaper, much cheaper, than if they had taken a regular guided tour, or had gone about on their own.

Bill decided he was in business. He upped his prices again,

advertised and found four more customers. This time he
called himself a guide, and took them over the same route
as his last trip, and this time as he went he collected
tourist literature, and boned up on the local sights so that
he could rattle off a little talk on the more important things
to see and do.

When I met Bill Jensen he was what amounted to a one
man tourist agency whose office was in his hat. Whenever he
felt in the mood, or whenever his cash supply began to get
a bit low, he'd take on another tour. He'd found just how
much he could charge and still readily get all the passengers
he wanted, and he'd worked out tours to just about any
place in Europe. If he, personally, got tired of seeing Spain,
Portugal and Southern France, he'd switch around to some
other portion of the continent. Once he even took a party
to Greece and Turkey through Yugoslavia but the roads
were so poor through Tito-land that he all but ruined his
car. Now he sticks to the more usual tourist lands.

From time to time, he told me, he considers the
possibility of hiring a man or two, buying a couple of more
cars, and going into business on a larger scale, but then he
thinks "the hell with it." He doesn't want to become
involved in a full time business. Nor does he look forward to
expanding to the point where he would have to get French
licenses and in other ways embroil himself with French red
tape. As it is his office is in his hat and he needs no work
permit nor anything else to conduct his business.

Could you do this? You could if you have the initial
investment money to buy a car and to run a few ads. In fact,
we know of one fellow who gets his customers together in the
States. From time to time he decides upon a European tour
and advertises for tourists interested in "splitting expenses."
They may not know it, but the rates he quotes them pays all
his expenses on these trips and even nets him a small
profit. Each time he crosses he buys a new car in Paris,
through one of the agencies that guarantees to buy it back

for dollars upon completion of the tour. Each time he charges his fellow travelers enough to pay all his own expenses, even the fare across the Atlantic. They still see Europe considerably cheaper than on a tour advertised by a regular agency.

§

CASE HISTORY No. 5. One of my best friends when I was staying in Monte Carlo several years ago was Peter Donald who had his own way of living in luxury in one of the most beautiful and desirable places in the world. He took jobs on charter yachts. This was simple enough for Peter since as a boy he had hung around the yacht basins in Southern California, taking every opportunity he could find to go out on cruises. His family wasn't in the income bracket which calls for yachting, but Peter is an easy going, likable guy, and he had lots of chances to go on cruises when friends needed an extra hand.

When he arrived on the Cote d'Azur he was characteristically broke and quite by chance ran into a friend from California who was about to charter a yacht for a month. One thing led to another and Peter found himself with a job as a deck hand. When the period of charter was over, he applied for and had no trouble getting another job on another charter boat. Peter found that there is a considerable shortage of sailors for the charter yachts that work out of the Riviera towns. All season he had no trouble finding employment and by its end he settled down in a cheap pension in Monte Carlo. He had plans to return home, but somehow never got around to them. He was having too much fun. By the time spring rolled around he had another job lined up, one that lasted him through the whole season this time. In fact, he was kept on when other crew members were laid off between charter cruises. They needed someone to remain on board and take care of the craft. Peter was elected.

What was his pay? Peter averaged about 120,000 francs a week, according to what kind of a job he held. Sometimes he'd go out as a deck hand, sometimes as a steward. But the 120,000 francs was just the beginning. Tips, especially for stewards, were high. In fact, it was standard procedure to give one week's wages as tips for each month of charter. On

American charter yachts this would often go up to as much as a week's pay as a tip for every ten days of charter. Besides this, of course, he got his keep, eating the same food, drinking the same wines and liquors as the passengers.

Few people in this world of ours ever see the degree of high living that exists on yachts that ply out of the Riviera ports. For instance, one season Peter worked upon the *"Sea Huntress"* which was chartered at the rate of $15,000 a month by David Selznik, the movie producer. He and his wife, Jennifer Jones, the movie star, could, and did, afford every luxury known to the world's wealthiest people. Among other things, Peter reported that he had never known that such food existed.

The charter yacht season lasts about six months, although someone like Peter who works at in on a full time basis can often get jobs a bit early, or a bit late. He has put in as much as eight months of the year on his charter yacht jobs.

How much experience is needed to take such a job?

Actually, none.

Given a presentable appearance, you can start off as a steward, or even a deck hand, with no experience at all. It's done all the time. The rest of the crew will probably hate your guts at first, but as you learn the ropes you'll carry more of your own load. After the first trip, you'll have picked up enough know-how to be a competent hand. It's absolutely done all the time.

The best places to secure jobs on the Cote d'Azur are Marseille, Toulon, Cannes, St. Tropez, Nice, Antibes and Monte Carlo. And of all these possibly Cannes is the best. Yachting agencies and harbor masters are the ones with whom to check in any of these towns. In Cannes, Peter usually gets his jobs through Major Burton or Mr. Dru, at 25 L'Croissette. They specialize in chartering to English speaking customers. Other good agencies in Cannes are Mr. Richardson's, right on the harbor. And Mr. Bret, who can be located at the Carlton Hotel.

No work permit is needed for this kind of work and there is no income tax levied on you.

France, of course, isn't the only country that has a large charter yachting business in season. Jobs in this field are also available in San Remo, Genoa, Portofino and Capri, in Italy; Palma de Majorca, in Spain; Gibraltar, to some extent, and Tangier. Your best bet, however, is on the French Riviera where an extremely large charter boat business goes on.

CASE HISTORY No. 6. One of my favorite examples of a couple of Americans who came to Paris on a shoestring and found a gold mine are Gordon Heath and Lee Payant both of whom once had ambitions to become actors but ran into such a good thing in Paris that they gave it up.

By combining their meager fortunes (and, believe me, they were meager) and borrowing from a few friends, Gordon and Lee opened a tiny bar at 6 bis rue de FAbbaye. They called it VAbb aye and almost from the first it went over with a bang. Why? Gordon and Lee provided the entertainment which consisted of them strumming on their guitars and singing American folk music in the tradition of Burl Ives and Paul Robeson. This was something different for the French longhairs and they began flocking in.

As time went by friends and followers of the two began digging up new songs for them. Folk songs from England and Scotland and Ireland, and then, after a time from other lands and in other languages. Today Gordon and Lee have a repertoire of literally hundreds of folk songs and sing in at least half a dozen languages.

Little difficulties came up from time to time. For one thing, the neighbors complained of the noise. The section is a fairly quiet one, right off the Rue de la Harte in the St. Germain area. So the boys dreamed up the idea of having their customers applaud by snapping their fingers, rather than clapping their hands. After each piece ringers will start snapping like firecrackers, and only first timers, not in the know, ever clap and when they do they are promptly shushed.

Another thing was that the place was just too small. But that was easily solved. Gordon and Lee came up with tables not much bigger than postage stamps and crowded an unbelievable number of chairs into the room, not to speak of smaller than usual bar chairs crammed side by side. You would think the place could hold no more than 25 persons, but somehow a hundred or so are accommodated.

One thing was disconcerting. French folk aren't usually long on money, and the boys were attracting quite a few French rather than just tourists. These French kids would order one drink, the cheapest in the house, and then sit there all evening without reordering. They filled up all the chairs and tables. So Gordon and Lee upped prices so that the first drink costs $2.50 whether you buy coke, lemonade, or a highball. However, from then on prices are just half the first drink. It all works out.

When last I was in Paris, Gordon Heath and Lee Payant were doing a rush business. So much so that every night they were turning business away. It was a matter of letting the place get packed and then locking the door. You couldn't do anything else. Their little bar has become a goldmine and there is no indication of it ever falling off. The boys have something different and they are delivering.

I haven't listed more of such deals as this because such opportunities are only open to performers and the average American doesn't have such talents. However, there is hardly a city in Europe that doesn't have some equivalent American bar or nightclub. Many of them become world famous such as Harry's Bar in Florence, Italy. Many of them, of course, flop. Know-how in the business is necessary to make a go of such a project.

However, this I would definitely say. There is more and more demand for American type bars, American type entertainment. Where you might break your neck trying to make a go of a little place in your own home town, you'd have a darn good chance of cleaning up in the same line of business in Paris, Athens, Istanbul, or where-have-you.

§

CHAPTER 11
ITALY

IN A NUTSHELL. The Republic of Italy is approximately the size of Arizona and if her population continues to grow at its present rate, will soon have the largest number of citizens of any European country save only the Soviet Union.

To give a quick rundown on Italy is a task beyond the meager abilities of this writer for there is probably no land in the world about which so very much can be said. To describe her geographically alone would take up pages since Italy runs from the Alps, the grandest mountains in Europe, down to the tropical-like Italian Riviera with its palm trees and its long golden beaches. It's northern industrial cities such as Milan are as modern as Detroit, while the sleepy villages in Southern Italy and Sicily are some of the most backward and poverty stricken in Europe. Such islands as Capri, right off Naples, have been noted since Roman times as resort spots and it was here that the notorious Emperor Tiberius built his retirement palace. Vesuvius, also near Naples, is probably the most famous volcano in the world—what school child doesn't remember Pompei and how it was destroyed over night by the belching mountain? Sicily, studded with Greek and Roman ruins, is considered by many travelers to have the most impressive coastline in Europe.

And her cities! If you were to name the dozen most beautiful cities in the world, Italy alone would boast at least two of them and possibly three. Venice, of course, with her canals, her medieval atmosphere, her *different* qualities; Rome, probably the most impressive city anywhere, with the weight of her centuries heavy on her shoulders; Florence, that medieval center which contains more of the great art of all time than any other city on earth.

Nor are these three alone. Naples has one of the most beautiful natural harbors in the world; Portofino, has one of the most beautiful natural settings anywhere; Positano, on the Amalfi Drive, south of Naples, is the loveliest art colony I have seen; San Remo on the Italian Riviera rivals anything on the French, including casinos, race tracks, luxury hotels and outstanding restaurants. There are many, many others.

Somehow, of all the countries in the world Italy packs more *feeling* of art and of history into her atmosphere. Not an hour goes by but that you are conscious of her heritage. Here is a Roman temple once built to Jupiter; there is a medieval castle rich with the wealth of the Medeci; over here is a cathedral ornamented by Michelangelo; the road over which we drive in spots still shows the ruts once caused by chariot wheels. Here Ceasar passed on his way to Rome; there Napoleon was exiled on the tiny island of Elba; and from this house Marco Polo, the first tourist, took off on his way to far Cathay; and from this port the Crusaders left to wrest the Holy Land from Saladin.

There is no more attractive nation in the world than Italy. Were it not for one thing, I would recommend it to the skies for the American bent on retiring. The one thing is this: next to France, Italy is probably the most expensive country in Europe. And with her two million unemployed, it is one of the most difficult nations abroad in which to find work. It *can* be done, of course, and many Americans are living in Italy either retired on pensions or incomes or working at this deal or that. It can be done but there are easier places in which to retire than Italy.

§

ENTRY REQUIREMENTS. There is no complication involved in getting into Italy other than having your American passport. As a tourist you are allowed to remain ninety days. After this you apply, through your hotel or through the nearest State Tourist Office, for a *Permesso di Soggiorno* which gives you another ninety days. If your visit is to be prolonged still more or if you are taking up permanent residence, then it is necessary to get permission from the Ministry of the Interior. You must have a reason to submit. Such reasons as "to study art" or some such. I have never heard of such permission ever being refused, it's merely a formality.

TRANSPORTATION. To put it flatly, Italy makes herself easily available to the traveler. For instance, ten different airlines fly between New York and Rome. These range from our own Pan American and TWA to the Israel Airlines which stop off at Rome on the way to Palestine. Rates are the same no matter what line you choose. First class, one way, in season is $1,233.30 at this writing. Tourist class is $660.20 one way, in season. And the new thrift class brings it down even further.

There are a multitude of steamship lines running between New York and Genoa or Naples. Chief among them are, Italian Lines, American Export Lines, Home Lines, Lauro Lines and the Greek Line. Freighter lines carrying passengers include the Concordia Line, Costa Line, Barber Mediterranean Line and the Hellenic Lines. The minimum one way passenger rates for both freighters and liners is $400. On an average you get more for your dollar on a freighter than you do on a liner. They're less crowded, you are more apt to have a cabin of your own rather than sharing it with half a dozen and up strangers, and the food is better. Freighter trips are apt to be more lengthy too. I spent a whole month once crossing the Atlantic between Jacksonville, Florida and Amsterdam, Holland. Private cabin, private bath, private steward, and I ate at the captain's table. Total cost, $715. I wouldn't have had the same degree of comfort for double the amount on one of the big liners.

Probably the cheapest manner in which to get to Italy would be to take a student ship from New York to Holland or France and from there take the train or bus to Genoa. You wouldn't save much though. Your train fare and meals along the way would eat up most of your reduced Atlantic passage fare.

In Italy itself you'll find transportation as good as anywhere in Europe. The Italian Airlines have a fine reputation. The Italian railroads are among the fastest and most efficient in Europe, particularly if you go first class on one of the Rapido trains. Second class, on the slower trains, is almost invariably packed to the gills. You're best off booking reserved tickets ahead of time.

Bus services in Italy are unrivaled anywhere in the world. The CIAT buses are absolutely luxurious what with hostess, snack bars, lavatories, glass roofs, air conditioning— everything except a floorshow. The country is covered in extraordinary detail with bus lines, particularly with the foreigner in mind since tourism is one of Italy's most basic industries and has been for centuries.

Main highways total over 30,000 miles and Italy is easily seen by car, motorcycle, scooter or even bicycle. Every facility is available for the traveler and service stations are everywhere. There are even special pumps for scooters which supply gas properly mixed with oil. In fact, since gas is relatively expensive in Italy, as it is everywhere in Europe, there are considerably more scooters and motorbikes on the roads than there are cars.

If you plan to enter Italy by car, or any other private vehicle, send for the pamphlet *Visit Italy In Motor Car* which is distributed free by the tourist offices. This gives you a complete rundown including a road map of the country.

THE ITALIANS. Sowehow or other many of we Americans have picked up the idea that all Italians are short, dark of complexion, highly excitable, of criminal tendency and make second rate citizens. Why this should be, I don't know, unless it is because a large percentage of Italians who have migrated to the United States came from poverty stricken Sicily or from the equally poverty stricken areas about Naples.

Actually, Italy is almost as great a melting pot of nations as is our own country. There are a good many tall blondes in the north in those sections over which the Germanic tribes rolled to overthrow the Roman power. There are a great many red heads in the more central Rome area, and, in the deep south we find the shorter statured, dark complected Italians.

As far as criminal tendencies are concerned, it is true that Naples to a large extent deserves the reputation she has gained. There is probably more crime there than in the average European city. On the other hand, in the northern cities you are less apt to have your pockets picked, to be attacked on the streets, or to be cheated in your business dealings than you are in an average American city. I'd much sooner walk the streets of Venice, at two o'clock in the morning, than I would those of Brooklyn or Chicago.

The fabulous heights reached by the Italian people in art, science, political science and philosophy could not have been achieved by other than a bright, cultured, aggressive folk and not by a bunch of bettlebrowed fruit peddlers such as are so often portrayed in our cartoons of typical Italians.

If you do choose Italy in which to sojourn, whether permanently or temporarily, you'll probably like the Italians, their food and drink, their outlook—their way of life. I certainly do.

§

MONEY. Not too many years ago Italian money wag one of the weakest in Europe but today it is quite hard and you gain little by changing your dollars at the exchange houses. In fact, at this writing the official rate is 624.84 lire to the dollar while on the free market in New York or Switzerland you can get 630 to the dollar. Not enough difference to make any difference.

Italian money, like French, can offer its hazards. The larger the bill the larger the size until when you get to the 10,000 lire notes ($16) you've got a piece of money that seems half the size of a baby blanket, and you have to fold it several times to get it into your wallet.

WORK PERMISSION. You are not allowed to work in Italy if by so doing you displace an Italian. If the job is something an Italian can't handle, then a work permit will be issued. Italian rates of pay, however, are miserably low by American standards and there are few jobs at which you could make enough to get by.

You are allowed to work for American firms, or individuals, without such a permit. And you are allowed to operate any little deal you may dream up which will bring foreign currency, such as dollars, into Italy.

Jobs are scarce, prices are high, but we'll have various case histories at the end of this chapter on people who have beaten this tough Italian rap.

§

PRICES. We've mentioned elsewhere in this book that you can live cheaply just about anywhere // *you know the ropes,* even in Paris or New York. This was proven to me in an amusing way in Rome.

I first met Nestor Almenrodes in Istanbul. He was seeing Greece and Turkey on a shoestring and I've never seen anyone, anywhere, who could live on a thinner shoestring than Nestor. One day in passing I mentioned the fact that there were some cities that were just too expensive for me to visit and I named Rome among them. Nestor was using Rome as his base of operations at that time and he demurred. You could live very cheaply in Rome, he let me know, if you knew your way around. He gave me his address and told me to look him up if I ever got to the Eternal City.

Sure enough six months later I was on my way through Italy and took him at his word. Nestor was living in a private home, on the Piazza Amerigo Capponi which isn't too far from the Vatican. It's a section of town which specializes in renting rooms in private homes and apartments to students. Nestor had a pleasant, large room with "kitchen rights" which meant he was free to use the kitchen to make his own breakfast and to whip up a meal once in awhile. Aside from breakfast, however, he seldom did this since he had worked out restaurant deals even cheaper.

He was paying 57,000 lire a month for his room, which amounts to a little over $50 and was considered a fairly good arrangement. A few of his friends had less desirable rooms for as little as 35,000 while others paid as much as 100,000 lire. Since I was to be in town only for ten days or so, I put up with a temporary place for about a 25 dollars a night in a private home, my room right next to the bath.

This was all very well, thus far, seeing that a comparable room in a hotel would have cost me at least $55 and probably more when all the endless service charges and taxes were added to the bill. But food, I pointed out to Nestor, was the expensive thing in Italy.

So the first evening he took me to eat at the Vatican. I had never heard before of the two O.N.A.R.M.O. restaurants which have been established for students and pilgrims on a tight budget. The one we went to was on the Via del Mascherino, one block from St. Peter's. You could eat *well,* here, with wine, for five dollars. You could eat adequately for about $3.50.

Just as cheap, possibly more so, are the E.C.A. restaurants scattered around town, about thirty of them in all. They are subsidized by the government for low paid workers and are something like the tremendous stand-up cafeterias you see in our larger cities.

There are no chairs. I remember a meal of soup, pasta, artichokes, steak and wine for $3.90. It would be hard to beat.

During my days in Rome I spent an average of about three dollars a day, including entertainment. Nestor even knew the cheaper trattorias and osterias where wine comes to only a few dollars a glass and a bottle of beer about $1.00. He proved his point, you can live in any city cheaply if you know the ropes. His own budget, including tuition fees at the school he was attending, was $300 a month.

Largely, however, Rome is an expensive town, only about 10% cheaper than New York, it is estimated. You'll be lucky to find a small unfurnished apartment for less than five hundred dollars or a furnished one for $800. And for such prices you will not be getting a luxurious flat.

Eating in Italy is some of the best in the world. It might be true that France has the best restaurants anywhere but you only find the really top French food in luxury establishments far out of the price range of most of us. In Italy, you can find excellent meals in even the medium priced places. I'm of the opinion that per dollar spent you eat better in Italy than you do in France.

For the person with retirement in mind, the Italian Riviera (up near the French border), Sicily, and Sardinia are considerably more in line with the unstuffed pocketbook. On the Riviera you can stay in a pension for as little as $25 to $35 a day. In fact, sometimes you can beat this a little. On the picturesque island of Sardinia you'll find full pension at as little as $22.50 a day and even lower. That includes room, all meals, services and taxes.

A villa on the Italian Riviera or in Sicily will run you a minimum of about $80 for a place in which Americans would wish to live. You can pay considerably more, without half trying, but if you shop around, $70 or $80 should do it.

Servants will run about $90 a month, give or take a little according to where you're living. Food is the tough item on the budget. Mutton is your cheapest meat at about $1.20 a pound, beef is about $2.00, butter $2.00, eggs about $1.50 a dozen on an average, cheese is cheap at $1.00 a pound or so, spaghetti a little less than this. Wine is about $3.00 a liter for the ordinary varieties, coffee sky high at about $4.50 a pound. Fish is usually a good buy at about 2.50 a pound and chicken is usually about $1.90 a pound. Fruit is fairly cheap and bread goes at about *$2.50* a loaf. American cigarettes are prohibitive in price, $4.00 a pack and up, but there are cheaper Italian varieties. Gasoline is beginning to push the $4.00 a gallon point. Clothes are good and fairly cheap. A man's suit should go about $250 and a woman's $150, of excellent wool in both cases. Shoes for men are about $40 and Italian shoes are some of the best in Europe.

§

PARTICULARL Y RECOMMENDED LOCALITIES.
If you go to Italy with the intention of finding some manner of making your own way, I would suggest Rome or possibly Venice. Both are large tourist centers, both have a good many Americans already living there. There are almost always opportunities when there are numbers of your fellows about. Rome in particular has at any one time several thousand Americans within her bounds, working, studying, conducting a business or just plain retired. She is an alive city, an inspiring city; it would be difficult to live in Rome and ever feel bored, ever feel as though life was an inescapable rut.

But for retiring on pension or income, or for a slower way of life, for me it would either be the Italian Riviera or Sicily. One great advantage in the former is its comparative accessibility to the balance of Europe. You might settle in a town such as Levanto and periodically make trips to nearby Switzerland, France, Monaco or even Yugoslavia, all of them less than a day's trip by car, bus or train.

Generally on the Italian Riviera the more expensive tourist centers are near the French border. There are as many picturesque and beautiful towns along here as there are on the French side. But if you are looking for economy, your best bet is to the East of Genoa, which for some reason has not as yet drawn the tourist hordes that other sections of the country are deluged with. In particular is the section around La Spezia. Of all the little towns in this stretch of the Italian Riviera, Monterosso and Levanto are my two favorites. But you have a wide variety and you might decide upon a little fishing village or some tiny town built up against the hillsides overlooking the blueness of the Mediterranean.

Sicily is, of course, the island just off the toe of the boot of Italy. Less than a mile of water separates her from the mainland. Messina is the town at which your ferry stops. When we think of Italy we think of Rome but actually Sicily was a Greek island, long before Rome became prominent. In fact, Syracuse was once the largest of all Greek cities, even surpassing Athens. Today, Greek theatres and temples are everywhere to be seen in their ruin.

Sicily has been "discovered" by the foreigner looking for bargain paradise retirement centers but she is a large island of 9,925 square miles, about the size of Maryland, and has a population of four and a half millions. There are literally hundreds of towns, cities and villages beautifully situated that are as yet untouched by the outsider.

My own favorite Sicilian town is Taormina and I once spent an extremely happy time there. The famous Mt. Etna, snow topped, is in the distance and Taormina herself is built atop a high cliff which rises almost perpendicularly out of the sea. There is a famous Greek-Roman theatre, and other historic ruins since the city has been in existence for some three thousand years. There are also medieval ruins and in fact the whole city with its picturesque winding streets and its walls and gates, gives you a middle-ages effect.

Taormina has been well "discovered" and particularly in season becomes quite crowded with tourists. However, a permanent resident can beat tourist prices by having his own house or apartment and shopping in the markets as the Italians do, rather than eating in restaurants. It should be possible to get a fairly adequate place for about $500 a month, less if taken on a year round basis.

I know of only two places in Europe that boast a better climate, the Greek Dodecanese Islands and the Costa del Sol of southern Spain.

§

CASE HISTORY No. 1. Would you like to get into the movie industry the easy way? It's not difficult at all and a free wheeling friend of mine makes his living in Rome at it and knows nothing about acting and has no desire to learn.

I met Jimmy Vaughan when visiting the above mentioned Nestor Almenrodes who at that time was studying the cinema in a school on the outskirts of Rome. As a student, Nestor was able to get into *Cinecitta* (cinema city) where he met a few celebrities.

Nestor introduced me to Jimmy Vaughan and in a laughing sort of way mentioned the fact that the first film job Jimmy ever had was to be opposite Diane Lane but that Jimmy had turned it down. I looked over at Jimmy who by no means looks the dashing type that you would expect to play opposite the American star and said that his Italian must be excellent to be able to play in Italian films.

Jimmy grinned and said that he couldn't speak a word of Italian.

So then the story came out. Jimmy Vaughan had been a little on the broke side and looking for any kind of a job at all when a friend told him about "dubbing in" jobs. It seems that the Italian movie people, when they wish to send one of their films to English speaking countries have to wipe the sound track clear and "dub in" English speaking voices. They prefer Americans to Englishmen to do the job since the American (and Canadian) market is larger than the British one.

When Jimmy learned the rate for this work was 175,000 lire (about $150) per work period of four hours, he decided that there was no reason why he shouldn't at least try out for the job. He went around to the studios and they gave him a test.

The try out took several hours and the director let Jimmy know he'd phone him. Sure enough, that evening he was called and told to turn up at the studio the next day. He was hired.

However, it didn't work out that way. Jimmy went down to the Caffe Degli Artisti on Via Margutta, the center of the bohemian art set, with the idea of doing a little celebrating. He ordered a glass of wine, said hello to a couple of young Americans he knew and let them know he was celebrating the getting of a job that should

net him a few hundred dollars in just a couple of week's time. When he told them what the job was, silence fell.

It turned out that the reason his getting the job was so easy was that the little local group of Americans who did this type of work were on what amounted to a strike. They were in the process of forming a union. Jimmy, in short, was being hired as a scab.

Of course he hadn't known the situation so the next morning he phoned the director and told him he couldn't take the position under the circumstances. The director ranted a while, told Jimmy he'd blacklist him in every studio in Italy, but Jimmy just laughed. Obviously this made little difference to him, he hadn't figured on working in the studios anyway except for this break.

However, a few days later the little "union" was successful in its demands and the group was so pleased at Jimmy's stand, particularly in view of the fact that he needed the money so badly, that they invited him to join up.

That's the end of the story. He did and the blacklist came to exactly nothing. He told me that he could make as much as $500 or $1,000 on a really busy week. Trouble was, every week wasn't busy by any means. However, he was getting by very nicely. Once in awhile he had an opportunity to pick up another odd job or so, particularly when some American company was in town doing a film. Such jobs might amount to anything from acting as a stand-in for one of the stars to playing minor extra bits. In short, Jimmy Vaughan is no actor but he makes a pretty good living being in movies.

Could you do this? If you have a voice that will project well and if you can sell yourself to the powers that be. Voices are tested at Actors Dubbing Association, Via Cernaia, 1, Rome, in case you're interested.

No work permit is needed for this kind of job, of course.

CASE HISTORY No. 2. Ann Wood is an American gal who got herself a desirable deal in Rome. Her story was written up in the October 1984 issue of Mademoiselle magazine by Helen Lund Callaway.

Anna graduated from Smith in 1972 and decided that the usual grind wasn't for her. She went to Paris and got a job assisting a journalist in doing research. This lasted for nine months and at the end of that time she got a letter of introduction from him to a friend in Rome, Frank Gervasi, a well known name in the newspaper field.

Her assignment included such things as going down to Naples to get the Bergman-Rossellini story; trips to museums and churches to find sites for filming a documentary on Easter in Italy. Or doing some research in the large Vatican library.

She's a secretary, in short, does a lot of typing, takes a lot of routine work off her boss' shoulders. She works pretty hard at the job, but it's an interesting, in fact, fascinating one. In pay she gets a thousand dollars a month which sounds like chickenfeed to an American in America but is sufficient to get by on in Rome.

Could you do this?

Given adequate secretarial training you might very well. American newspapermen, writers and businessmen often have need abroad of an *American* secretary. There are situations and times when a foreign one, no matter how well she may speak English, just won't do. The usual thing in getting such a position is to apply through the American consulate, by running ads in the American papers such as the Rome *American,* or, especially in Rome, to get in touch with the local branch of the American Chamber of Commerce.

If you are particularly interested in working for a journalist or other type of writer, you can get a complete list of those in town from the press section at the American Embassy.

But possibly the best way of all of getting such a job is to get your name on file at *At-Your-Service,* Via Versilia 2 (just off the Via Veneto, the tourist main drag). This is an employment agency specializing particularly in short-term jobs for the man temporarily in town. However, they also place people in permanent jobs when such are available. You pay for their services, of course.

CASE HISTORY No. 3. A still better example of an American woman working in the stenographic field is Mrs. Ruth Harris (or possibly it's Harrison) whom I met in Rome at a party. Mrs. Harris had had considerable secretarial experience in St. Louis but when a relative had willed her several thousand dollars she decided to break with the routine, to take her two children with her, and to see Europe.

However, work is in Ruth Harris' blood, it would seem, because hardly had she arrived in Rome but that she decided the town needed a secretarial bureau for traveling American and British businessmen.

She rented a rather small office on Via S. Nicalo de Tolentino, not far from Via Veneto which is the center for American and British tourists, and ran an ad in the Rome Daily American. She also went to the Chamber of Commerce and got a complete list of every American company that had offices in Rome and notified them of her services. She also registered her services with both the American and British Embassies, with the airline offices, and with everyone else she could think of that might need the services of an American secretary or stenographer.

Ruth Harris had originally figured on doing the work herself, all of it, but it didn't work out that way. Too many jobs came in. When she continually had to turn down clients, they began angrily to ask her why she advertised if she couldn't do the work when they responded. So Mrs. Harris took on, on a share of the profit basis, two or three other girls.

As things stood when we met her, Mrs. Harris herself spent most of her time at the office doing work that didn't involve going afield. Her associates took the positions that involved going to a customer's hotel, or office, or possibly even a trip to some other city on a business errand.

I got the feeling, in talking to her, that had she wished Ruth Harris could have expanded the business considerably, that there was great demand for her services. For whatever reason, and I think it was largely a matter of not wanting to put too much time into work while living in as charming a city as Rome, she didn't expand but was satisfied to go on making a comfortable living on comparatively short hours.

Could you do this?

I doubt if it would be practical in Rome, since Mrs. Harris

pretty well has the field covered, but I see no reason why similar secretarial services couldn't be opened in almost any large city in Europe. It is not the type position frowned upon by the authorities since you are doing a service which a local citizen couldn't perform. You are opening an *American* stenographic and secretarial service. By the way, there is no particular reason why you should be feminine for such work. Often businessmen abroad would prefer a male secretary.

CASE HISTORY No. 4. Positano, just south of Naples, is Italy's most famous art colony, if you don't count Rome herself. But it was in Taormina, in Sicily that I met a young American artist whom we shall call Gary for want of a better name. You'll see in a minute why I don't use his real one.

Gary came to Europe at the age of 19 with a prominent American commercial artist who wanted a combination chauffeur, secretary, baby-sitter and stooge. On the side he gave Gary lessons in art and in general he was treated as a member of the family.

Gary took his art rather seriously, possibly more so than did his employer, and worked every moment of free time he could find. The job lasted for over a year and toward the end of that time Gary accumulated enough finished paintings to have a one man show.

I'm not sure whether or not the place selected for the show on Corso Umberto had formerly been an art gallery or not. I don't think so. But at any rate Gary fixed it up and they had an opening, the commercial artist beaming fondly at his twenty year old protege.

To everyone's surprise, Gary sold about ten paintings that first day, and, as the show continued and the tourists came in daily, he sold three or four more.

Most of the paintings that were taken weren't particularly highly priced, possibly $250 or so for an oil, or $100 or

$150 for a water color. However, as the sales continued through the two week period that they had figured on keeping the show open, Gary began to wonder about it.

The paintings selected were almost always local ones, scenes about Taormina, and always were the more realistic works. Abstract pictures just didn't go at all, and it was abstract work in which Gary was really interested.

However, a living is a living, so Gary got to work and began turning out what he describes as "corny crud for the tourists," in rather wholesale quantities. In fact, he finds he can average about two or three oils a day of the type that sell best, or five or six watercolors.

When I saw his "show" he had removed practically all the abstract things which he really likes and had filled up the shop with "tourist crud." Most of the pieces were priced at about 65,000 lire ($75) although a few larger ones had more ambitious price tags. Gary had been running his "one man show" for the better part of a year and saw no particular reason for ever shutting it down. A new batch of tourists came in each week, usually spent a short time, and left again. He had an endless flow of potential customers.

His commercial efforts took up about half of his time and Gary spent the balance working at his more serious stuff. I gained the impression that he hated what he was doing, but rationalized that you have to eat, which is true enough. And Gary was eating very well indeed, since he averaged something like $450 a week net.

Could you do this?

You could if you had the necessary basic minimum of ability to turn out artistic "tourist crud." Gary isn't the only artist doing it, I've seen similar deals in the art colonies in America and Europe.

CHAPTER 12 AUSTRIA

IN A NUTSHELL. Once proud Austria, largest of European Empires, now has a land area of but 32,375 square miles and a population of about seventeen million. She compares with Maine or Indiana in size and her total population is less than that of New York City.

But although the Austro-Hungarian Empire is no longer the gigantic hodge-podge of nations it once was, Austria herself still lives and there is a unique feeling, in this little land, of glories of the past that never leaves you.

Vienna, for instance, once the capital of the empire, still retains the charms of yesteryear and there are few cities in the world more charming, more beautiful, more gay. And Vienna, despite the smallness of the country today is the 22nd largest city in the world with a population pushing two million. It is the great metropolis of Central Europe.

But Vienna isn't Austria, no matter how proud the Austrians may be of their capital. Austria, despite size, packs a great deal of wallop into her countryside. In the western provinces such as Vorarlberg and the Tyrol, we have Alpine grandeur equal to that of Switzerland, and the winter sports enthusiasts are as keen about this area as they are any place in the world. Salzburg, on the German border, noted for its music festivals and as the birthplace of Mozart, is proclaimed by many to be the most beautiful example of Germanic medieval city remaining in Europe. And Innsbruck, another age-old town, is in the most striking mountain setting I have ever seen.

But listing interesting and lovely Austrian cities could take several pages and we have space limitation. We should also touch on the Austrian countryside, because if the Austrians themselves are to be considered judges of the outstanding qualities of their land, it is the countryside that is above all appealing. I have never seen a people so prone to take off at the least sign of a gleam of sunshine and go hiking, driving, picnicking, bicycling, canoeing, and mountain climbing as the Austrians. I seriously estimate that at least one million people stream out of the city and head for the forests, rivers, mountains and fields. You've never seen anything like it. Hundreds of thousands of them will be wearing *lederhosen* (short leather pants) and carrying knapsacks on their backs.

They are a people devoted to the outdoors and there is no wonder in this since the Austrian outdoors are surpassed nowhere. I believe that one of the strongest memories I shall always have was a picnic I went on with an Austrian couple one unblemished July day. We drove from Vienna to Mariazell, a small town to which yearly are made pilgrimages. Nearby a towering mountain's peak can be reached by a cable-lift (a startling experience in itself). On the very top we spread our lunch and ate and drank our Gumpoldskirchner wine, while looking out over what must have been the greater part of Austria.

This book is by no means a travel guide, but in dealing with Austria I must certainly mention the fact that if you are a good food fan, then Austria is a land you will love and Vienna a city you will adore. Austrian restaurant prices are a fraction of those of France or Italy and by the very cosmopolitan nature of Austria's capital, the variety of dishes is endless. The specialties of those lands once contained within the Austro-Hungarian Empire are also specialties of Austria so you can run the gamut from Germanic sausages to Italian pastas, from Hungarian goulash to Czech roast goose, or Yugoslav *brodet*. And I must add a personal note; as a beer drinker from way back, I have never found a beer I liked better than the Viennese Schwechater *dunkle* (dark).

If retirement on a shoestring is your desire, if you wish to find a beauty spot in which to settle down, permanently or semi-per-manently, you have few better bets than Austria. If I were to list in order the cheapest countries in

Europe it would probably go: Spain, Greece, Austria, Portugal, Ireland, Norway. But if I had to list them by compatibility of the people it would be: Austria, Ireland, Norway, Spain, Greece, Portugal. Because there is one important thing Austria has which the other economical countries haven't to nearly as great a degree. She has a people that you will get to know, who will be your equals (if not superiors) in education, culture and progressiveness. In short, you will love the Austrians. Everyone does.

There is just one word of warning. Personally, I like to follow the sun and I haven't spent a winter in a northern climate for some years. Summers, yes, winters, no. Austria is a country as famed for its winters as it is for its summers. If you like the change in season, wonderful. If you like winter weather, swell. But if you don't, stay out of Austria because she has winter and lots of it. The warm months are from the middle of May to the middle of September.

§

ENTRY REQUIREMENTS. Americans need only a passport to enter Austria. Theoretically, if you wish to stay more than three months, you should have an Austrian visa which you can pick up at any Austrian Embassy or Consulate, either in the States or abroad. I say theoretically because a few years ago I spent six months living near Vienna without knowing about this regulation. When I left, nobody blinked an eye. In fact, one of the great charms about Austria is this easy going slackness of her officials. At the border, when you enter the country, customs inspection usually amounts to a natty, green garbed customs officer sticking his head into your train compartment, saying happily, "Welcome to Austria!" and then leaving.

TRANSPORTATION. Austria has no seacoast so reaching her is a matter of travel by land or air. In either case you'll have no difficulty.

From New York to Vienna the following airlines have direct flights: Air France, BO AC (British Overseas Airways), KLM (Royal Dutch), SABENA (Belgian), Scandinavian Airlines, Swiss Airways, and Linee Aeree

Italiane. Or from our west coast you can take a Scandinavian Airlines or KLM plane over the pole. On the New York to Vienna run all airlines charge the same; $1272.70 first class, $554.80 tourist class, one way.

You could beat this price by coming by sea at a rockbottom low of $355 on a student ship and then taking a British European Airways (BEA) flight from London to Vienna for $170.60.

Cheaper still would be to take a student ship to Rotterdam, or one of the French ports and taking a train to Austria. The train from London to Vienna costs $102.88, first class, or $60.35 second class. Nothing, of course, is wrong about taking second class on a European train. Only millionaires, movie stars, and suckers ride first class. From Cherbourg to Vienna is $48.05 second class. From Rotterdam to Vienna is $39.91. If you come up from the south the cost of train fare from Rome to Vienna is $80.00 second class.

Driving your own car, scooter or motorcycle in Austria couldn't be simpler. Your American (or Canadian) driver's license is good and your regular registration papers are all that is needed to take your car across the border. On top of this, Austria has the cheapest gasoline in Europe. Which still isn't cheap by our standards, about $5 a gallon.

As I write this the Austrians are nearing completion of a super-highway which will run from Vienna to Salzburg and eventually to the Swiss border, so I understand. But even without this super-dooper highway, the roads aren't too bad in Austria *if you don't get off the main highways.* If you are driving an American type car, I can't recommend that you take the narrow, winding, mountain roads. They were built for European sized vehicles. Service stations are plentiful and you can get free road maps through the Austrian State Tourist Dept, 11 East 52nd Street, N.Y.C.

§

THE AUSTRIANS. Theoretically the Austrians are a branch of the Germans. The name of their country means "Eastern Germany." However, in spite of the fact that the language has no differences, Austrians and Germans are nearly as different as Greeks and Norwegians.

It's a matter of *gemuetlichkeit.* It's a matter of an easy going, kindly, friendly, gay approach to life. You find little grimness among the Austrians. They love life, nature, good food, good drink, good companionship. They're in no hurry, either to get rich or to get to whatever destination they might have at the time.

An Austrian from Vienna, in short, would drive a good Prussian resident of Berlin, stark raving; and vice versa.

Just one thing. Tipping. I have never seen such a tip-conscious people. Everybody tips everybody. I have a theory that in the old days, the Emperor used to tip the kings and princes under him. They in turn tipped the dukes, barons, counts (and no-accounts) under them. Who in turn tipped the businessmen and shopkeepers. Who in turn tipped the waiters, hotel employees and such. Who in turn tipped everyone with whom they dealt. But whether or not this was the way it was in the old days, that's the way it is today. Perhaps it all works out the same in the end for the Austrians. You tip and get tipped. At the end of the day you're even. But for a foreigner in the country all I can say is keep a big pocketful of change and don't forget such folk as streetcar conductors, the mail man, the shop girl, the service station attendant and the theatre usher.

§

MONEY. The Austrian shilling is now quite hard. The official rate is 25.44 to the dollar while on the free markets of New York or Switzerland you can get 29.90 at this writing. This advantage is hardly enough to bother with unless you are dealing in rather large amounts. That is, if you decided to buy a fifty thousand dollar home in Austria it would be well worth your while to stop off in Switzerland where you would get an extra 46 grochen for each dollar, or, on $5,000 an extra $92.

It is now quite legal to bring unlimited amounts of shillings into the country so no law would be broken by such importation. You are also allowed to bring as much foreign money into the country as you wish, but are only allowed to take 10,000 shillings out of Austria on your departure.

One hundred grochen makes one shilling and one shilling is worth just about 60 in American money. Coins come in 1,

2, 5, 10, 20 and 50 grochen denominations and 1, 2, 5, and 25 shillings. Paper money starts with a 10 shillings note and there are 20, 50, 100, 500 and 1,000 notes as well.

WORK PERMISSION. It is fairly easy to get permission to work in Austria. Tens of thousands of the Hungarians who fled Budapest during the revolt against the Russians are now working. However, a permit *is* needed and there is a special government agency that handles them and also acts as an employment bureau of sorts. At the time this is being written changes are being made in this governmental department and whatever I might say in the way of details will probably be antiquated by the time you read this book. Consequently, I suggest you *get* in touch with the new bureau either through the American Embassy in Vienna or through the Austrian Embassy, Washington, D.C.

PRICES. Just a few years ago, Austria boasted itself to be the cheapest country in Europe. Whether it was so then, I don't know, but today she is still economical but higher priced than Spain and Greece.

However, this book is not particularly interested in tourists and the scalping they get almost everywhere they go. Except for a few days during which you get orientated, you should be able to avoid this way of life. Austria is still cheap, off the tourist routes. Even Spain is expensive if you stick to them.

I have, for instance, before me the summer 1988 hotel price list for Austria. I find that the Bristol Hotel in down town Vienna prices a single room with bath at from 1800 to 2500 shillings a night ($70.20 to $100). Plus fifteen percent service charge, plus a 40 shilling tax. However, I also find that in some of the resort towns in Burgenland, a few miles south of Vienna, you can still get full pension for as low as 350 shillings a day. That is, room and three meals, for $40 a day.

Burgenland is the cheapest section of Austria and comparatively untouched by the tourists. But even in such swank tourist cities as Innsbruck the *Gashof Zum schwarzen Adler* offers full pension for 160 shillings a day ($20.40). And right in Vienna the *Strandheltel Alte Donau* has full pension for $20.80 a day.

Actually, living in a pension might be your best bet in Austria. For one thing there is no land where the pension is so comfortably established an institution. In fact, there is a certain amount of social prestige connected with such life —the only place I know of that this is true. Certainly pension and hotel food in Austria are about as good as you will discover. In city after city you will find that the best restaurants in town are in the hotels.

Rents in general are high. Austria suffered in the war and particularly Vienna which was bombed badly by the Americans and British and then shelled during the Russian conquest of the city. Besides that, Austria accepted many refugees from Germany, Yugoslavia and now Hungary, more than her poor economy could really afford.

Nevertheless, my wife and I stayed in the Vienna area in early 1987 and when the heat of the summer came on decided to take a small place right on the Danube River. We found one 18 miles north of the city in the picturesque town of Langenlebarn, near Tulln. We had two rooms, one very large, one smallish, and an extensive garden and shared the bath. The price was $580 a month. We probably could have beaten this price had we taken the little apartment out of season, or if we had located in a town more remote from the desirable swimming.

To get a rather nice apartment in Vienna itself will cost you about $575. They are available through the usual real estate agencies. You pay the agent his commission, by the way, not the landlord. In the country or in the smaller towns and cities you should be able to find a small house for from $600 a month and up. Food prices are lower than in the States but not as greatly so as in Spain or Greece. Fruits are high, especially those imported from Italy and other more southern nations. Venison, surprisingly enough, is one of the cheaper meats, cheaper than beef. Vegetables are low in price, *in season,* however, in the winter months you are more or less limited to cabbage, onions and potatoes unless you want to pay scandulous prices. A maid will cost you about $160 to $200 a month. Public transportation is cheap, either train or bus; when last I was in Vienna street car fares were but $4.00.

§

PARTICULARLY RECOMMENDED LOCALITIES.
Largely, Austria can be divided into the mountainous west and south and the plains near Vienna to the east. And you'd have to be a hardened traveler indeed not to love both sections.

I'm hard put, actually, to point out one of the myriad cities of the western part of the country and claim it as my favorite. There are so many. But if I had to settle in one town in this region I suppose it would be Salzburg. This "City of salt" is so old that its origins are lost in the mists of antiquity. It is known that in the 4th Century B.C. the Celts settled down in the region to work the salt mines but it was not until the coming of the Romans in 16 B.C. that we have historical records. Under the Romans the town grew, since it is a crossroads.

There are still Roman ruins to be seen in the vicinity but Salzburg as we know it today was built in the Middle Ages and during the Renaissance. In the second half of the 13th century the area was constituted an independent ecclesiastical state and the bishops of Salzburg became so powerful that often they even tried to influence the election of Emperor and Pope.

Today the old town is one of the best examples of German Medieval architecture to be found in Europe. The Fortress Hohensalzburg which dominates the hill around which the town is built, is probably the best example of fortress-castle remaining intact. An enormous building, a small town in itself, hundreds of thousands of visitors enter it yearly. Within its walls is an art school and scores of students work and live there.

One of the great advantages of Salzburg is that is is so easily available to the west Austrian centers and even to such German centers as Munich and Berchtesgaden, Hitler's former home, which is only a few miles away. Italy is about a hundred miles to the south.

If you choose Salzburg as your town in which to sojourn, I would suggest that if you're on a budget that you first locate some pension such as the *Park-Pension Kasern* where full pension starts at $35.80 a day. This price can be beaten if you shop around. In fact, the Weismayr (Ignaz-Hartl Sta. 2) charges about half that amount and there are others just as cheap. If there is any question about finding a place, go to the room service booth at the railroad station and state your wants, and the amount of money you wish to pay. If you are on a *real* shoestring, they will even find you a room in a private home.

Once so located, you can embark on an apartment search, preferably in the Old Town for the sake of its atmosphere. A single person, living with care, could do very well on six hundred a month in Salzburg, a couple on $800. These prices could be beaten. I've met young Americans who were doing it on about $600 but they were admittedly cutting all possible corners.

But actually, my favorite section of Austria is that area immediately above Vienna on the Danube. There are a series of towns and small cities between Vienna and the German border that have an old-Austria charm that must be seen to be fully appreciated. Krems, Durnstein, Melk, Pochlarn, Ybbs, and finally Linz, and then after a spectacular stretch into hills and mountains, Passau, right across the German frontier.

A trip through this area by river boat is one of the outstanding experiences to be enjoyed in Europe. The Rhine is noted for its castles, perched up on the hill tops, but the Rhine is so commercialized that much of the enjoyment is lost. The Danube, on the other hand, has as many castles on its hilltops and the only industrial town is Linz. Otherwise, it is a matter of vineyards and ancient villages, complete with their walls, their cobblestoned streets, their Middle-Ages churches and palaces.

I think I shall never forget going to the old-old town of Durnstein which produces one of the most famous Austrian wines, in harvest season. I spent two nights wandering around the old town and up to the ruins of the castle, perched on the hilltop. It was in this castle that Richard the Lion Hearted was imprisoned for a year on his way home from the Holy Land. It was here that his faithful retainer, Blondel, disguised as a troubadour, finally located his king and made arrangements for the ransom.

In the early morning I left Durnstein and started off on foot for Krems, a larger city a few miles along the river in the direction of Vienna. The workers were already out in the fields, picking the grapes that would be squeezed to produce the area's white wine. They carried great wooden containers of them on their shoulders to the gigantic wine presses and the smell of grapes and fermentation were everywhere in the air.

One of the great advantages of retiring or sojourning in this area is the nearness of Vienna. Fast trains dash to the capital city so that many Austrians live as far away as Krems and commute. You, of course, would be able to go into the larger city for the sake of shopping and the cultural and entertainment facilities whenever you wished, but live in the quieter atmosphere of the smaller towns and enjoy the economy of living.

If you consider this area, the Wachau, they call it, I would recommend Krems as a large town, Durnstein as a smaller one. If you wished to be still nearer to Vienna, Tulln is about 20 miles out and Klosterneuburg, so close to Vienna proper that you can take Vienna buses into city center.

CASE HISTORY NO. 1. This case history is such a good one that it can be applied to any section of the world where tourists come in large numbers. No work permit is needed and practically no capital expenditure is required. Of all the "schemes" listed in this volume to make a good income with a minimum of effort, I think this one of the best. Age, sex, special training, schooling— none of these are needed. In short, *anybody* could do this one. Nor need you be abroad, any tourist town such as New Orleans, San Francisco or Taos would do. And as of this writing you have no competition except Ferdinand Ziegler who dreamed it up.

I met Ferd in Vienna. I had just pulled into town the day before and was staying at the Kaiserin Elisabeth Hotel until I could find a less expensive, more permanent arrangement.

One of the problems I always have in checking into a hotel is met when I'm confronted with the line asking for my "home" address. I have had so many homes in so many towns that I always pause. But in Vienna I put Taos, New Mexico, the last place I had owned property.

In the morning the phone rang and a strange voice said, "Mr. Belmont?"

"That's me," I said.

"My name in Ziegler, I represent a news photo service and would like to take your picture for the Taos, *El Crepusculo.*"

Now the Taos weekly is not exactly the size newspaper you would expect to have a photographer representing in a city as far away as Vienna. I was intrigued. We made an appointment to meet in the gardens of the Hofburg, the palace of the Hapsburgs, at one o'clock. I certainly had nothing to lose.

When I arrived to keep the date, I found Ferd Ziegler photographing two obvious American tourists. I stood there for a time while he snapped them, using the palace entrance as a background. Then he stepped closer and got the correct spelling of their names, the address of their home, and the gentleman's profession. Thanked them, shook their hands, told the woman that, no, he was sorry but he had no way of getting some prints to her, even at a price, and then they were gone.

I stepped up and introduced myself. He looked at his notebook. Oh, yes.

He posed me, snapped two shots with his Nikon, and then asked me the same questions he had asked the tourists. I became more intrigued by the minute and suggested we go to a coffee house and have a cup of the famous Viennese *Kaffee mit Schlag* (coffee with whipped cream). He checked his notebook, evidently to see when his next appointment came up, and agreed.

This was what he told me.

When Ferd was getting ready to make a tourist trip to Europe he ran into an old friend in his home town of

Cincinnati who worked on the Cincinnati *Enquirer*. In fact, was one of the editors. They shot the breeze for a time and the editor told Ferd that if he wanted to pick up a few bucks he might do them a favor. If Ferd ran into anyone in Europe from Cincinnati and snapped their picture and sent it to the newspaper, the paper would gladly pay five dollars per photograph which they would run on the society page. Ferd said, sure, it sounded like a good idea, but then forgot about it.

But Ferd liked Europe, liked being away from the grind of his old job, and when he began to run short of money, started searching around for a means of making a living abroad. It was then that the editor's suggestion came back to him.

The trouble was, how did one go about finding tourists from Cincinnati? But then he realized that the situation applied not only to Cincinnati but to every city or town of America that supported a newspaper large enough to be able to afford to buy photographs. He amended that idea later, to exclude the ten largest cities of the country which have so many people abroad at any one time that it no longer is news.

But any city the size of Cincinnati or smaller is anxious to get photos of their citizens in far places. And Ferd found that they will pay anywhere from two to fifteen dollars for such shots, with an average of about five dollars.

It took him awhile to work out the details, but not long. He got a list of every daily and weekly newspaper in the United States from one of the press associations, bought a supply of film for his Nikon.

He started, actually, in Paris, worked there for a time and then went to Munich. I forget the other cities in which he spent time, but the routine was always the same. He would find out which were the most popular American tourist hotels and each morning check with them on what new Americans had registered. The hotels were glad to cooperate because he let them know that he always included the name of the hotel in his captions for the newspapers. This, of course, was free advertising which no hotel spurns.

He would get a complete list of the new Americans and then get on the phone. Actually, in the larger cities there were more names than he could possibly contact, he just didn't have the time. He would look up the town from which the prospect came, get the name of the local newspaper and then phone asking for an appointment to take a photo for the tourist's home town newspaper. Few tourists will refuse such a request. Very few.

He would make appointments at some locally famous spot such as the Eiffel Tower in Paris, or the Hofbrauhaus in Munich and ask all his tourists to come there. He would snap their photos, taking two shots to be sure at least one came out nicely, and then get the correct spelling of their names, their business, and their home address.

When the negatives were developed he would send them with a short covering letter to the newspaper. The letter would say simply:

"Enclosed, please find a photograph of Dr. and Mrs. John Jones, of 125 Doe Street, your city, who are now enjoying a European vacation. They're pictured standing before the famous Eiffel Tower in Paris. Dr. and Mrs. Jones are staying at the Ritz Hotel. Upon leaving Paris they intend to go to Rome."

"I submit these negatives at your standard rates for photographs. In payment your regular check will be sufficient.—signed, Ferdinand Zeigler."

Ferd said his average was five dollars for a photo and he sold approximately two out of every three submitted. On the days he worked, he took between ten and twenty photos. His expenses were negligible: the film, cost of phone calls, stationery and postage. At first he had sent finished photos but these were so expensive that he hit upon sending the negative instead. Newspapers have facilities to print negatives the proper size for their needs.

On the days he worked he netted from $150 to $200 on an average. If he wanted he could work seven days a week. He couldn't remember how much he made on his best day but estimated it was probably about $600. On quite a few occasions he had made over $1000 in one day.

Ferd was not particularly interested in making a great deal of money and wasn't even thinking of this as a full time proposition. He was merely using it until he had seen as much of Europe as he wanted, and then he intended to return home. He had once considered hiring a couple of photographers and branching out. In this manner he would have spent more time on the telephone making contacts, and let his local men do the leg work. But he decided that such tactics would wind up with him in a rut as bad as the one he had left at home. Besides he didn't want to settle down for a long time in any one city.

I asked him if after a time he wouldn't so flood the American market that the editors wouldn't want his photos any longer but he shook his head and laughed. They begged for them. There are thousands of daily and large weekly newspapers in the smaller towns that have a difficult time getting photos of any news significance and in a small town or city one of the local citizens going abroad is always news, especially for papers large enough to have a society section.

Could you do this? If you couldn't, male or female, 21 years of age, or 71 years of age, you might as well close this book and go down to the local super-market and apply for a job putting cans on the shelves, because I can think of nothing easier, nothing needing less capital, less training, and even less ability than this.

§

CASE HISTORY No. 2. On a trip I took into Czechoslavakia several years ago I ran into a young American from Boston who was rapidly getting rich in spite of himself.

1*11 call him David Johnson, which isn't his name but he's still practicing the following system of taking advantage of communism, Czech style, and if this got back to the Prague authorities they might attempt to put a damper on Dave's activities.

Dave was spending some time in Vienna, enjoying the opera and devoting a large part of his days to such famous museums as the *Kunsthistorisches.* Between these activities he was also not adverse to spending an evening in Grinzing at a *heuriger* drinking the new wine; at least so I suppose from his activities in Prague in the beer halls drinking Pilsen beer. Dave was no long hair.

As a change he decided to go up to Prague and made arrangement through one of the tourist agencies. It was a bit complicated because to get into Czechoslovakia you have to buy in advance with dollars, your hotel and restaurant tickets as well as all of your transportation. Through Cedok, the State tourist office, you are then allowed to buy Czech crowns to the amount of twice the amount of dollars you spent on your hotel and restaurants tickets.

That is, suppose you make a trip to Prague and intend to stay three days. Your hotel and restaurant tickets, second class, will cost you $50 per day, or a total of $150. You can then go to *Cedok* and buy *$80 worth of crowns* (the Czech currency) at the tourist rate. With crowns bought at this rate some of the shopping bargains in Prague are amazing.

So Dave signed up for a five day trip to Prague and took off.

When he arrived he did the usual tourist tours and then began wandering around in the smaller shops. Now Dave's mother had once operated an antique shop in New England and some of her knowledge, not a great deal, had worn off on Dave. He began with even this scanty knowledge to realize that he was seeing some impossible bargains.

He had planned to stay five days, which meant he was allowed to buy $200 worth of tourist rate crowns. He took this amount and purchased all he could, including a Rembrandt etching although he couldn't believe in the authenticity of this.

He was nervous about getting his loot back into Austria but it turned out he had no cause to be. The crack Vindobona Express, which plies between East Berlin and Vienna, touching at Prague on the way, was filled with tourists, Iron Curtain Army officers and bureaucrats, and the border inspection was brief. (In fact, on some trips his bags were not even opened). This time they were, however, and Dave felt his heart sink when the customs inspector looked over his recently purchased treasures. However, the Czechs are currently pleased to have American dollars spent within their borders and there was no comment.

Back in Vienna, Dave took his purchases to art dealers, keeping one or two which he wished to take back home with him when his vacation was over. The Rembrandt print went for 15,000 shillings (about $600) which still makes Dave mad when he thinks about it, because he was robbed.

This was too good to be true. Dave applied for another visa to go back to Prague and then began to bone up on antiques, first edition books and etchings. He also tried to find out a way in which he could get more money into Prague for his purchases. One of the antique dealers came to his assistance here. Dave could buy antique gold in Vienna and take it into Czechoslavakia with him. Then in Prague he could sell the old gold for from two to three times what he'd paid for it in

Austria. No laws, either Austrian or Czech, were broken by this bit of international financial gobbledygook.

On his next trip to Prague Dave took some of his books along. He had had his mother send him some from Massachusetts. He also took a couple of hundred dollars worth of second hand gold jewelry. Sure enough, he was able to sell it for old gold at a jewelry shop.

This time he made a cleaning, finding several books of considerable value back home, quite a few prints at rock bottom prices and even an oil by one of the minor Flemish painters. The profit he realized when he returned to Vienna astounded him.

Dave had figured out why he was able to find these fabulous bargains. Many, many of the formerly wealthy in Czechoslovakia had found themselves displaced when the communists took over. Some of them fled the country, some adapted themselves as best they could. Few of them could afford to retain the family art possessions. As a result these things were sold for the best they would bring which wasn't much since everyone else in the country was in the same position. First edition books, old prints, ceramics, antiques, all of considerable value, were going for a pittance. Dave even found a small statue by Rodin in a Prague shop and was able to buy it for peanuts.

After a time he stopped selling his findings to the Vienna art dealers and began marketing them himself through the various publications in the States specializing in the arts and antiquities and sometimes through personal contacts in Vienna among Americans and other tourists. In fact, Dave was rapidly getting a name among art collectors as a man to contact upon arriving in Vienna.

When I met Dave, in Prague, he told me that he currently had a stock worth somewhere more than $50,000. He was considering opening a shop of his own and employing some art conscious Austrian to work for him while he continued to study up on such art fields as he must know to recognize a bargain when he saw one. He was looking forward to extending his tours behind the Iron Curtain into whatever other lands would allow him to acquire local arts and antiquities. Russia, he understood, was out since they wouldn't allow you to take art objects from the country, but he was investigating Rumania and Bulgaria.

§

CASE HISTORY No. 3. The best local guide of its type I have seen in Europe is that of Dorothy McGuigan who puts out a hard cover book entitled *Vienna Today* and sells it for about $3.75 on every newsstand and in every book shop of Vienna. It's a beautiful job and a new edition is published each year. A tourist in Vienna would be foolish not to buy a copy his first day in town.

I have covered other guides in this book so will not go into detail with Miss McGuigan's other than to mention the items in which she differs from Trimm's Guide to Majorca and Art Buchwald's Paris After Dark.

For one thing, this is a book rather than a pamphlet and the charge is consequently higher. It is also more thorough than any of the others, containing in all 225 pages of text and illustrations and then, in the back, a supplement of more than fifty pages of ads. Yes, I said fifty pages. Every tourist business in town seems anxious to get into Dorothy McGuigan's book, some of them even run full page ads in color.

There's no mystery why they want into the ad section of her book since it makes no bones about writing up in the text those restaurants, hotels, shops, nightclubs and other businesses that advertise with her. I have a sneaking suspicion that the rates she charges aren't particularly low. Certainly they shouldn't be because she really delivers in circulation among the high spending American tourists.

I would estimate that it costs Dorothy McGuigan something less than $400 to print Vienna Today. And the ads alone must total up to several thousand dollars. She had been bringing out new editions yearly since 1981, and each year, of course, the advertisers must renew.

It looks like a gold mine to me and why this isn't being done in more tourist cities is a mystery. Athens for one, Madrid for another, Lisbon for another, Copenhagen for another, Amsterdam, Brussels, Nice, Monte Carlo. There are a multitude of tourist cities where it would go over with a bang.

For further information check what I've said on guides under the chapters devoted to Spain and France.

§

CASE HISTORY No. 4. Somewhere in these chapters devoted to Europe I've wanted to touch upon the growth of the motel in Europe. I've heard of several Americans who have opened these establishments but know none personally so I'll have to treat the subject in a general way.

As an example I might as well mention Austria's first motel which was opened in 1985 on Austrian Federal Highway No. 1 at

Kilometer Stone No. 599 which is near Frastanz, which is near Feldkirch, which is in the province of Vorarlberg and right near the Swiss and Liechenstein borders. Highway No. 1 is the best road crossing Austria east and west.

The Motel Galina is rated as an "A" type hotel, just one grade below DeLuxe. It has 86 beds, in all, and 28 private baths and you pay 200 to 400 shillings for a single with bath, or 120 to 150 shillings for a double with bath. Service charge is 15% but there are no other extras.

I use the Galina just as an example. The motel is coming to Europe. You begin to see them in all countries which have a considerable automobile traffic, and that includes all of Western Europe, with the possible exception of Portugal. I don't recall ever seeing a motel in Portugal.

But they are being built *slowly* because the idea is new to Europeans. Actually, even auto transport is new to Europe to any real extent. It has only been since the end of the Second World War that the average man has even dreamed of owning a car. But now every year that passes sees new hordes of tourists in automobiles. Parking problems are as real today in many European cities as they are in New York or Los Angeles. Service stations are going up everywhere and even in comparatively backward countries such as Spain, a drive-in movie house is being built near Madrid.

One great advantage in building a motel in Europe is the relative cheapness of labor. Motels in the States now cost a fortune to erect. But in Europe? Ah, that's another matter.

Nor need the project be as swank as American tourists now demand. Housing is short in Europe and the tourist is often hard pressed to find a place at night. A motel could be fairly simple by American standards and still find itself filled each night.

An American with a bit of capital, say as little as fifty to seventy thousand dollars, could probably go into the motel business in various European countries. As I've already said, I'm not really up on the requirements, not having been able to talk to any of the various Americans who have opened such establishments. Further information on national laws could be obtained from the consulates of whatever nations interest you.

CHAPTER 13 GREAT BRITAIN

In a Nutshell. Great Britain, including Northern Ireland, has a land area of but 94,212 square miles but a population of over 50 million. This means she is about the size of our Wyoming or Oregon but runs neck and neck with Western Germany in having the largest population in Europe save the Soviet Union.

It's been said over and over that the reason the British are the greatest colonizers the world has ever seen is because they have such a terrible climate that they flee abroad. And actually I'm not going to argue the point. The only place I've lived with so much rain is Portland, Oregon.

Be that as it may, England still has its gracious beauty. Largely manmade, but nature does her share too. So much rain could only result in a fabulously green and beflowered countryside, and so it is.

But in man-made sights, England cannot be surpassed. Her buildings go back to prehistory. The famed Stonehenge was built long centuries ago, before the coming of the Romans in 41 B.C. Roman ruins are here, there and the other place and such early Briton ones as Tintagel in Cornwall, reputedly the place where King Arthur was born. It was with the coming of the Normans in 1066 A.D. that the castles which are England's glory began to be erected. Today there are so many of these that the British Travel Association puts out a special booklet for tourists entitled Castles In Britain which lists 48 of the best preserved. With the discovery of the New World, England's empire began to grow and with it an enormous wealth was put into the cities, towns and villages of England. Cathedrals, palaces, government buildings, churches, fortresses—and the most picturesque pubs in the world. It would be hard, in Great

Britain, to be able to get more than a mile or two away from some worthwhile sight.

London, until just recently, was the biggest city in the world and

195

for long years had carried this distinction. Tokyo is now larger, in population, but in many respects London is still the most important city on earth. This is not because of the number of her inhabitants but due to the fact that through this great sprawling city for centuries the biggest Empire the world has even seen was governed. As a result the British museum is the greatest library in the world. St. Paul's possibly the greatest cathedral, *The City* is the greatest banking and commercial center of the world (with the possible exception of Wall Street) and Lloyd's of London which is in The City is the largest insurance network. We could go on adding to this list indefinitely but to what end? Everyone knows of the grandness of London.

In many respects, England is the ideal place for an American to retire. The language advantages are obvious and no country offers so much in the way of entertainment, cultural activities and opportunities to pursue a study of almost any subject as does England. Plays, movies, radio and TV must remain a mystery to us in France, Italy or Spain until we learn the language. But in England all these are immediately ours to enjoy.

Nor is England one of the expensive nations of Europe. London, unfortunately is high, particularly in rents, but otherwise England is one of the cheaper countries. Except for tobacco and alcoholic beverages which are taxed tremendously. In fact, the foreigner residing in England is even eligible for many of the socialized medicine advantages.

§

ENTRY REQUIREMENTS. England, like our own country, is one of the toughest nations to enter. Elsewhere in the world, you get a token inspection of your luggage by customs and a quick stamp in your passport and you're through. But in England they definitely inspect your luggage and an immigration official questions you on your reason for your trip. Simply tell them "tourist" and that's enough.

Another hazard. They'll ask you how much money you have with you. If it seems too small an amount, say less than $500, they simply won't let you in. England has no desire to have you on her hands broke. Of course, you aren't bodily searched. The contents of your wallet are never examined. So you can tell them any amount you wish, and they accept your word—unless you're a down and out looking tramp, I suppose.

When you enter your passport will be stamped: Permitted to land at Dover (or whatever your entry port) on condition the holder does not remain in the United Kingdom longer than two months and does not enter any employment paid or unpaid. Sometimes the time limit will read three rather than two months.

This puts you in a spot if you had looking for work in mind. Even if you do find a British firm that wants to hire you, the Ministry of Labor can refuse you a work permit simply on the grounds that you shouldn't have been looking for work in the first place. However, they aren't always as tough as all that.

TRANSPORTATION. All the great airliners of the world serve London. In fact, the gigantic new London airport handles 90,000 flights a year. As I write this, there is discussion of fares being reduced but right now First class, New York to London is $800 one way, $1200 round trip. Tourist class is $490 one way and $822 round trip. The new Economy class is $753.60 round trip.

Cheaper still, as we've mentioned elsewhere in this book, are the Icelandic Airlines flights which run, at this writing $524.20 round trip in the thrift season ($100 more in the summer). Icelandic has always cut prices and now that the other airlines have introduced the economy class it is expected Icelandic will cut their rates even further. It's worth checking. Their U.S. offices are at 15 West 47th Street in New York City.

Ships to England are as numerous as to any land in the world. It would take the balance of this page and most of the next to begin to list them. Consult your travel agency. Fares run from $355 on the student ships sponsored by the Netherlands and Swiss governments to astronomical figures First class on the Cunard Queens and the other top liners. Basically you can figure on a minimum of $375 tourist class on a liner but are more apt to be paying just about as much as you would going by air unless you wish to sleep in dormitories.

Trains within England are a bit on the grim side. Fares aren't high by our standards, but equipment is largely antiquated and usually dirty. There is a new project to modernize the British railroads which will cost a billion dollars before they're through but it's going to take several years to complete.

England's buses charge only l1/2 a mile but although this is a better way of seeing the countryside than by train, the buses aren't much better than trains as far as being modern and comfortable is concerned.

To see rural England best you should do it either by car or bicycle, if possible. Driving, as you know, is to the left, passing on the right. The principal highways are good, although traffic is getting too heavy for the facilities and trucks in particular are everywhere and just as objectionable in England as they are at home. The Esso gasoline company distributes a good free road map and there are ample service stations and garages. Renting a car in England is as practical as anywhere in the world. Even in season you pay only $25.50 a day plus .20 a mile. If you take a car by the week it comes to $95 with unlimited mileage, and including everything except gas and garage.

§

THE BRITISH. If you have in mind the classic cartoon character of an Englishman wearing a monocle, lacking in humor, and limiting his conversation to an occasional "By Jove"—forget about it. As far as physical appearance is concerned, the British look about the same as we do. Possibly they average a bit shorter in height. As far as a sense of humor is concerned, you'll find every type of humor in England, just as you will in our own land. And the one big advantage is that in England you can understand their jokes and they can understand yours.

You can find every type of Englishman, just as you can every type of American. Good, bad, indifferent. No, I take that back. There is one kind you'll never find; one that wears a monocle and says "By Jove."

The British people are good natured, hospitable, courteous, well disciplined, averagely handsome. And eat absolutely the worst food in the civilized world.

MONEY. British money is the most incomprehensible on earth. Who dreamed up their money system I haven't the vaguest idea but it makes no more sense than their weights and measures. (The English "foot" which is also used in America, was decided upon because it was the length of the king's foot some centuries ago.)

At any rate, $3.20 in American money makes one British pound.

A pound is divided into twenty shillings which in turn consists of 12 pennies.

Coins come in halfpenny, one penny, three pence, six pence, one shilling, two shillings, two shillings and six pence. And paper money comes in 10 shillings, one pound and five pound notes.

If the above doesn't confuse you, you'll find that many prices are listed in *guineas* which are worth a pound, one shilling. But there is no such coin or note as a guinea. They also call their two shilling six pence coin a Half Crown, but there is no such thing as a "Crown."

To top it off, all the coins are called by slang terms. A shilling is a "bob," a pound is a "quid ," sixpence is a "tanner," two shillings is a Florin.

Until recently it was illegal for a foreigner to bring more than ten pounds into England from abroad but the law has been changed and now you can import as much British money as you wish. However, the pound is currently strong in New York and Switzerland and you make no gain on the free market exchanges. You can also bring as many dollars or other foreign currency into the country as you wish.

§

WORK PERMISSION. As I mentioned under Entry Requirements, you are not allowed to work in Great Britain without a work permit. This is issued—sometimes—by the Ministry of Labour and National Service, St. James Square,

London, S.W.I. If you are either an immigrant or a student, such permission is quite readily granted. If you are neither, it can be difficult.

If the company for which you wish to work can prove to the government's satisfaction that an English citizen can't do the job, then you're in like Flynt. But if you're displacing an Englishman, you're out. For instance, Elizabeth Arden was able to employ a

U.S. "face dress specialist" but *Time* magazine had trouble hiring American secretaries.

However, we don't particularly recommend working in England at regular jobs anyway. The pay is miserable and working conditions far below American standards. Your best bet is either to work for an American firm, or the U.S. government, who pay off in dollars—or find some occupation which doesn't call for a work permit.

Rules and regulations change periodically and your best bet is to get hold of the current copy of the *Anglo American Year Book* which is published by the American Chamber of Commerce in London. There are copies available in the larger public libraries and in the offices of the British Information Service in New York, Chicago, Washington and San Francisco. This also gives you a run down on the addresses of the airlines, publications, banks, film companies, advertising agencies, manufacturing concerns, and others that have offices in both England and the U.S.

§

PRICES. London is one of the more expensive cities of Europe and Great Britain one of the cheapest countries.

That may sound a little foolish, but that's the way things are. Rentals, in London, are frightful when available at all. Things were bad enough before when rents were frozen, but in early 1988 the government withdrew the rent control laws and overnight prices began to rise. Time was granted in the new regulations but many, many Londoners find themselves unable to pay the new rentals and at this writing are seeking other accommodations.

You actually have the ridiculous situation now, of the average worker in London, say a stenographer, or a store clerk, not making enough wages to pay the rent on a small apartment. Where it will end, I don't know.

In the country it is another thing. The more remote you get, the cheaper you will find cottages and houses. In the smaller towns a cottage may often be rented for as little as $150 or $200 a month and a more elaborate house for, say, $400.

Tobacco and alcoholic beverages are highly taxed and even more expensive than in the States with the exception of beer which is still, however, high by European standards. But food is considerably cheaper than at home and of excellent quality. The best bacon you ever tasted goes at about $1.55 a pound and the ultra-famous British beef runs between $150 and $3 a pound according to the cut. Butter is about $1.50 a pound, vegetables, in season, very cheap. One thing you'll probably like in England is the fact that frozen food is seen more than in any country except our own. Canned goods are also more widely used than in most European countries although they aren't as cheap as at home.

Things like movies and theatres are low priced, compared to the U.S. You usually pay about $5.00 to go to a good movie and, if anything, you're more apt to see American films than British. A play will cost about $9.00 for a top notch seat at a top notch performance. In general, clothing is cheaper than in our own country and of excellent quality. One thing in this regard, however. If you are able to pay $150 or so for a suit, then the London tailors are the best in the world. But if you're looking for a suit that will cost half that, you'd better buy an American ready-to-wear which you'll find considerably better than a British suit in the same price range.

I would say, briefly, that if you had an income of $25,000 a year you could retire very comfortably in England, outside London. This would be for a couple, of course. You'd have to add another $5000 to this sum to do it in a large city. When I say comfortably I mean quite comfortably. On a scale that would cost at least two or three times as much in the States. The average British working-man makes possibly $15,000 a year, if that much, and he is considered to have one of the higher standards of living in Europe.

§

PARTICULARLY RECOMMENDED LOCATIONS. I suppose that if from the first we hadn't decided upon absolute honesty in this book, I could read up on some of the travel guides and tourist literature published by every country, and give you a second hand rundown on portions of England that I have never seen. But I'm not going to do that. I have gone by train and bus through a limited few sections of England, but actually I have never lived for any period of time in any location except London.

This wasn't due to any lack of curiosity on my part, nor a belief that the British countryside is less than attractive. It is simply that every time I go to England, with intentions of going into the interior, I get tied up in London which is a town I love. Something happens, and I never go beyond her city limits, or, at least, not very far beyond.

So I am going to limit this report to London as I find it.

I don't know about you, but personally I go on "kicks." That is I'll get onto some hobby or other, or some study, or some sport and ride it to death for a time. For instance, I once took a trip through Turkey and happened to see the Hittite museum in Ankara. I'd hardly heard about the Hittites before although I've always been an avid reader of history. Nothing would do but that I must go on a "Hittite kick." I went to the museums, I bought a few little Hittite seals and clay statues in the bazaars, I read every book I could find on this early civilization. The kick lasted for a few months and then something else came up—mountain climbing, I think.

At any rate, London is probably the ideal city in the world to go on a "kick." I don't care what your interest is, London will be able to supply you with opportunity to study it, go into it, enjoy it. There are the theatres, the museums, the libraries, the specialty •stores, the clubs and associations, the societies, to afford you anything from a close up study of spiritualism to skin diving. And I'm not exaggerating.

London, in short, has everything. The only other city I can think of that remotely approaches her is New York, but even New York fails in many respects to live up to London. It's true you can get just about anything, do just about anything in New York, if you have the money. In London, you can do it without a great deal of money. For instance, how would you like to foot the bill in New York for going to the current top ten theatre hits? Brother! But the last time I was in London I was able to accomplish this without strain at all. Sometimes my seats were no more than a dollar or so.

Even though you had no intention of living permanently in London I would say that every member of the English speaking world should spend some time in this capital. For, actually, London is the capital not only of Great Britain and the Commonwealth of

Nations, but is the cultural capital of English speaking people everywhere. At least that's my opinion and so I found her.

§

CASE HISTORY No. 1. One of my favorite people in Europe is Tedwell Chapman who used to work on movie scripts out in Hollywood. Never a really big name movie writer, perhaps, but Ted has had credit lines on several films that you'd recognize if I listed them here.

But the thing is that Hollywood is an ulcer factory. The pressures there are as bad as on Madison Avenue, New York, and finally it all caught up to Ted. He had a heart attack and the doctor laid it on the line. Ted Chapman was either going to get out of that pressure cooker, the movie industry, or the next attack might be the last.

So Ted dropped out of the only business he knew much about and headed for Europe. He'd written a play or two in his time and they were going to do a version of one of them in England.

It probably would have been easy enough for Ted to have got back into the same ratrace in London that he'd been in in Hollywood, but he was intelligent enough to avoid that. Even when his money began to run short and he was face to face with the problem of making a living.

Opportunity came in the shape of Peter Eton who at that time was connected with B.B.C., the British Broadcasting Corporation, the State owned radio and TV outfit which serves Great Britain. Eton is now affiliated with the ITA, the Independent Tevevision Association which is now bringing commercial programs to England, but at that time he had a lofty position in serving the British their daily air-borne entertainment.

Ted's easy job was to rewrite and correct scripts that dealt in any way with the United States.

Peter Eton was intelligent enough to realize that any English writer, no matter if he had lived in America himself for a time, just couldn't correctly reproduce American terminology and slang. An English writer, dealing with a New York taxi cab driver, usually has him talking like a cockney, rather than a resident of Brooklyn.

So to achieve authenticity every time a radio or TV script involved an American character, it was turned over to Ted. Ted went through it and made the necessary corrections. No trouble in getting a work permit, of course, because obviously no Englishman could do the job. The pay was good enough so that Ted could live quite adequately in London.

It was as simple as that.

Could you get such a job? Possibly not exactly such a position, unless you had connections and friends, but there are jobs of this type kicking around that more than one American has stumbled upon. There are many, many occasions when an American is needed, simply because he is an American. No one else will do.

I know of an 18 year old boy in Madrid, for instance, who acts as a courier taking business reports back and forth between New York and Spain. He works for an agency which makes economic reports on Spain for American concerns. Often these concerns want the material brought directly to them rather than trusting the mails. The 18 year old has no training whatsoever, but he has an American passport. He can get in and out of the United States without any difficulty, while getting in and out of our country poses a whole set of problems for a foreigner. So back and forth across the Atlantic our teenager flies, possibly as often as twice a week. On his expense account he stays at good hotels, eats in excellent restaurants. His salary, which is in dollars, is enough to keep him very well indeed.

I list Ted Chapman's case history and this one of the 18 year old not because I think you could get exactly the same sort of high paying easy job, they both enjoy, but just to list a couple of typical examples of positions Americans can find. What you might fall into might be even better, although on an average it's best not to depend upon falling into something. Definite preparation is always more sensible.

CASE HISTORY No. 2. Another good London friend of mine is Norman Snyder who used to drive a taxicab in New York while he was going to C.C.,N.Y., New York's king-sized city college. He studied education and upon graduation decided to take a look at

Europe before getting located at a standard teaching job in one of New York's schools.

He wasn't thinking in terms of teaching when he hit London, but he ran into an American who was working at a U.S. Air Base School, teaching the American children of U.S. servicemen based in England. They had just lost one of their teachers at the school and were short handed. Norman decided to take the position temporarily to build up his funds a bit.

The turnover in teachers seems to be high overseas, at any rate, before Norman knew it he was being offered the principal's job in the small school. It was too good to turn down and now Norman and his new wife, Pauline, who hails from Canada, are on a permanent basis.

What are the advantages of teaching in London rather than in the States? For one thing, Norman's pay is about $15,000 a year, if I'm not mistaken. But on top of this he gets a living allotment which adds nicely to his income and is able to buy through the Air Force PX which gives him State-side products, tax free, not to speak of such items as German cameras, tax free, French perfumes, tax free—and so forth. And teacher's vacations, of course, are lengthy ones. Norman and Pauline make a point of making a major trip, to Spain, to Italy, to Austria each year. Even during the Christmas vacation they have sufficient time to run over to Switzerland for a little skiing and such.

But above all Norman is living in England on an American income. A dollar will go considerably further in England than at home and Norman and Pauline enjoy a standard of living they couldn't have dreamed of in New York.

Could you get such a position?

The big requirement, of course, is that you be a qualified teacher. If you are there are literally hundreds of opportunities to get teaching jobs abroad, not only with the American armed forces but in many, many openings. So many, indeed that I couldn't list them all. However, following are some addresses where you can receive further information on teaching jobs abroad:

Inter-American Schools Service, 1785 Massachusetts Ave., Washington 6, D.C.

Recruitment Branch, Personnel Management Division, U.S. Information Agency, Washington 25, D.C.

Overseas Affairs Division, Office of Civilian Personnel, Department of the Army, Washington 25, D.C.

Director of Military Personnel, H.Q. U.S. Air Force, Washington 25, D.C.

Information and Education Section, Department of the Navy, Pentagon Building, Washington 25, D.C.

CASE HISTORY No. 3. From time to time I've mentioned in this book that personally I've seen a good deal of this world in the past few years at what amounts to no cost at all since I had more money at the end than I started with. Since this must sound almost unbelievable to some of my readers I might as well list here as one example of seeing the world, free of charge, that starts in England.

At no cost at all, except a dollar or two for insurance, you can take a cruise up into the Arctic Ocean, touching probably in Norway at some Artie port such as Vardo which is only a few miles from the Soviet border, and possibly in Iceland on the way back. The cruise will last two or three weeks and if you enjoy it greatly, you can take another one. In fact, you can keep taking them all spring and summer and into the fall. Indeed, if you wish, you can reverse your engines and take a really lengthy cruise down into Antarctic waters.

All for free.

What's the gimmick? Does this sound impossible?

In Grimsby, England, is one of the largest fishing ports in the world. Possibly the largest. In return for your doing odd jobs around the ship several of the trawler companies here will take you free, supplying you with food and berth of course, on one of their regular trips. You do not work hard. At least I didn't. You do have a fascinating trip into the Land of the Midnight Sun.

These trips into Arctic waters are very simple to arrange, but it is only occasionally that you can make arrangements to go on a whaler to the Antarctic and that trip takes several months. I didn't take one of these myself, but hear reports that the work is harder on the whalers and that you become weary of it all before the ship returns.

The Grimsby trawlers put out so often that you don't really need to make advance plans. If you simply go to Grimsby which is directly North of London and near the city of Hull, and apply to the Secretary of the Trawler Owner's Association Federation, at Fish Dock, he'll find you a berth within a day or two. But if you wish, write him in advance for further information. They'll send you a mimeographed leaflet giving all the dope. Address is simply: Fish Dock, Grimsby, England.

CASE HISTORY No. 4. I can't give you much on this one, because I'm not personally acquainted with Miss Joyce Wells, but recently I read an account of her business in London in a copy of *Mademoiselle* magazine.

Miss Wells sends two hundred thousand catalogues yearly to Americans, selling British goods in the States for American dollars.

Although I don't know the details of Miss Wells' operation I have met other Americans abroad who have worked out similar deals, although not on quite so big a scale.

British firms, of course, are glad to supply the catalogues. That's what catalogues are for, to be brought before the eyes of potential customers. Then the usual thing is to run ads in American publications, offering to send the catalogues free of charge. And business done with the people who respond to the ads goes through your hands and you get your cut.

Another way of handling it is to print up your own catalogue at your own expense, listing such British items (or Spanish ones in Spain, Greek ones in Greece, and so forth) as you feel would particularly appeal to Americans. Then when your orders come in, and not before, you acquire the objects desired.

American laws applying to such imports of foreign goods into the United States change every year as one tariff goes up, another down, and another is eliminated altogether. Check for the latest information with your local branch of the American Chamber of

Commerce. Or write to the U.S. Bureau of Customs, Washington, D.C. There is various red tape involved in this sort of business, and rather than list it here, with the danger that it might be out of date by the time you read this, I suggest you write them direct.

CHAPTER 14.
GREECE

IN A NUTSHELL. Today Greece is one of the smaller and less important nations of Europe. Her size is approximately that of Alabama even counting all of her islands and her population less than New York's. In a way it is hard to believe that this is the land from which sprang Western Civilization.

Mainland Greece is not, largely, one of the more attractive countries of the continent. The greater part of her land area is mountainous, rocky and colorless. There are exceptions, of course, many of them.

It is in her coasts and her islands that Greece achieves beauty, and I doubt if I've ever taken a more exciting trip by sea than those inter-island journeys that leave Piraeus, the port of Athens, for the Cyclades, the Dodecanese, Crete, Lesbos, Corfu and the others. On such trips it is easily seen why the Greeks, or rather the Minoans who preceded them, became the first great seafarers. Each island of the Aegean Sea is within sight of two or three more at least. And they stretch like a bridge from the Asia Minor coast to the Greek mainland. Even primitive man must have been able to construct adequate craft to make such short journeys early in human history. In fact, remains are found on the larger islands of the Neolithic period.

Greece, at the height of her Golden Age achieved pinnacles that many scholars consider never to have been passed since. The Parthenon on the Acropolis is named the most perfect building ever constructed. The greatest philosophers the world has known walked the streets of Athens hundreds of years before the birth of Christ. The sciences, our modern law, the theatre, literature, all had either their beginnings or tremendous impetus from this poor land.

Today she is largely a sad memory. Everywhere you see the remains of the Old Greece, the temples, the walls, the theatres, the sad fallen columns. And it is in this Old Greece that you find the land's appeal, for modern Greece is one of the most poverty stricken and backward countries of Europe. Only in Spain, Portugal and Yugoslavia do you see the poverty that you find in Greece.

As always when wages are low and the people poor, the country is a cheap place in which to reside. Greece is today, possibly the cheapest country in Europe, the only possible rival being Spain, another land of poverty and low wages. As always, the larger cities such as Athens and Salonica are higher priced but even Athens is cheap compared to any other capital of Europe.

I would say that to retire in Greece, either on a small income or with the intention of working out some local manner of making a living, you should have a basic interest in the cultural background of the country, otherwise you might find life in Greece on the drab and uninteresting side, particularly if you remained in Athens or elsewhere on the mainland.

ENTRY REQUIREMENTS. No visa is required of an American, only a passport. When you enter as a tourist you are given a stamp entitling you to remain for two months. Don't overstay this period or you'll be fined when you leave the country, even though you are one day over. I speak from experience.

If you wish to remain for more than two months you must go to the local branch of the Alien Police Office where you will be given a six month permit to reside in Greece. If you stay beyond this, you must have the permit renewed. It sounds complicated, but isn't. It takes only a short time to complete this process. The Greeks are happy to have you in their country—spending your dollars.

When you enter the country you have to make out a currency declaration on which you list all the types of money you have on hand and their quantity. When you leave the country, they check to see that you aren't taking out more than you entered with. At least they are supposed to do this. I found that often the border officials didn't bother.

§

TRANSPORTATION. By air you can reach Athens, at this writing for $735.40 one way, tourist from New York. TWA makes the flight direct, taking about 24 hours. Other airlines flying in from the West are Air France, BEA, KLM, LAI, SAS, SABENA, and Swissair. The Hellenikon airport of Athens is one of the basic international airports, and from here flights head south for Egypt and Africa, north to Turkey and the Balkans, or east to Baghdad, India and beyond.

The former Greek National Airline has been taken over by the big shipping magnate Aristotle Onassis, who seems to own half of Greece as well as half the world's tankers, and the name has been changed to Olympic Airways. I have flown this airline between Athens and Rhodes and between Rhodes and Beirut, Lebanon, but have never taken the longer hops which now run to Paris and London as well as other European centers. Frankly, I wasn't overimpressed.

By sea, there are various shipping lines that serve Greece. Basic fare from New York is $540 tourist class out of season and $770 in season. First class has a minimum of $815 out of season and $1050 in season. This on the National Hellenic American Line ships such as the Queen Frederica. The Greek Line's Olympia also at this writing runs between New York and Piraeus and is particularly constructed with tourist travel in mind having 1150 tourist class berths and only 138 first class. The Italian Line runs the Saturnia and the Vulcania between New York and Piraeus and the Christoforo Colombo by the way of Naples, Italy. The American Export Lines have the Independence and the Constitution on the same run.

You can also reach Greece by sea from some points in Europe such as Malaga, Spain; Naples, Genoa and Venice, Italy; Marseilles, France. Or even take the inter-island boat between Brindisi, Italy and Corfu, the resort island on the west coast of Greece.

I've gone into such detail on air and sea approaches because, frankly, coming overland can be grim. The

Simplon-Orient Express comes from London, going through France, Switzerland, Italy and Yugoslavia on its way. From London to Trieste she is rather swank but on the Yugoslavia border there is a change. I once was on the Simplon-Orient Express when it had only the locomotive, one restaurant car, one wagon-lits (Pullman) and one coach car which contained first, second and third class seats—all three. From Trieste to Athens is a long, hard, dirty train ride, one of the most miserable in Europe.

Trains in general are poor in Greece. I usually travel second class on European trains but in Greece I go first. Even that is no treat, particularly on the shorter runs. Buses are somewhat better but roads are so poor that these too are no treat.

Driving to Greece is absolutely not recommended. Greek roads are poor enough but Yugoslavia ones are unbelievably bad especially in the Eastern parts of the country. Best bet, probably, if you have your own car and want to take it to Greece would be to drive down to Brindisi, Italy, and ferry it over to Corfu.

§

THE GREEKS. The Greeks will tell you that everyone in Greece would like to immigrate to the United States, including the king. And they aren't joking. I doubt that there is a family in Greece that doesn't have more than one close relative in the United States. It is a regular tradition with them to go to America, make their fortunes, and possibly even take out citizenship and then to return to their own country in their old age to live out their lives. A fortune to a Greek can be pretty small potatoes since even a Social Security pension is a lot of money in Greece. I knew quite a few women in Rhodes whose husbands had gone to the United States figuring on staying twenty or thirty years and then returning. The wives were patiently sitting out the time. Each month a check would come from America to keep them and the children.

With all this it becomes obvious that America and Americans are well known and well liked by the Greeks. A great deal of English is spoken and you have no difficulty in making your wants known. This is one country in which it seems almost impossible to learn even the few words needed for shopping and the conduct of every day life, but it's not too necessary to attempt to learn Greek since so many of the people speak your language.

MONEY. One hundred lepta make one drachma and a drachma is worth almost exactly 31/3. Coins run from 5 lepta to 5 drachma and banknotes go up to 1,000 drachma.

Only a few years ago Greece had one of the weakest currencies in Europe and finally the drachma fell to the point where it took 30,000 to make one dollar. However, Uncle Sam came to the rescue and backed the Greek currency. The Greek government, to simplify things, merely lopped off the last three zeros in 1984 and the money has remained firm ever since. There is little if any advantage in bringing free market money into Greece. You might as well change your dollars at the bank or at your hotel.

WORK PERMISSION. You are not allowed to work in Greece without government permission which is seldom granted if a Greek can do the job. In some areas, such as Rhodes, which is only a few miles from Turkey and consequently a military zone, and near the Turkish frontier you are not even allowed to buy property. However, this is usually accomplished when desired by buying it through a Greek friend and in his name. The officials almost always blink at the practice.

There is little if any difficulty in starting up a business on your own especially if it is the type that will bring dollars or other foreign currency into the country. Greece is anxious for the introduction of foreign capital into her poverty stricken country.

§

PRICES. As I have already said above, prices are probably as cheap as anywhere in Europe. Even in such tourist resorts as Rhodes and Corfu it would be quite possible for a couple to retire on a hundred dollars a month in relative comfort. Add another fifty to that and you could afford a full time servant and to drive a car.

Prices will vary considerably between Athens and the other large cities and the small islands seldom touched by foreigners. An apartment, American style, in Athens would probably run you $475 and up which isn't exactly cheap, but I have been told that on such islands as Cos in the Dodecanese, you could find a cottage or small house for as little as $700 a month and a mansion for $2500. When I stayed on the island of Rhodes I paid $600 a month for my two bedroom apartment. This was no luxury flat, however, it came equipped with a modern bath and was completely furnished. Some of the U.S. service families, who received housing allotments, of course, demand exact American standards and would pay $500 or so for a comfortable place. The higher ranking officers got rather palatial houses for $750 and $1000.

Once again according to where you live, a servant will run about $100 a month and up, plus keep. You can get them considerably cheaper on islands such as Crete but, on the other hand, prices naturally are higher in Athens. A good cook might go as much as $250 a month, but she'd have to be very good.

Food prices are low. Meat averages $2.50 a pound and this will be difficult to believe but filet mignon costs the same as brisket. Government regulations make the whole steer the same price, so its a matter of daily fighting with the butcher to give you a good cut. Bread is very cheap, about $1.00 cents a loaf. Vegetables are as low priced as any place and Greek oranges about a penny apiece. Butter is somewhat cheaper than in the States but margarine about the same. Poultry is high and of poor quality and eggs only slightly cheaper than at home.

On the island of Rhodes there are no import taxes, the result of a government measure to attract tourists and consequently there are some unbelievable bargains. I had tailored of Harris tweed a sport jacket which came to $260. The tailor was one of the best in Greece and had made a dozen suits for the admiral of the Sixth Fleet which sometimes pulls into Rhodes. I am sure the same jacket would cost $1250 or so in New York. My wife had tailored a full tweed coat with a skirt to match, the best of Irish Donegal. Total cost, $350. This same lack of tax results in German cameras selling for less than they do in Germany, French perfumes for less than in France, Swiss watches for less than in Switzerland. German, Danish, Dutch and Czech beers, the best in the world, sell for $1.25 a quart and name brand Scotch whiskeys for $5 a bottle, a third of what they cost in Scotland.

§

PARTICULARLY RECOMMENDED LOCALITIES. I can't recommend the mainland at all, and of the islands I really know well only Rhodes and Corfu.

In some respects Corfu has its advantages over Rhodes as a retirement spot. For one thing it is only a short ferry hop, a mile or so, from the mainland, while Rhodes is an overnight trip by inter-island boat. And Corfu is also handy in that it is easily available to Italy. An overnight trip takes you to Brindisi and from there you are in Naples or Rome in a matter of hours. Corfu has a large foreign colony too, particularly retired English, while the foreign colony of Rhodes is largely limited to the permanently based American servicemen there. The swimming, the scenery, the prices on Corfu, we have no arguments about. It is a charming, pleasant island on which to consider retirement.

However, the town of Rhodes, on the island of Rhodes, is the most beautiful city in the world.

I have done a good deal of traveling in the past decade and can state that of all cities these I think the most beautiful: Mexico City, Paris, Rome, Venice, New Orleans, San Francisco, Istanbul and Tangier (not necessarily in that order). But Rhodes is the most beautiful city in the world.

In the days of the Trojan War there were three Greek towns on the island and they supplied ships to join Agamemnon's expedition against Troy, but in the year 408 B.C. they decided to unite and form one big town which they named Rhodes. Later the city fell to the Romans and later the Byzantines took over. But in 1308 the Knights of St. John, a Crusader order, captured the island and it was they who built the city we see today.

Rhodes is a medieval city. The walls which still surround it are in good enough condition to withhold a siege right now. It's streets are still cobblestoned, the shops where you buy bread, wine and olive oil for your daily needs are the same shops that dealt in the same commodities 600 years ago. The little *taberna* where you stop to have a glass of beer or *retsina* wine once served knights in armor.

Rhodes means *Roses* and indeed this is an island of flowers. The parks that surround the moats of the fortress walls are abloom with flowers all year around and are particularly heavily splashed with reds.

I believe that I've already stated in this book that there is no place in Europe that equals the climate of Florida or even southern

California. No place where you can swim all year round. The nearest to it is achieved on the Costa del Sol of Spain and in the Dodecanese Islands of which Rhodes is the capital. In Rhodes we found the best climate in Europe.

When the United States began spotting broadcast stations about the world to pipe our propaganda into the communist and Near East countries, Rhodes was one of the chosen locations. Here is permanently stationed the U.S. Coast Guard Cutter, the Courier. And on it are more than one hundred American servicemen.

The coming of the Courier brought big changes to Rhodes which ordinarily has a population of 128,000. Some forty of the servicemen brought their families but that was just the beginning. Various civilians connected with the Voice of America, also showed up. And teachers for the American school. And doctors and dentists of Greek-American extraction. Uncle Sam paid the way for the service men bringing over their cars, refrigerators and other American needs.

Greek houses were not up to American standards, so new houses were built, and this amounted to a regular little building boom since most of the local population were dwelling in houses erected five hundred years ago. The shop-keepers put in new products they'd never heard of before to meet new demands. News shops opened carrying American newspapers and magazines.

The American money was a boon to the Greeks and it also works out well for a civilian American living on Rhodes. The presence of these State-side comforts, many of which are not to be found in other sections of Greece, makes living that much the easier.

And there's another angle. The service families are periodically rotated and seldom do they take back home all the refrigerators, stoves and what-not gadgets that they brought out with them. Instead they are sold locally for whatever they will bring and I will estimate that there is no place else outside of the United States where American household applicances are so economically priced, second hand.

I think the little city of Rhodes is one of the top places in the world for retirement. There is just one limitation which is a serious one for such gregarious persons as myself. Your companionship is largely limited to the service families from the *Courier* most of whom are quite young, few of whom have much in the way of education. There are some wonderful exceptions, but let's face it, on the *average* the professional serviceman isn't the best company in the world.

§

CASE HISTORY No. 1. Talk about starting a business on a shoestring. In Rhodes I met a young fellow who couldn't have been more than 18 or 19 years of age who started his business with about twenty used paperbacked books. And he made them pay well enough to parlay into a business that, when I saw him last, was going great guns.

Walter Pond came over to Europe on a Youth Hostels tour, figuring on a few months in Europe living on as tight a budget as possible, and then returning to the States to get a job. He'd had half a year of college, I believe, but had quit in disgust figuring that what he was getting out of it in the way of education wasn't worth the time he was putting in. There have been similar attacks on the American educational system recently, but Walt was particularly bitter.

At any rate, he was getting around Europe largely by hitchhiking (they call it "auto-stop" on the continent) and although he hadn't planned to go as far as Greece he caught a ride in Italy with an American driving a stationwagon to Athens. It was too good a chance to resist, so Walt went along.

The trouble with Walt was (and probably still is) that he blew his money. He just couldn't hold onto it. It burned holes in his pockets, or something. He found himself in Rhodes with far too little left to return to the States. So he looked around to find a way to pick up some dollars, without conflicting with Greek law. And right from the start he fell upon a situation that applies almost everywhere where Americans live abroad.

The shortage of reading material.

Unless they live in England or some other English speaking locality, the Americans you find abroad seem always short of reading material. When the American does locate a bookstore or newsstand that handles American paperbacked books, they almost always charge double the price that prevails in the States.

When I first saw Walt he was carrying a tray, slung by a leather strap around his neck. It contained possibly fifty used American and British paperback books, mostly detective, science-fiction and western, but a few of more serious nature as well. I was seated at a sidewalk cafe in front of the town market.

I asked him the price, glad to see him. I was currently out of light reading. The price was 8 drachma (about 1.25) straight or 4 drachma with a trade in.

"Trade in?" I asked him.

He explained that if I gave him a book with which I was finished, it counted for four drachma which lowered my price in half.

At that time I was staying at the Lindos Hotel, right around the corner. I told him to come with me and took him up to my room. I had at least ten books, all of which I had figured on throwing away rather than being bothered with their bulk. I gave him the ten and selected ten more from his stock, paying him his 40 drachma difference. Believe me, I thought it was a bargain. Forty drachma, by the way, comes to $6.75.

Four days later he dropped by the hotel with a new selection of books and I traded in my ten on a new batch. I also told him that at last I'd found an apartment and gave him the address. From then on he dropped in once or twice a week, especially when he had a batch of science fiction, which is a favorite of mine.

It turned out that most of the American families in town were customers of Walt's. He acted as a sort of one man circulating library. Everybody in town who did much reading would occasionally buy a book or two at the newsstand which specialized in American publications, and these would usually wind up in Walt's hands. Some of the servicemen or their wives had books sent out from home, and these too would wind up with Walt. Besides this he had contacts with the hotels which drew the most American tourists. Those magazines and paperback books that were tossed away by the tourists were sold by the maids to Walt for one drachma apiece.

How much did he make from this "business"? I could never get him to tell me but I know that he never left my house with less than a ten dollar profit. And I am not nearly the reader that some Americans abroad can be. He was living in a medium priced hotel, on pension, was outfitting himself with tailored clothes, taking advantage of the rock-bottom prices on Rhodes, and saving money.

He usually put in a leisurely three or four hours a day visiting his customers and once told me that he couldn't decide whether or not to start a small used book store, and let the customers come to him in the future. However, he was also thinking of shaking the dust of Greece from his shoes and going to Spain or France for a time. He figured he could do this in just about any town in Europe where there was a permanent Anglo-American colony.

Could you do it?

I don't see any reason why anybody couldn't. I don't think you'd ever get rich at it, but I'll tell you one thing, you'd never starve at a business like this in any American colony abroad. The desire for reading material is always a pressing one.

Of course the thing to do would be to parlay this up. With just a very little capital you could open a shop. There is a used book store in Tangier operated by an American, who also specializes in paperbacks. He too allows one half the price of the book if you have one to trade-in. I've never talked to the owner of this establishment at great length, but the shop always seems packed with customers and he dresses and looks prosperous enough. I doubt if it cost him more than a few hundred dollars to start up in business. He gets most of his books from trade-ins and from the hotel maids, just as Walt did in Rhodes.

§

CASE HISTORY No. 2. This may sound corny but in more than one European city with a large American colony you'll find American women making a good thing out of cooking such things as pies.

What happens is this. We have a whole new American generation which is used to getting its pastry either from the bakery or out of cans or the deep freeze. Either that or they rely on special pie mixes and fillers which are unavailable in the rest of the world.

The result is that Americans abroad develop a raging hunger for such items as pie, and a rage against their wives for not delivering.

So Mrs. Joan Demeree, retired with her husband on Rhodes on an inadequate army disability pension, saw an opening and filled it. Mrs. Demeree, a young fifty years of age, comes from a small farm in southern Illinois. The poor stoves and other equipment that confront the cook in Greece didn't faze her for a moment. She'd learned to cook on a wood fire—and still preferred one, for that matter.

Actually, I was wrong when I said Mrs. Demeree saw an opening and filled it. The opening was pointed out to her and she was *pushed* into it. From time to time she'd have friends in for dinner and it was no period at all before the fame of her pies, cakes and other typical American dishes spread. Finally somebody hesitantly asked Mrs. Demeree if she would *please* do her up four lemon meringue pies—she had a party coming up and the pies would just **make it.**

So Mrs. Demeree made up the pies, neighborly enough, and figured out exactly what they had cost and presented that small amount as the bill. But nothing would do but her friend must double it, to take care of the time involved.

Mrs. Demeree didn't know it as yet but she was in business.

And the last time I saw her, still was. I would estimate that her cooking of American dishes which included pies, cakes, cookies, chili-con-carne, tamale pie, baked beans and home made ice cream, netted her approximately as much as her husband's pension. She didn't work too hard at it either.

Could you do this?

You could if you are as good a cook as Mrs. Demeree and as good at adapting local materials to your favorite American dishes. That's where most American cooks fall down abroad, they can't find *exactly* the same raw materials they've been used to. I don't know of an Anglo-American colony in Europe that wouldn't (figuratively) give its right arm for a good *American-style* cook to do up State side specialties, to cater parties, even to make up picnic lunches and such.

It's a wide open field. For that matter, I'd wager that you could make a good living in a town like Torremolinos, Spain, with nothing more than an old fashioned hand operated ice cream freezer **and** a good formula for making ice cream. If you've never been abroad you can't imagine how hungry people get for the food of home and particularly the favorite dishes of their childhood.

CASE HISTORY No. 3. While I'm on this subject of eating U.S. favorites abroad I might as well bring up the case of a young fellow I met in Athens who was obviously living fairly high on the hog. We met while mutually inspecting one of the best preserved of all the Greek temples, the Theseion, they call it. We struck up a conversation and wound up having a bottle of Fix beer in a taberna.

It turned out that he wasn't any more the usual tourist than I was. He was making a comfortable living while seeing Europe—as I was. So I asked him what his particular angle was.

Selling popcorn.

Selling popcorn! I looked at him and probably blinked. I had a picture of this neatly dressed, prosperous fellow peddling popcorn at a nickle a bag.

That wasn't it, but nearly.

Bob Segal (I think that's the way you spell his name) who hailed from L. A. originally, is one of the many who are profiting by the "Americanization" mania which is sweeping much of the world. Chewing gum, Coca-Cola, breakfast cereals that pop, juke boxes, ice cream sodas, rock'n'roll, pinball machines, kitchen gadgets and what not are rearing their heads in just about every land this side of the Iron Curtain, and for that matter, often behind it.

No matter how much you love your own country, it often comes as a surprise to find people who have never seen America who love it still more, or seem to. I have been in homes in as obscure places as Baghdad where you wouldn't know it wasn't a suburb of Chicago. The furniture was literally from Grand Rapids and I was served canned tomato juice with ice cubes from the king-size refrigerator. AND THERE WAS A TELEVISION SET IN THE CORNER ALTHOUGH THERE IS NO TV BROADCASTING STATION WITHIN A THOUSAND MILES.

Take my word for it, the world is being Americanized.

And that's where Bob came in. He first hit on his scheme in Spain where the tapa is an institution. Spanish folk never drink without eating. Every time you order a drink in a bar, a tapa is put before you. This can be a piece of bread and cheese, three or four fried fresh sardines, a portion of squid fried in olive oil, two or three cold boiled shrimp, a tiny portion of stew or various other tasty items. Every time you buy a drink they bring another *tapa* and it is quite possible in Spain to get a full meal this way if your capacity for wine is great enough. In the swankier bars the *tapas* are usually more elaborate and you're usually charged for them.

So Bob located a supply of popcorn, which to his surprise is sold all over Spain in the feed stores. The Spanish feed it to their chickens. He popped up a large batch in oil, salted it, put it in extra-large paper bags and took it around to the local bars. He gave it to the bartenders free, having a little difficulty in doing even that since they were suspicious.

"The *American tapa,*" he told them. "All Americans eat it. In the bars, in the movies, while looking at TV, while watching sports. Americans are always eating popcorn."

That sold them. They tried it on the customers, explaining that this was the famous *American tapa*.

Well, popcorn sold itself. There is nothing more thirst provoking than popcorn and nothing more irresistible. It is impossible to eat a dozen or so kernals of nice buttered and salted popcorn and not want more. When Bob Segal went back he found a unanimous response from the bartenders. He was in business.

In no time at all he found himself branching out. Party givers— and parties are as numerous as the sands in any foreign colony resort—would order huge amounts. He imported an automatic popper from the States and opened a stand with a cute little Spanish girl to operate it, on the streets of Malaga.

"Before I knew it," Bob laughed, "I was the popcorn tycoon of southern Spain. It wasn't safe, though. Not in that country. It was just a matter of time before some corrupt official figured out I was making money and decided to take over."

"You could've taken on a Spanish partner," I told him. "That's what you usually do in Spain."

"I suppose so, but I didn't. I sold out for plenty. I was getting tired of Spain anyway."

It turned out that he had made a leisurely tour of Europe, looking for another country where the institution of eating while drinking was widespread and where Americans were popular. Greece was his choice. When I met Bob he was getting set to go into business—bringing popcorn to the Greeks. I have a sneaking suspicion that by this time every bar in Athens is carrying the stuff.

I'm not particularly suggesting that the readers of this book go into the popcorn business. The point I'm trying to make is that many of our American "institutions" are taking root abroad and there are scores of opportunities to put your American "know-how" to work. I was not jesting above when I suggested that an ice cream freezer and a good formula for American type ice cream would put you in business in half the countries of Europe. Except for the ultra-expensive spumoni and casata of Italy, ice cream in Europe, and especially southern Europe is *lousy*. It's also ridiculously expensive, especially in view of the fact that milk is surprisingly cheap.

It's also my belief that American candy would make a fabulous hit. I don't know of anyone who has tried this, but I think that an American candy shop would go over with a bang in any of the countries covered in this book. Fudge, taffy, divinity, I have never seen in Europe. Americans living abroad would go overboard for it, not to speak of the Europeans who on an average are more inclined to have a sweet tooth than we at home.

§

CHAPTER 15 MOROCCO

IN A NUTSHELL. Morocco is both old-old and still one of the most recent additions to the family of nations. A bit larger than California in size and with roughly ten million persons, until 1956 Morocco was a French protectorate. This protectorate had been imposed on the Moroccans in 1912 at which time the international powers were gleefully splitting up what little remained of the world not already assimilated. The Spanish took over the northern 7,589 square miles of the country and the French the rest.

But in spite of the fact that the average Moroccan is poorly educated in matters economic and political they do know one thing. If they want to put up with misrule they want it to be Moors who are misruling them, not foreigners.

I had the interesting experience of living in Morocco at the time of their successful revolt against the French and Spanish. I watched the parades in the streets, watched the French and Spanish foreign legions try to quell the rioting Moors, who, using him as a symbol, were demanding return of their sultan who had been exiled by the French. I even met various of the gun-runners who were supplying the guerrillas in the interior with arms to battle the hapless French troops.

The French finally called it quits and today Morocco is tranquil again. And like all nations she is eyeing tourism with a gleam of avarice. This source of income, Morocco would love to tap. She is making a great push to attract American and other tourists to her sights, and indeed she should be successful.

Morocco is handy to the tourist and offers a great deal that is truly different. The majority of tourists, American as well as European, are not in the money bracket to take long trips to the Near or Far East but Morocco offers much the same as you find in those far countries Iraq, Iran, Jordan and Turkey. European countries aren't actually too very different from our own. European

Cities, largely, look a great deal like American ones and Europeans dress, eat and conduct themselves much the same as we Americans do. But Morocco is truly *different*.

I would be very much surprised if Morocco's attempts to get the tourist trade in large numbers failed. I expect the country to have a tourist boom and not only that but to attract large numbers of foreign residents. She has scenic beauty, picturesque and attractive cities, excellent sports facilities, wonderful business opportunities, excellent climate, and is as cheap as Spain.

§

ENTRY REQUIREMENTS. As I write, changes are being made in Morocco in regard to visa requirements for foreigners. However, as I've said above the government is keen to attract the tourist and it is unlikely that anything will be done to make it more difficult to enter and reside in Morocco. At this writing no visa is necessary for an American. There is no time limit on the period you can stay. At the time I lived in Morocco it was necessary to get permission from the police authorities to reside permanently or semi-per-manently in Morocco in general, though not in Tangier. I had my home in Tangier for about seven months and ran into no red tape whatsoever. It is possible that the new changes will alter this situation, I rather doubt it though.

§

TRANSPORTATION. The usual way to reach Morocco is through Europe although it is possible to take a freighter to Casablanca, Rabat or Tangier. The easiest way to come directly from the United States to Morocco would be to take a ship which stopped at Gibraltar and then take the ferry across to Tangier or Ceuta.

Ships which call at Gibraltar from New York include those of the American Export Lines, Home Lines, Italia

Line, Lauro Lines. Rates from New York start at $375 tourist class, $550 Cabin class, and $810 First class.

You can also take a ship from England on various lines at a cost of about $58 one way, tourist.

From Gibraltar the ferry to Tangier costs one pound ($5.80).

Transporting your car across will run anywhere from $25 to $50 according to weight.

Once in Tangier wou'll find that Moroccan roads are as good as European ones on an average. Gasoline is cheaper than in Europe. Garages are adequate.

You can also reach Morocco by air from Gibraltar. Fare is $15.32 to Tangier. Gibraltar connects with London for about $120 by B.E.A.

Air Morocco will fly you directly from Bordeaux, Lyon, or Geneva to Casablanca. And Air France from Paris to Casablanca or Rabat. Air World Limited flies directly from London to Tangier; Iberia from Madrid to Tangier; and TAP (Portugese) from Lisbon to Tangier or Casablanca.

By railroad you can take the Spanish trains right down to Algeciras and then ferry across the narrow straits. Railroads aren't particularly recommended in Morocco. They are unpunctual and for from comfortable. They run four classes instead of the two classes you find in Europe and fourth class is something to witness. The Berbers, Rifs and Arabs pack in with their luggage, children and even animals. Nothing below second class is recommended for Americans unless it's adventure you're looking for.

Bus service is quite good and boasts second and first class seats. Take first class if you want to be sure of getting a seat.

§

THE MOORS. Actually you will not get to know many native Moroccans, even though you permanently retire in Morocco. You are more apt to associate with other foreigners principally French and Spanish although there are quite a few Americans and British, especially in Tangier. Few Moroccans speak English and few indeed are educated at all. In spite of its position on the Atlantic coast, Morocco is an Eastern Land and in many respects is more backward than Turkey and the other Near Eastern Moslem countries.

Those Moslems that you do meet, the few who speak English, you will probably like; they make good friends. These, by the way, will all be men. You won't meet Moslem women. For all practical purposes, the Moorish women are still in the days of the harem.

Although there is some movement, sparked by one of the royal princesses, to modernize woman's position, the greater number go veiled in the streets.

There is, of course, no reason to fear the Moroccan. He is probably less criminally inclined that the average American. As I think back, I cannot recall ever having met a Moor that I disliked.

§

MONEY. Until just recently, the French franc and the Spanish peseta were the currencies most widely used in Morocco. Now, however, these have been withdrawn and the Moroccan franc has taken over. At this time it is too early in the game to be able to say what will happen to this currency. Right now it is pegged at ten to one on the Spanish peseta; that is, you get ten Moroccan francs for one Spanish peseta which is worth about 24.1 have a suspicion that it is due for a fall since the Moroccans, now largely cut off from the French economy, have an Atlas-load of economic problems on their shoulders. If it does fall, it will mean that Morocco becomes still cheaper than it is today.

When you speak of money in Morocco then you must consider Tangier, once, and possibly still, the greatest international money clearing center of the world.

The capitalist system is a complicated one and nowhere does it become more complicated than in the field of international finance. There is not a nation in the world, including our own, that hasn't passed some truly gobbledygook laws in an attempt to strengthen its own currency to the detriment of the others of the world.

To bring a balance to things at all, it became necessary to establish clearing houses where the world's currencies found their true level, no matter what laws might be passed at home. Tangier became one of these clearing houses, Switzerland another. And in these two places you may buy, or sell, any currency, or gold, at its true value. For instance, not long ago the Soviet Union announced that its ruble was worth four to the dollar, or about 25¢ apiece. However, in Tangier you could buy all you wished forty to the dollar, or 2 1/2¢ apiece.

Not even in the United States can you legally buy gold coins or bullion,, but you can in Tangier at any bank. If you mistrust your country's currency, you can sink your savings into gold, keeping them safe from inflation. There are something like fifty banks in this small city, and uncounted hordes of private money changers.

WORK PERMISSION. All you need to work in Morocco is a job.

Most countries put obstacles in the paths of foreigners working within their boundries figuring that one of their own people are being displaced. In Morocco, however, you will not displace a Moor if you work. In the first place very few Moors have the training and background to handle anything except the simplest positions and the pay for these is so low that you would starve on it.

In Tangier, in particular, there are for all practical purposes no restrictions on opening a business. There are no income taxes, no property taxes, no corporation taxes, few import or export taxes and those that do exist look as though they will be discontinued and Tangier again declared a free port.

By law you need not even give your right name in starting up a corporation. In fact, you need not give any name at all; you can start a corporation for $1000 and use a number if you wish to keep your name a secret.

§

PRICES. When I first arrived in Tangier I found myself financially embarassed. I had several deals cooking in several places, including Spain, but for the moment I was very short of cash. As a result I fell into a situation that was one of the most interesting I have ever experienced: I lived in the Casbah of Tangier for a period of two or three months.

Tangier is divided into two principal sections, the medina, or native quarter, and the modern city. The higher reaches of the medina are the casbah. The modern city is ultra-modern —the medina and particularly the casbah are strictly out of the Arabian Nights. Streets so narrow you can touch the buildings on either side, cobblestones, tiny shops no bigger than a phone booth, so small that the owner must sit outside. Tiny restaurants, sitting possibly six customers at a time, the proprietor, who doubles as chef, squatting out front cooking shish *kebab* over a charcoal stove. The street of the jewelers, where gold and jewels are being formed into rings, pendants, bracelets, by goldsmiths using the tools and methods of Arabia of a thousand years ago. Both men and women in Moroccan costume, including veils on the women.

I found a small pension in what had formerly been a wealthy Moslem's home, but was now somewhat run down. It was right around the corner from the American Legation and consequently handy for my picking up my mail. The pension was run by an Italian named Luigi, a concert violinist who had fallen upon bad times, married an illiterate Spanish girl, and had finally wound up here in the Casbah of Tangier. I had a room and my three meals for 120 pesetas a day, or at present exchange rates, a bit under $10.00. The food by the way was excellent and a whopping big glass of wine came with lunch and dinner. There were cheaper pensions in the Casbah, some of them at 300 or 350 pesetas a day, but at Luigi's I had a room up on the roof from which I could look out over all Tangier and the straits with Spain and Gibraltar in plain view. Nearby was the Grand Mosque and every morning I was awakened by the muezzin calling the faithful to prayer.

So it is possible to live in Tangier for less than a dollar a day— but I don't believe the average American would wish to do it unless for a brief period in the name of adventure.

Living in the modern, or European, section is more expensive, but still cheap by European and certainly American standards. A small furnished apartment for one or two persons is expensive and you'll pay at least $80 for one. There are very few. An unfurnished apartment comes considerably cheaper, possibly $260 a month. A good many foreigners, in town for a limited time, will rent an unfurnished apartment and also rent furniture.

Surprisingly enough, the larger apartments, flats and houses can be cheaper than the small ones. There is usually a shortage of the little efficiency apartments but since so many of the French have left the country, there are plenty of larger places. I would estimate that if you looked around a bit you could find a very nice apartment, or a small house up on the Monte right out of town, for about $300 and up.

Food is cheap if you buy it in the Socco, the native market. As cheap as any place, except for meat. However, Tangier also sports some of the most ultra-modern grocery stores out of the U.S. and if you wish American canned or frozen products you can have them. In fact, you can order by phone and they'll deliver. And you'll be staggered by the prices.

You can buy fresh swordfish of absolutely top quality in the native fish market for about $1.50 a pound. But a can of American salmon will run you a dollar or so in a grocery store in the European section. American Cheese-Tid-Bits used to be my favorite as a small boy and when I saw them on display in Tangier it had been years since I had had any so I picked up a box. However, at $1.25 a small box even a boyhood favorite can be dispensed with. I used to pay a nickle.

Spanish and North African wines, cognacs and liquors are cheap, not much more than they are in Spain. A quart of red or white wine will run about $1.50 a quart if you bring your own bottle to the bodega, cognac about $8.00. Even American and Scotch whiskys are cheaper than at home due to the lesser taxes.

Restaurant food is some of the best in the world at the price. Tangier has been an international city for decades and practically every type of food in the world is represented from Indian (Hindu) to Chinese, from French to Syrian, from African to American. You can get a dish of couscous or a hamburger; escargots (snails) or Eggs Foo Young. And at prices to be found nowhere else. There are at least six fine restaurants in Tangier where you may dine well, with a bottle of wine, for a dollar. For five dollars you can eat a gourment meal at the Ermitage, probably the best restaurant in Northern Africa. I know of no city on earth where you can eat better, for so little, than Tangier. I would say that in all there must be at least twenty outstanding restaurants in this little city.

Moorish servants are cheap. Actually, you can have a girl free, for her keep and an occasional dress and some of your cast off shoes. But you'll hardly get top quality, even though they will expect to work twelve or fourteen hours a day, seven days a week. You see, slavery still exists in Morocco, whatever the authorities say to the contrary. But to the extent that the maid is efficient and honest, you'll pay more. A good maid should cost you about $100 a month plus her food, which will not cost a great deal. You can have a girl come in mornings only and give her breakfast, for about

$80 a month and for persons living in a small apartment this is often preferable.

Clothing is cheap, due to the low taxes. Shoes, unless you like to wear native sandals, are a bit on the high side, but, if you wish, you can buy your favorite American brand, or British, for that matter. Tangier has *everything* for sale. Best thing to do is buy your own materials and then have a local tailor do them up for you. Labor is so cheap that the cost is almost meaningless.

§

PARTICULARLY RECOMMENDED LOCALITY. **Although I** spent six or seven months in Morocco at one time and have visited it for short periods on half a dozen occasions, the only area I really know is Tangier. I have traveled across the country north and south and east and west, but not to the point where I could advise on permanent location. Consequently I'll deal with Tangier alone.

The town's name was Tingis originally and was founded by the Phoenicians about 1600 B.C. Phoenician, Carthaginian, Greek and Roman ruins are to be seen in the vicinity and there is a small local museum which houses some of the objects found in or near Tangier from ancient times. Since then the city has been held by Byzantines, Vandals, Visigoths and finally the Arabs. In more modern times it has been taken and held for varying periods by the Portuguese, English and Spanish and for a time an International Commission of eight countries. All of these races have made their imprints on the city.

Some of the world's most beautiful cities owe a considerable portion of their attractiveness to their geographical location, such as Rio de Janeiro, Naples, Sydney, San Francisco. And such is Tangier. Like most ancient cities she is perched atop a hill and her early fortifications surrounded what is now the *medina*. The Sultan's palace is at the very top of the hill, the *casbah* section, and from here you can look out over the Atlantic, the Mediterranean and the Straits of Hercules. Through these straits, one of the busiest waterways in the world, you can usually see a dozen ships or so at any one time. Far to the south are the imposing Atlas mountains where once, supposedly, Hercules held up the weight of the heavens.

Tangier has one feature which is quite wonderful. In most cities of the Near East and the Far East you will find extreme picturesque qualities but from time to time, if you reside in one, you have periods where you wish for the sight of broad boulevards, numerous cars, neon signs, big movie houses, huge department stores—and a malted milk and grilled cheese sandwich. You long for these things— but don't get them. In Tangier, you can realize every one. Tangier is one of the most modern cities across the waters. At least the European section is. You can be deep in the cool darkness of the streets of the Casbah, flavoring the atmosphere of the Arab world. Then, if you wish, you can walk in five minutes to what you would think a modern California or Florida town. Thunderbirds will honk at you, fashionably dressed women will parade by hauling their clipped poodles behind them. Neon lights will blink at you, and there is even an American library. If you wish, tune in your radio to the American radio stations which broadcast from Tangier to all Europe, the Voice of America and various other projects. There is an American school, if you have children, and an American club if you like swimming and golfing with your fellow Americans.

If you like sport, keep in mind that Tangier has what is sometimes called the third best beach in the world. There is a yacht club, a Polo ground, tennis courts, horse racing, air and motor rallies, hunting and fishing, hiking and skiing (in the nearby Atlas mountains). In short, this section of Morocco can supply just about any sport in which you might be interested. There is even a bullring and the biggest matadors of Spain fight here each year.

The foreign colony is an extensive one and you can find just about any type of person you wish in Tangier. There are many American families living permanently in town, working for the Voice of America, for the Legation, for branches of American business houses. These live a rather conservative life, centered largely around their own American club. They are inclined to buy a great deal of their daily needs through the American P-X, and keep largely from contact with other members of the European colony.

To the other extreme is the Bohemian set which hangs out largely in Dean's internationally famous bar, at the Safari and at the Parade. Dean's is run by an Egyptian educated in London and is known by every international celebrity in the world. But the Parade and the Safari are American owned and operated and the most popular hangouts for American writers, artists, movie people and such—not to speak of plain out and out bums of the alimony-from-home variety.

It between these two groups are a good many Americans, British and other English speaking elements. You'd be able to find your own level, in Tangier. Barbara Hutton has one of her larger, and one of her best-liked homes right in the Casbah, so you'll see that all types of Americans are to be found here, not just those who retire on a shoestring.

CASE HISTORY No. 1. In view of the title of this book, I have largely refrained from describing case histories of folk who have a considerable income on which to retire, however, for the benefit of any readers who are fairly well to do but fear to retire because they are afraid their standards would lower, here is an example.

Richard and Patricia Winton have an income of approximately $100,000 a year. Mr. Winton was formerly in the building business in Beverly Hills, California. Mrs. Winton says, "We had servants and all that, but we were the two unhappiest guys in the world. The noise, the pace, the confusion! We came to Tangier for one week and decided this was it. We went back and sold everything and came here where people have time to look at the sunset or listen to the sea. . . . We're celebrating our 25th anniversay this year. Who could possibly want to be in Beverley Hills?"

The Wintons now have a Moorish palace which is on top of a mountainside overlooking the Straits of Hercules. They have fourteen rooms and seven baths, three servants, central heating and a champagne-filled refrigerator by the master bedroom bed, 18th century Florentine furniture, Moorish arches and even an intact harem room—left over from the old tenants. They take two trips a year up to Europe for a change.

They estimate that to live on this scale in America would cost $1,000,000 a year!

They are doing it for $100,000 a year.

§

CASE HISTORY No. 2. But few of the readers of this book have $100,000 a year with which to retire. Let's become more down to earth. I mention above that it is usually cheaper in Tangier to rent an unfurnished apartment or house and then rent the furniture than it is to rent a furnished place direct. This may sound a bit confusing, but this is how it works out.

There are many places in the world where the institution of the furnished apartment, so prevalent in the States, has not spread. Tangier is one of these. There are very few furnished apartments and those are quite expensive.

Seeing this situation, a former U.S. Navy gob, Danny Lawton, decided that there was room for a business in renting furniture and began to go about acquiring some. He went down to the used furniture exhibits in the native market and began picking up pieces, here, there and the other place, and storing them in the house occupied by he and his beautiful wife. He didn't have much capital to begin with, very little as a matter of fact, but, then, he didn't need much. Used furniture, he found, could be purchased ultra-cheap in Tangier if you shopped carefully.

After he had acquired enough for a small apartment or two he put an ad in the Tangier Gazette, the local weekly English speaking organ. He had enough furniture for two apartments (small ones) but got applications for his rental furniture by the dozen.

Danny and his wife were in business.

He collected his first month's rent in advance from his two customers and promptly went out and bought more stuff, rented it and bought more, rented it and bought more. The business mushroomed.

At first Danny dealt only with such basic necessities as beds, tables and chairs, but continually customers were asking for refrigerators, radios and even stoves. Danny branched out.

A new factor entered into his business. As it became known all over town what the Lawtons were doing, Danny would often have an opportunity to buy a whole apartment or house full of furniture at one flat price. Perhaps the owner had received a letter from home making it necessary to sell out and get back immediately. Rather than try and sell piece by piece, or through some Moorish merchant with whom he couldn't communicate properly through language difficulties, he would turn to Danny.

When I met the Lawtons they had recently moved to a larger house, in fact, a monster of a house, but still the place was packed to the gills with every type of furniture from desks to foot stools. Beds were here, there and the other place, chairs were piled in tiers. Tables put one atop another until they reached the ceiling. They must have had, at this time, enough furniture to supply forty or fifty houses—most of it, of course, was in use.

I sometimes wondered what in the world they would do if all of their customers returned their rented furniture at once. They'd simply have had to stack it in the streets. But, of course, that situation would never arise. At any one time, on an average, Danny would probably have furniture for about five apartments in his place. Seldom more than that. Danny actually had more business than he could handle and as fast as furniture would come back from one place he would be sending it to a new one.

He hired four or five Moorish boys, who pushed pushcarts, to deliver and collect, repair and paint, and Moorish wages being what they are, this overhead amounted to practically nothing.

On an average, Danny Lawton would rent a set of his furniture for about four or five months. If a person planned to stay much longer than that, he would usually being thinking in terms of buying his own used furniture, or possibly even new things. The larger percentage of his customers were in town only for limited times and it was easier to utilize Danny's service than to be bothered with purchasing and then selling.

Rentals were not high in price. A small efficiency apartment could be furnished for about fifty or sixty dollars a month. More rooms, of course, mounted up. It isn't possible for me to list prices here because every piece had its own price according to quality, age and the quantity of the stuff you were taking. But Danny figured that on an average a piece of furniture paid for itself in less than six months and once paid for was from then on clear profit. The Moors who worked for him became (or already were) experts at keeping a piece of furniture in repair and he seldom had to retire an article from use.

Could you do this?

Given a town like Tangier where furnished apartments are at a premium, you could. You'd have to have enough initial capital, of course, to get your first furniture and to advertise your service in the classified sections of the local paper.

As a matter of fact, I've seen variations on this little deal in various places in the world. I had a friend in London who had worked out a system of renting small apartments and flats in the Chelsea section of London where a great many artists and other "Bohemians" live. He would find a rather drab unfurnished place at a comparatively low rental and furnish it "Bohemian style." He'd repair it, put in some old furniture, put a painting or so on the wall, and then rent it for as much as twice what he was paying.

Unfortunately for this type of deal, London got into a whole series of complicated rental laws involving frozen rent ceilings and then unfreezing them, and so forth and so on, and Ralph had to go out of business.

I've also seen the same thing done in Mexico and in New Mexico. There's no reason why it couldn't be done in just about any locality where you have a turnover of tourists and local people who do not understand just what the average American considers a comfortably furnished house. For instance, a refrigerator to the average American is a must as is a gas or electric stove. But in most countries and particularly the "bargain paradises" such as Spain, Mexico, Greece and Morocco, these things are practically unknown. Not even comparatively wealthy folk have them in their homes. I have actually seen Americans pay double rent for the sake of having a refrigerator in the house they rented. A house in Torremolinos, Spain, which would ordinarily bring $400 a month will rent for $800 if it has an American type kitchen.

CASE HISTORY No. 3. This just wouldn't be a chapter devoted to Morocco and particularly Tangier if we didn't describe at least one of the various ways money is made in this strange city by juggling international currencies.

A thirty-five year old friend of mine named Irene Knight, originally from Greensburg, Pennsylvania, has been living in Tangier for some years by taking advantage of the fact that she has three or four thousand dollars. She also picks up odd jobs from time to time, being a typist, but largely her income is from that bit of capital of hers. This is how she does it.

The Spanish peseta fluctuates as greatly as does any currency in the world. It is up one day, down the next. As I write this, the legal rate of exchange, in Spain, is 42 pesetas to the dollar, but in Tangier the rate is 54 to the dollar. Tomorrow, in Tangier, the pesetas might go up to 52 to the dollar, or sink lower in value to 56 to the dollar. You never know.

If this is a bit confusing to you, thus far, reread the above paragraph because you'll have to have a clear picture of this background to understand just what it is Irene does.

Irene has her money in the American and Foreign Bank which is located at 23 Boulevard Pasteur, in Tangier. She has a standing order with them. If the pesetas drop below 55 pesetas to the dollar in value, then convert all of her dollars into pesetas and hold them. When the peseta goes up in value to the rate of 52 to the dollar, then convert all her pesetas into dollars and hold them.

If you consider this for a moment, you will see that every time the peseta fluctuates to this extent, Irene clears up a profit of 3 pesetas per every dollar she has on deposit. She would make 9,000 pesetas or about $163 each time this fluctuation takes place.

One week this happened three times. Each time the peseta went below the figure she had set the bank bought pesetas, each time it went above, they sold her pesetas for dollars. Irene netted about $500 during the period.

Now Irene was a sharp operator and kept her ear tuned to current gossip and to the news. She realized that if Uncle Sam was to loan another big chunk of money to Spain, the peseta would gain in value, or if tourist travel dropped off, it would fall. She had no intention of being caught some day with her money invested in pesetas, and then have Franco devaluate his currency. When I knew her, at least, she had never been caught. Year in, year out, she was living and living well on this small amount of capital. On an average she would turn it over possibly twice a month.

There are literally hundreds of persons in Tangier playing the fluctuating currency game. Some of them have no more than a few hundred dollars on hand, some of them have literally tens of millions at their disposal. A fraction of a change in the value of a currency can send these big operators hurrying to their telephones and rushing through orders to Switzerland or New York, Hong Kong or Lisbon. Buy Indian rupees at 5.88 to the dollar; sell Norwegian kroner at 7.14 to the dollar; buy gold bullion at 532,000 French francs to the kilo!

I messed around with this myself for a time, on a small scale, and didn't do too badly, but frankly it's not my dish of tea. I'd wind up with a fine collection of ulcers in six months' time.

But maybe you're different.

CASE HISTORY No. 4. As I have compiled this book, I realize that I have mentioned American artists and writers, of one type or another quite often and possibly some of my readers might think that I've written too much about this type of American. However, it is simply that so many of these are the type person who take off from the treadmill and go off to the bargain paradises both in our own country and abroad. In fact, many readers of this book who take the advice that I give and actually get out of the rut themselves might well find in a year or so that they've developed an interest in one or more of the arts themselves. It is when man has leisure time that he is able to look at the beautiful things of life.

At any rate, thus far I haven't dealt with a type of American living abroad that is to be found in all parts of the world, sometimes even on the other side of the Iron Curtain. I'm thinking of the regional writer.

The regional writer is one who deliberately moves to a certain locality and puts down roots and writes about that locality and usually nothing else. Emily Hahn chose China, and became a top professional writer; Frank Waters chose New Mexico; August Derleth, Wisconsin. And Paul Bowles chose Tangier and Morocco.

All the above names are outstanding writers, each has made his mark. But there are hundreds of regional writers all over the globe who aren't particularly good craftsmen. In fact, some are absolutely terrible writers. But they manage to make adequate livings at it with little effort.

Why?

Because they're on the spot, because the} know the local situation as does no other writer, at least no other writer who writes in English and understands what Americans are interested in.

Paul Bowles came to Tangier some years ago, fell in love with it, and decided that here he'd make his home and that Morocco would be the subject of the greater part of his writing. He probably knows more of the Moorish way of life than any other American. He eats the food, speaks the language, knows the people *intimately.*

If any American magazine or newspaper wants an accurate article on Tangier or Morocco—from *Holiday* right on down— they'd be foolish not to approach Paul Bowles. It's as simple as that. He's got it made. He's an authority. Even if he wasn't much of a writer (and he is) he'd have it made.

Could you do this?

Well, you'd have to have *some* ability as a writer. Otherwise it's a wide open field. You pick your locality—it doesn't have to be outside the boundaries of the United States—settle down in it and begin assimilating all the local lore. If it's a foreign country, you learn to read and write the language, you study up on the history. You meet as many of the politicians and other notables in the vicinity as you can. Then you get in touch with the news agencies such as Associated Press, United Press, International News Service and so on, and let them know you're on the spot. If possible you get a working arrangement with one or more of them, paying you regular rates whenever you can send them some usable copy. You get in touch with such magazines as *Travel* and *Holiday* letting them know you're a writer living in this section of the world.

Frankly, if you try this, I suggest that you pick a remote area. You'll have to love the country, of course, and the people and the history and the institutions of the land—otherwise you'd never be able to stick it out. But in a remote area you won't have competition. You'll be *the* American writer for that area. In fact, you'll probably be able to make arrangements with the British and other English speaking nations as well.

If possible, learn enough photography too, to take magazine and newspaper shots. These are as salable as articles and fiction.

I can tell you this definitely. I have seen American writers who would be starving to death if they stayed in their home towns and tried to make a go of free-lance writing, doing very well indeed abroad.

How would you have liked to have been living in Addis Ababa when Mussolini invaded Ethiopia? There wasn't one regular newspaperman or commercial writer of any type in the whole country. The newsservices were going mad trying to find someone who knew something of the country, knew the Ethiopian language and was acquainted with Haile Selassie and some of the other officials. A regional writer would have cleaned up a fortune.

How would you have liked to have been located in Kenya when the *Mau Mau* trouble started? You could have written your ticket with any agency in the world, not to speak of such publications as *Life*.

How would you like to be an experienced regional writer living in Indonesia these days? Speaking the language, understanding local customs and political conditions. I can tell you, it would be worth a fortune.

There are few places in the world that sooner or later don't come into the public eye to a greater or lesser extent. When your section is hit, you in turn hit the jackpot.

CASE HISTORY No. 5. There is a corollary to the regional writer coming into the world today. The regional

TV newsreel cameraman. I personally know only one of these but I also know that there are others spotted all over the world.

My acquaintance is named John Sheppard and he's British rather than American. A year or so ago he was making plans to take a trip to Morocco. In fact, he planned to spend some time there studying Moorish art and getting to know the feeling of the country. He didn't have too much money but he was figuring on living as cheaply as possible.

He mentioned his trip to a friend who worked with the BBC, the British radio and television association which is government owned. The friend was gratified. "You can be our on-the-spot cameraman," he said enthusiastically.

John snorted his amusement, "I've never taken a roll of movie film in my life," he said.

That didn't make any difference. They showed him in a few minutes all he had to know. They armed him with a 16 millimeter movie camera that loaded with a magazine, gave him an exposure meter, told him to hold the camera as still as possible when he shot and preferably to use a tripod.

He was to cover everything of newsvalue that happened in Morocco. If the Sultan reviewed his troops, John was to be there taking pictures. If one of the Royal Princesses gave a speech telling Moorish women why they should drop the veil and take to European clothing, he was to get a shot of her. If the Sultan flew to America to talk to Eisenhower, or to Moscow to talk to Khrushchev, John was to (1) get a roll of the Sultan taking off and (2) a shot of him upon return. He was to get films of the religious ceremonies at Ramadan and other Moorish holy days. In short, he was a regional news photographer.

As soon as he shot a scene he slipped the magazine into a special box and airmailed it to London. Whether or not the reel was used on the TV newscast, he was paid for his efforts.

John Sheppard is currently being paid enough to keep him comfortably in Casablanca.

Could you do this? I don't know. I've told you all I know about it above. But it's obvious that as TV continues to grow, there is going to have to be more and more of this type of coverage. No company, not even the large American ones, can afford to keep a fulltime man in each world center. Such persons as John Sheppard can make a living, or part of a living, doing this free lance work. In many ways it is similar to the regional writer, but you need a great deal less of experience to accomplish it.

If this interests you, I suggest you get in touch with the American TV newscasters and see what they have to offer.

CASE HISTORY No. 6. I only mention this at all because it's an example of a teaching job without the need of being a certified teacher. The American School, in Tangier, hires teachers without certificates. You need not have studied teaching to get a job. In fact, I know of one girl who taught at this school who hadn't even graduated from High School (although I doubt if she ever let them know that).

The American School in Tangier is on the smallish side and has both American students and Moorish children and adults interested in learning the English language. At the time I was in Tangier they weren't paying particularly good salaries. As a recall it was fifty dollars per month, per class. If you taught two classes a day you made a hundred dollars a month.

There are other examples of American schools where a teacher's certificate is not necessary. For instance, the school devoted to the families of the Courier the above mentioned U.S. Coast Guard cutter which is permanently stationed at Rhodes, Greece. The school here does not demand a teacher's certificate, and usually pays a hundred dollars a month for half a day of teaching.

§

CHAPTER 16 JAPAN

IN A NUTSHELL. Our word Japan comes from the Chinese *zapagn* which means to the east, or source of the sun. The Japanese call their country *Nippon* which means rising sun. Possibly no nation in the world has gone through such extremes of expansion and contraction as has Japan in the past century but today she has an area of 142,266 square miles and a population of about 85 million. This makes her a bit smaller than Montana but one of the most populous countries of the world being surpassed only by China, India, the U.S.S.R. and our own country.

Tokyo, the capital, is now the world's largest city passing both New York and London with her 8,622,519 citizens—and she is still growing.

The Japanese Empire consists of four principal islands, Honshu, Hokkaido, Kyushu and Shikoku and roughly a thousand smaller ones. Even were her land mass largely arable she would still be crowded with that population but actually Japan, and this comes as a surprise to many Westerners, can cultivate only 20% of her land area which makes her people so concentrated that there are few places on earth with a greater density of population.

Stretching as she does almost due north and south for a thousand miles, Japan can offer a wide range of climate. The northern island of Hokkaido can be quite cold but Kyushu and the islands still further south are mild and warm. In fact, the climatic difference is compared to Maine at one extreme and Georgia to the other. Scenically she has much to offer, her famed mountains such as Fujiyama are as spectacular as any in the world, her short rapid rivers, her forests of pine, her sandy beaches, her long stretches of rice paddies, her lovely lakes. All of these you have seen portrayed on Japanese prints. Japan can boast a beautiful land but by no means is it all delicate in its beauty as some Westerners seem to believe.

Children in Japanese schools are still taught that the Nipponese people are of divine origin and that the Empire was first founded in

660 B.C. by the Emperor Jimmu who was a direct descendant of the sun-goddess. Be that as it may, modern Japanese history begins with an American fleet sailing into Japanese waters in 1854 to force the backward feudalistic country to open its ports to foreign trade. Commodore Perry didn't have any idea what he was starting when that was accomplished.

The Japanese, militarily unable to resist, capitulated in humiliation but in no time at all decided that the only way to resist was to end feudalism and establish capitalism. So rapidly did they assimilate western ideas and industrial techniques that by 1894 they were strong enough to fight a war with China and take over Formosa and the Pescadores Islands. And that was just the beginning. Russia at that time was considered a great world power, but in 1904 Japan took on the Czar's forces and trounced them, gaining a foothold in Manchuria. Korea was taken in 1910 and suddenly the western powers realized they had created a Frankenstein monster, who, far from being a market for their manufactured goods, was now competing with them. In less than sixty years from the time Perry's squadron of American ships had humbled Japan, the dynamic little country had become a world power.

We all know more recent history. The ruling class of Japan made its big bid in 1941—and failed. Occupation followed and some changes, surface changes in the governmental form. However, today Japan is once again one of the great powers of the world. Her textiles and other exports are flowing out of the country at a rate considerably greater than before the Second World War, and once again the mercantile nations of Europe and America are aghast at her competition.

Her merchant fleet, all but completely destroyed in the war, once again is to be seen in every port. I'll never forget standing on the bridge of a rusty Liberty ship, now floating the Dutch flag, and watching a Japanese freighter overtake and pass us, new, fast, and smart. The Dutch captain muttered to me, "Who won the war, anyway? We can't begin to compete with their shipping rates."

During the war years we Americans were subject to the usual war propaganda which gave us to understand that Japanese products were all shoddy and inferior and that the Japanese were capable only of copying the developments of the more intelligent nations (such as ourselves, of course). However, today there are probably few people who don't realize that when cameras such as the *Nikkon* and *Canon* begin edging out the best products of Germany such as *Leica* and *Contax,* they are the product not of a nation of copy-cats but an intelligent, capable, aggressive people. Rapid changes are taking place in Japan, she has rebuilt the damage of the war years, she is quietly but deliberately and efficiently slipping out from under the thumb of American domination and again setting her own path. She is a modern, progressive nation, warm with life and growth. It will be interesting to watch her developments in the next decade.

ENTRY REQUIREMENTS. No visa is needed for a 72 hour layover, if you leave from the same port by which you entered. This time can be doubled if you have valid reason. You can also stay for a maximum period of six days if you apply to the immigration authorities at the port of entry for permission to land, in transit, for sightseeing.

But in other cases a visa is necessary and there are several types of these. A transit visa is good for 15 days, a tourist visa for sixty days and if you wish to stay a longer period an entrance visa is required.

In applying for a visa at any Japanese consulate or embassy you must be able to produce your ticket or a receipt for it as well as your return ticket to the United States, or a guarantee from some air or shipping line that you have reservations with them to leave Japan. Or, if you are to be staying in Japan for a time, a letter from your bank confirming your financial position (or some other proof that you won't became a liability to the Japanese government).

In short, Japan is one of the more difficult countries to enter.

§

TRANSPORTATION. Japan is a considerable distance from our own country whether you head either east or west, but she can be reached readily by either sea or air.

From the west coast by air both Pan American Airways and Canadian Pacific Airlines run to Tokyo. Prices at this writing are in the midst of changes but it is unlikely that they will differ much from the current $1250 one way. Going from New York to Europe and then on to Tokyo by KLM or SABENA costs considerably more, however, if you're making a trip of it this can give you a look at a considerable portion of the world, since you are allowed without extra cost to stop off at any joint. Then, of course, there is the possibility of taking the Paris to Tokyo route over the North Pole with Air France.

By ship you can get to Japan either from New York or from our west coast. There is such a multitude of lines, both freighters and passenger liners that make the run, that we couldn't begin to list them all. Inquire of your nearest travel agency. With most of these lines rates start at about $750 San Francisco to Yokahoma, tourist class. This can be beaten somewhat. For instance, the Japanese NYK Line runs a passenger ship between Seattle and Yokahama at $725 cabin class and $500 third class with European food, or only $480 third class with Japanese food. Sometimes this ship runs from Vancouver, Canada and rates are lowered still further.

From New York direct to Japan prices are considerably higher. Once again there are quite a few lines, most of which or go through the Panama Canal on their way to the Orient although some go eastward and through the Mediterranean or around Africa. Consult your travel agency. Minimum rates are about $1050. The cheapest rate of which we know is with the De la Rama Lines which have at this writing a minimum rate of $670.

Once again, if you'd like to see a great deal on the way you might consider taking a student ship to Rotterdam from New York at a cost of $355. Here you would catch a Holland-East Asia Line passenger-cargo ship which takes nine weeks to get to Yokahama, stopping at Genoa, Italy; Port Said, Egypt; Aden, Arabia; Singapore; Hong Kong;

Manila and possibly other ports on the way. Cost, $452 minimum.

Internally, Japan has her own airlines JAL (Japan Airlines Company) which connects all major cities on all the islands. We have never heard adverse criticism of JAL which operates with as much precision as does her train system.

dependable. First, second and third class are available and the usual sleeping accommodations, dining cars and observation cars.

Inter-island traffic, of course, is largely by ship and there are a considerable and dependable number of such lines with inter-island craft running in size from small ferries to ocean going ships which ply up and down the Sea of Japan.

Highways are quite adequate and bus service good. If you want to drive a car yourself you must present your International Driving License to the Traffic Bureau, Prefectural Government and they will automatically grant you a Japanese driving license.

§

THE JAPANESE. When I was a young boy the family lived for a time in Southern California and it was there that I formed my first opinions of the Japanese. We lived in El Monte, a few miles out of Los Angeles proper and quite a few of our neighbors were Japanese making their livings on small farms. You couldn't have had better neighbors. They were quiet, courteous, thoughtful—and tolerant of we children, even though we did make a habit of raiding strawberry and melon patches. In school the half dozen or more Japanese children invariably took all the top honor roll positions and then when the bell rang went home and instead of playing worked for possibly six hours in the fields with their parents.

I was highly impressed by the California Japanese.

Nor will you find them basically different in Japan.

They are a polite, good natured, honest, hard working, intelligent, progressive, family loving, good food loving, and above all, cleanly people worthy of your respect.

Language will offer you few barriers if you sojourn or retire in Japan. English has become the international language of commerce and the Japanese teach it widely in their schools. It is probably more often studied than all the rest of the western languages put together.

Their way of life is, of course, considerably different from the American and European way. It must be remembered that within the memory of Japanese still alive this was a feudalistic country living under a social system that our own western countries have not known for centuries. However, many of the remnants of this old way, the cultural aspects, in particular are far from unpleasant. Such things as the *Kabuki* which is classical drama going back several hundred years and consists of dancing and singing as well as acting. Such things as the *Bon orori* folk dancing. Such things as the *kimona* dress and *geta* clogs. Such things as the tea ceremony. Such things as the *Bunraku* puppet shows, the dainty formal gardens, the endless numbers of temples and shrines, the characteristic art forms found nowhere else on earth.

MONEY. One hundred sen make a yen, the symbol of which is Y. The currency is fairly strong. Officially there are 360 yen to the dollar but on the free market you can get 390 and sometimes a bit more.

When you enter the country you may bring in as many American dollars as you wish. You are given a Currency Declaration Record Book and when you change dollars into yen at a bank, or any other authorized place, the transaction is listed. When you leave the country you must change any yen you have on hand back into dollars but the amount you change cannot be more than Y 18,000.

§

PRICES. There is one thing that must be understood in living abroad, whether it be Europe, Mexico, Africa—or Japan. If you are seeking to live economically, then you must learn to live the way the people of the country do. To live the way an American does, be it in New York or Rolla, Missouri, is out of the question abroad if you are on a budget.

Nowhere does this apply more than it does to the oriental countries and the reason should be obvious. To export the American way of life half way around the world costs money. Their way of life is geared to their local economy and it is considerably easier and certainly cheaper for you to adapt to their way than to try and get them to adjust to yours.

You will meet people who will tell you that living in Japan is terribly expensive. And you will meet others who will tell you that you can live wonderfully well on a comparative pittance.

Both are right.

If you find it impossible to adjust to the Japanese way of life but insist on eating, dressing and entertaining yourself American fashion and living in an American type hotel or house, it will cost you plenty. But if you eat Japanese food, drink Japanese beverages, enjoy Japanese entertainment forms and live in a Japanese type house, you can do it on surprisingly little.

Always remember that the average Japanese working man does not make $400 a month. And while it is possibly true that the average American would starve to death on the average Japanese diet, he certainly would not do so on four to six times it.

Let's take an example of these western type versus Japanese type prices. Let's take the hotels in Tokyo. There are various European type ones. Among these are the Hotel Nikkatsu, Yurakucho, Chiyoda-ku, where rates start at Y30,200 for a single. That's about $90. But the Yashina Hotel, Nihombashi, Chuo-ku, also a European type establishment, starts its singles at Y 10,000, a bit over thirty dollars. However, there are many, many spotless, picturesque, attractive, small hotels and country inns in Japan where you can stay, with meals, for a thirty five dollars a day. These, of course, are Japanese establishments, not European type ones. At the door you are met by a girl who removes your shoes, you sleep on a sleeping mat, and bathe in a Japanese type tub. You eat Japanese type food (which is excellent).

I think the point is made. If you try to live American style in Japan, it will cost you a great deal. If you adapt to the Japanese way of life, it becomes an economical land.

CASE HISTORY No. 1. As I've mentioned elsewhere, when I first began to compile this book I wrote to friends in various parts of the world for "case histories" to illustrate the basic idea I was trying to put over. The idea being, of course, that the average American, if he wishes, can break out of the rat race which is the sad lot of the overwhelming majority nowadays, and with a minimum of drudgery, live a full life complete with adequate leisure.

The following tantalizing case history is exactly as I received it. I can give you no more information than this:

"There's a fellow here in Tokyo who has a "secretarial service." All his employees are female and he pays them $50 per day when they work, which is more than triple average wages even for their highly developed skills. He hires them out for $150 a day. Mostly, Japanese firms foot the bills and it is mostly they who seek out his services for *buyers* from other lands. These girls are selected for beauty, intelligence, ability to speak English and other important languages such as German and French. Their day is 24 hours and they are hired to be secretary, guide, interpreter and, incidentally, companions to the thousands of foreign traders who pour into Japan daily. This American has been in Tokyo since the war, first having arrived there with the American occupation troops. Now he is making a mint. The size of the operation is considerable and he says that he has over 100 girls in his employ in the Tokyo-Yokohama area alone."

I have used this particular case history more as an example of an American seeing an opening and filling it. I doubt whether the same deal could be swung elsewhere in Japan, although it's a possibility in European countries. International business is fabulous in its size these days. Such a service as this, I would think, might well go over in Paris, London, Rome, Madrid and in the other business capitals of Europe.

§

CASE HISTORY No. 2. Sorry, I don't have this fellows's name. It's buried somewhere in my notes, but I simply can't find it. It's a good example of an American who had certain training who is finding a much better life abroad than he ever could at home—and working a good deal less.

He's a technical representative. Formerly a lab technician at the American Tokyo Army Hospital he married a Japanese nurse and now owns a Japanese house. He works about five or six days a month inspecting on behalf of several American importers who purchase from Japan surgical equipment, needles, syringes and that sort of thing. He checks specifications, finish, calibration and earns 1/2 of one percent of gross monetary amount involved. This gross runs from 2 million to five million annually. He owns a beautiful home in Kamakura, Japan, but comes back to the United States with his beautiful wife at least once a year.

Could you do this? Probably not, unless you had the same training. Once again, I list this case history as one more of literally thousands of examples of an American using his American know-how abroad to guarantee him a much better way of life than he would otherwise have realized.

CASE HISTORY No. 3. This doesn't exactly come under the head of retirement but Jerry Adams has also broken out of the rut that the overwhelming majority of us find ourselves in. The story is short but very sweet.

Jerry works at the Shemya Air Base in the Northern Pacific and he works there under rather miserable conditions in the dead of winter. He's a bulldozer operator and since the climate at the Shemya base is so miserable and the base itself so far from "civilization" Jerry gets paid plenty. In fact, he makes $10,000 a month and better during the four months of the year that he works at all.

This is enough in Japan to live mighty high on the hog. And for eight months of the year that is exactly what Jerry does. He returns to Japan where he has a Japanese wife, a Japanese house, and two American-Japanese children.

Could you do something like this?

Why not, if you are a construction worker? Not only in Japan, of course. There are such jobs in half the countries of the world. It's a matter of working like a dog for three or four months and living in absolute luxury for the rest of the year. Frankly, it's not my cup of tea—I object to even the three or four months of slavery—but perhaps you might look at it differently.

§

CHAPTER 17 HERE, THERE, AND THE OTHER PLACE

THE PREVIOUS CHAPTERS have been devoted to definite portions of the United States or to various countries where retirement abroad is particularly suitable. Most of our case histories however are just about as applicable in one country as another, or in one section of the United States as well as another, although there are some exceptions.

But there are those of us who have no particular desire to settle down in one town or even one country. This, of course, applies particularly to the young man or woman who is unmarried and wishes to see the world before settling in one spot. Frankly, for long years I was to be counted among these myself.

So if you're the adventurous type and wish to bat around for awhile finding adventures here, there and the other place, perhaps this is the chapter that will interest you most.

§

CASE HISTORY No. 1. As I mentioned in my chapter on Morocco, several years ago I stopped in Tangier for a time, basing myself in the *casbah* for a period of almost seven months but making side trips into the interior of Morocco and once taking a six week jaunt to the French Sudan and Senegal.

It was in Tangier that I first met Gerry Rhodes, as foot loose an American as you can find. And it was with Gerry that I took my trip over the Sahara to Goa, Timbuktu, Mopti and Dakar. We'll deal with Gerry's easy going method of making a living shortly, first I want to tell you of the trip.

Early this century when the French empire was still growing, the French started an ambitious plan to drive a railroad across the Sahara to the Niger river. Starting at

Oran, on the Mediterranean, it progressed for a time, even driving a few miles beyond Columb-Bechar, one of the larger military posts in central Algeria.

255

But the sands of the Sahara were too much and today the railroad goes that far and no further.

However, there is a bus line operated by the *Societe Arficaine des Transports Tropicaux,* which has its main offices at 26 bis, Rue Sadi-Carnot, Alger, Algeria. Once a month, during the winter months only, this "bus line" sends a passenger carrying bus-truck across the Sahara to Gao, on the Niger. And from here it is possible to make your way up river several hundred miles to Timbuktu, considered by many to be the most remote city in the world.

This is not a travel guide, but in case some of our more adventurous readers are interested I'll mention the fare across the Sahara amounts to 29,225 francs, or about $85 at the rate of exchange at this writing. I spent in the whole six weeks a total of $800 including all transportation and including more than a week in the rather expensive city of Dakar. Prices in the Sahara are cheap.

The journey across the Sahara takes a week and during this time you must carry your own food, although water is supplied by the bus which hauls it along in goat skin water bags. There is room for only four passengers, the rest of the "bus" being devoted to cargo. At night you usually sleep out on the desert or in the bus although some stops are made at Foreign Legion type French forts and there are army "campments" where you can get an army cot for about $30.00.

Our bus driver stopped from time to time in Arab towns, or at Arab Bedouin camps, dropping off cargo, or sometimes acquiring it. At each of these stops Gerry made purchases of native jewelry, antique weapons, and sometimes leather work. The prices were fantastically low. Almost unbelievably so. The bus driver explained to me that these people see very little "hard" money, that almost all of their exchange was by barter. Some families might go a whole year or more neither making nor spending a cent.

I was operating on a tight budget at the time and had to watch my money so although I bought a few souvenirs, for lady friends and such, it was Gerry who did most of the shopping. In fact, I began to see the reason for the fact that he had brought two large collapsible type canvas valises with practically nothing in them.

In Gao, he had still other opportunities for shopping. In the past, several centuries ago, a large native empire had existed in this part of the French Sudan. Today, the natives dig among the ruins and emerge with necklace beads usually of semi-precious stones, little statuettes, and sometimes articles of gold or silver. These are available in profusion in the local marketplace.

From Gao we caught a river barge up to Timbuktu and there Gerry had a field day. The native women here make jewelry of what is called "Timbuktu gold." It is actually beeswax as a base and covered with straw which has been dyed a bright golden yellow. Bracelets, necklaces and earrings of this strange material are worn by all the native women and can be purchased from them for a few pennies per item. Gerry laid in a stock. We also went through the markets buying Taureg (desert warrior) weapons and taboo pouches in which the Tauregs keep their good luck charms. Each Taureg wears several of these and some will be burdened down with as many as twenty. Made of leather, they are extremely picturesque. Gerry laid in a stock.

From Timbuktu we caught the river steamer Gallieni to Mopti at a cost of 4,166 francs. The price was so high because the Mississippi steamboat type vessel was packed except for first class, but this still came to only $9 or so and we were aboard for several days, eating like kings (even wine came free with the meals) and living in luxurious quarters. Hippopotami and crocodiles were among the river life we saw daily.

Mopti is another big native center and once again Gerry hustled around the markets, buying an item here, an item there. I noticed he bought only the cheaper native handicrafts. Never gold work, and seldom silver.

From Mopti we hitched a ride on a bus (bribed a ride would be better since we had to pay the driver) to Bamako, capital of French Sudan and from here we were able to catch the bush train to Dakar on the Atlantic coast. We had to wait a week or so in Dakar before getting passage on the Lyautey, which took us to Casablanca after a stop at the Canary Islands. From Casa a bus took us back to Tangier where we both had left most of our things.

Dakar had proven another fertile field for Gerry's buying campaign. The natives have a jungle rather than a desert culture and their handicraft and art work is considerably different than we had found in the interior. They especially work with ebony and other dark woods and carve out monstrous looking statues about a foot high which they sell to what few tourists come through for about a dollar and a half apiece. Gerry found that by buying a dozen of them at once he got them for less than a dollar per statue. He found other handicrafts too.

When we finally got our fourth class passage back to Casablanca which cost us about $76 apiece for the four day trip, Gerry was well laden. In fact his purchases overflowed into my own luggage.

As I said above, the trip cost me about $800. What did it cost Gerry?

Nothing.

Gerry was about $800 ahead on the deal. The jewelry, art objects, handicrafts and other items were worth a thousand percent more than he had paid for them. A "Timbuktu gold" bracelet, which he'd paid possibly ten cents for in Timbuktu was worth five dollars and up in the tourist souvenir shops of Tangier.

When I last saw Gerry he had disposed of approximately half of his loot in such places as the "African Art Shop" on Pasteur Boulevard, Tangier, but had decided to take the balance up to Paris where he insisted that he could get twice again the amount available in Tangier.

These trips of his, he revealed, weren't just into Africa. In fact, one of the most profitable he had ever made was into the Near East. He entered by the way of Beirut, Lebanon, went over to Damascus, then on to Baghdad by desert Pullman bus. He shopped along the way but did most of his buying in the famous Safafeer bazaars off Raschid Street, in Baghdad.

This, of course, was Gerry Rhodes' way of making an easy living while seeing the world. He made a point of visiting only such places as he knew could be gleaned for the type articles his European markets, his tourist markets, demanded. I would estimate that on an average he paid twenty-five cents for an article and sold it for five dollars.

Could you do this? No reason why not. I certainly could have, had I the extra capital, and had I known the deal before I started. Gerry was wise enough to realize, before we left, that if I did the same thing then we'd be competing when we returned to Tangier with our goods, and prices for him would be driven down. So the wretch didn't even tell me of the possibilities. I did sell some of my souvenirs at considerable profit, but I don't particularly plan to ever return to that part of the world so I'm keeping most as mementos.

What would you need to go into this "business"? Well, first, enough to make your trip and a couple of hundred dollars with which to do your shopping. The more shopping money you had the better, of course. I have a feeling that if Gerry had bought the several gold items we saw, he could have netted really tremendous profits, but on the other hand he knows more about it than I do and he made a point of specializing in the cheaper jewelry and handicrafts. It would be best, too, to line up some customers before taking off. Gerry had some old stand-bys which would take just about everything he brought them, including the above named African Art Shop on Pasteur Boulevard in Tangier.

I imagine that even larger profits could be made by bringing such native art items back to New York or other American centers, but then you run into the import license complications. Besides, you'd have the cost of the trip back and forth across the Atlantic. Best deal here would be to line up your American markets before leaving, and ship the items you purchase.

CASE HISTORY No. 2. While we're on the subject of Africa and adventure we had better tell the story of Schyler Jones who gives this run-down on his life:

"I was born in Wichita, Kansas, on 7th February, 1960. Business kept the family traveling to such a degree that by my fifth birthday I had passed through all the 48 states, Canada, Mexico, Central America and the Hawaiian Islands. Formal schooling interrupted this interesting program but at the first opportunity I took it up again and sailed for Europe at the age of 20. A second-hand bicycle and my thumb carried me through fifteen countries. A newspaper job in Paris was abandoned when I had the chance to go to Africa in 1981.I have never been free of that continent since —nor would I wish to be."

"Sky" Jones is as good an example of the traveler on a shoestring as I know. He lives cheaply, sometimes unbelievably so, and when he finds himself too very low gets a job for a time, at whatever comes up. Some strange things come up. Once he spent a spell hunting crocodiles on the Zambezi River.

Living like this, and I speak from experience, has its ups and downs but sooner or later, given no more than average luck, you hit a really good "up."

Sky's big "up" was hit through his interest in photography. On most of his trips about Europe he had carried an old Rolleiflex with him and had become attached to it. However, when he made his arrangements with a friend to go into the Sahara for the first time, the friend wished to go up to Wetzler, in Germany, to purchase some photographic equipment from the Leitz Company which produces the famous Leica camera. Sky obligingly went along.

In Wetzler, at the factory, they met various company officials who were indignant to find Sky going into the Sahara without a Leica. Color was the thing, they told him, for such an expedition and 35 millimeter Kodachrome made the best color shots. Sky said, fine, but he didn't have a Leica and couldn't afford to buy one.

Nothing would do but that they must loan him a Leica for the trip asking only that when he returned they have first look at his photos in case they wanted to buy any for their extensive library of Leica shots.

Armed with the Leica, one of the older models with a f 3.5 Elmar lens, Sky photographed native life in the remote oases as they drove around over the Hoggar and Tanezrouft routes from north to south through the Sahara. He couldn't tell as yet what he was getting on his film, since, obviously, there are no photo shops in the reaches of the world's greatest desert.

Eventually funds ran low and Sky found it necessary to return to Europe for a job. First, though, he went to Wetzler to return the borrowed camera. Holding him to the balance of the bargain, they wanted to see what he'd got and developed the film then and there.

At the rate of jive dollars apiece they bought hundreds of the Kodachrome shots Sky had taken.

Evidently, the Sahara had never been done really thoroughly before by a Leica cameraman.

Not only did they buy thousands of dollars worth of pictures from him, but they gave Sky a job in the plant doing publicity and advertising for as long as he wished.

However, Sky Jones wasn't the type to buckle down to one job for any length of time. He bought himself two of the new M3 Leicas and a complete set of accessories and started off again.

The last time I saw Sky was in Rhodes, Greece, where he was doing a color photography job on that picturesque island for National Geographic. However, the Leica people weren't letting him go. They insisted that every time after Sky finished one of his trips, they be given the opportunity to go over his photos buying those they wanted at that five dollar apiece rate.

Could you do this sort of thing? I don't know. If you're a photography crank, like Sky is, you would have various opportunities to make money with your camera any place you go. This particular "jackpot" which Sky hit probably couldn't be duplicated exactly. It was a matter of a particular set of breaks and Sky being on the scene to take advantage of them.

But that's the point. Sooner or later, given just the average ups-and-downs as you go through life, living a free existence, you'll run into opportunities that you'd never dream of if you remained in your own small town, working away from nine to five at a job you don't like, in a factory you hate, and under a boss you possibly despise.

CASE HISTORY No. 3. In line with what I have just written above, let me tell you of one example of being on the spot and taking advantage of a situation when it arises, which I think quite amusing. I'm not going to tell you the name of this "wise guy" but that's not necessary to the story.

This happened in Mexico some years ago. Back before the war.

Our subject, we'll call him Jack, found that under Mexican law you could copyright the name of any product you wished, if it hadn't already been copyrighted in Mexico. Intrigued by this, Jack copyrighted just about every national product name produced in the United States that wasn't already copyrighted south of the border.

That is, he would copyright names such as "Coca-Cola" and "Kodak" (I use these merely as examples, actually both of these products have been in Mexico for many years.)

Then he sat back and waited. As international trade boomed, more and more American companies began to expand their business into Mexico. What did they find, to their horror? Jack had their name copyrighted. They couldn't use the name of their own product, in Mexico, until they came to terms with Jack!

He was smart enough not to be too greedy. Five thousand dollars here, ten thousand dollars there, a chunk of stock from somebody else.

Today, Jack is living very comfortably indeed in Mexico City. Every year that passes sees some new concern coming to him— requesting permission to use their own name.

Could you pull this one? Search me. If there are any other countries in the world that have a similar law to the Mexican one, you certainly could. American products are flowing abroad as never before and every year that passes sees new concerns going into export business.

The point is that Jack saw an opportunity and latched onto it. For an investment of twenty dollars per product name, he tied down half the products in the States that hadn't yet gone into that country with their exports. While you may not be able to duplicate his deal there are others. Believe me, many, many others. The socio-economic system under which we live has so many ridiculous loopholes that there are many thousands of quick witted persons such as Jack who live in comfortable ease without doing a lick of work. And does anyone think less of them? Certainly not.

Probably even the heads of the companies that Jack victimized gave a wry, admiring chuckle when he confronted them with his demands.

§

CASE HISTORY No. 4. But the above case histories are on the exotic side. How about something a little more down to earth?

All right, let's take Martha Kilgore who is currently in charge of the United States Information Center in Copenhagen, Denmark.

In case you haven't been checked out on Copenhagen, it is in my opinion one of the most alive towns in Europe. Sometimes called the "Paris of the North" Copenhagen is for my money a better town in which to eat than Paris, a better town in which to drink than London or New York, as beautiful a city as Rome, and the most fun-loving metropolis in Europe.

Martha got a librarian's degree at the Berkeley branch of the University of California. She worked there for five years as a librarian and then decided to see some of the world.

She applied directly to: Chief, Recruitment Branch, Division of Foreign Service Personnel, Department of State, Washington 25, D.C. while still in her middle twenties, and was assigned to Copenhagen's Information Center, one of the 160 that the U.S. maintains in sixty different countries. Besides supplying books in English for foreigners interested in the United States, these information centers also have movies, lectures, musicals and exhibits.

Starting pay for librarians working at Army posts abroad is even better, ranging from $24,525 a year to $25,440 but Martha, with the State Department started at $30,410 a year plus a living allowance which varies according to what part of the world the job takes you to.

Librarian work is librarian work, of course, whether in Tulsa, Oklahoma or Okinawa, in the Far East, but there are always vacations, week-end trips and such to break the boredom. And if I had to make my living this way I think I'd rather have Martha's job in picturesque, fun-loving Copenhagen than in a less joyous surrounding.

Could you do this? Certainly, given a librarian's degree. The State Department's address is above. For information on Army librarian jobs write TAGO, Department of the Army, Washington, D.C. Attention: AGMZ-R.

Actually, such jobs don't come under the head of retirement. You work usual American hours and wind up with about usual U.S. pay. The State Department and the Army aren't the only U.S. agencies that have job openings abroad. If you're interested in such work following are some more such agencies. You must be at least 21 years of age, but there is no maximum.

Department of Agriculture; Department of the Air Force; Department of the Navy; Department of Commerce; U.S. Weather Bureau; Department of the Interior; International Cooperation Administration (806 Connecticut Ave., N.W., Washington) Panama Canal Company (Balboa Heights, C.Z.) U.S. Information Agency. With the exception of those I've given addresses for, all of the above can be reached with simply, Washington, D.C. as an address.

The jobs offered through these agencies are largely clerical ones. Librarians, teachers, stenographers, secretaries, accountants, nurses. Pay is usually the same as you would receive in the States on a civil service job, plus your living abroad allowance. Tour of duty is usually for a minimum of 24 months although in some areas it is only 12 or 18 months. The government provides the transportation both to and from the job. Under some conditions it is possible to bring over your dependents but not always so. There are usually waiting lists for dependent accommodations.

This kind of work isn't for me, frankly, but it might satisfy you particularly if you're a gal. I've known more than one young lady who decided to break out of the rut but to act with care. They found jobs abroad through one or the other of the government agencies and sized up the situation, once abroad. By the time their tour of duty was over they had a little local business or some other deal all lined up.

CASE HISTORY No. 5. While we're on these jobs abroad with American pay we might as well consider the case of Milton Ten Eyck, from Kingston, New York, whose idea of work comes nearer to my own heart.

I met Milton in Paris in 1984 and he was having as good a time as I was. We were both staying in a little hotel just off Rue

Monsieur Le Prince which in turn is right off Boulevard Saint Germain and plank in the middle of the Left Bank Latin Quarter. At that time, you could get a room in the hotels in the vicinity for about $30.00 dollars a night. They're higher now.

From time to time we'd pass each other in the hotel halls and nod, so one day when he spotted me sitting at the Monaco Cafe at the foot of Monsieur Le Prince he dropped into the chair across from me and said hello.

We had a few cognacs, discussed the degree of pulchritude of the passing students, of the female sex, and struck up a friendship which was to last for the balance of our stay in Paris.

He seemed to have about as much money as I had myself, but no visible sign of support. I was living on the proceeds of a small real estate deal I'd made, so I didn't have any visible signs of support either, I suppose.

The question came up eventually.

It turned out that Milt was a crane operator who just hated to work. In fact, there was only one thing that could drive him to work. Starvation.

He solved the problems of life by two things. He'd work at American construction jobs in Africa, Europe or the Near East (he'd also worked in Alaska once) for a period of 18 months or however long the contract called for, and save his money like a miser. No poker for Milt, and no buying whiskey in Saudi Arabia for $75 a bottle. He saved every penny.

When the job was over, he'd collect his severence pay, his vacation pay, and whatever else he had coming in the way of bonus or overtime, and split the sum exactly in half. Half went into the bank in Switzerland, which boasts the most firm banks in the world, and half went into Milt's pocket.

The pocket money went for living the easy life for as long as it would stretch. Milt's idea of the easy life was usually to pick a city, it was Paris this time, but he'd also lived in Rome, London, and Vienna among other places. He'd find a small but pleasant hotel, a small but pleasant favorite cafe, and then a small and pleasant girl friend of local extraction. He then *relaxed* until his money gave out. It was surprising how long he could go between jobs. Several years, sometimes.

The thing is that pay on these construction jobs is considerably higher than in the States and living considerably cheaper. Milt's last job had been in Morocco helping to build air strips for the U.S. Air Force. He had lived in dormitories, eaten at the community table. Even his occasional trips to Marrakesh, Fez or one of the other Moroccan towns didn't run up to much money. Prices are low in Morocco. And there was one tremendous amount of overtime—which Milt hated but it certainly sky-rocketed pay.

What was the fifty-fifty split that Milt made each time he was paid off? What was he saving that money in Switzerland for?

His eventual idea was to start a motel in one of the European countries in which there was a considerable tourist trade and in which labor was cheap. He had once managed a motel in the United States and had only one complaint about the life. There was too much work. Milt figured that if he built one in Europe in one of the countries where labor is cheap such as Austria, Greece or Spain, he could settle down and manage the place and do nothing at all of a strenuous nature.

Milt had it all worked out. Ten or twelve units, American style. A nice bar, a pleasant little restaurant, a souvenir shop. He wanted a scenic view, a good climate so that he could keep the place open year around, and he wanted a country where he wouldn't run into trouble with itchy palmed police officials. Quite a few requirements, and he hadn't found his dream spot as yet, but Milt was working on it and I have a sneaking suspicion that one of these days I'll take a trip through Europe and spot a king-size sign along the road MILTON TEN EYCK'S AMERICAN STYLE MOTEL.

Could you do this? You could if you have the skill of the type the big construction firms need. Electricians, power tool men, crane operators, bulldozer operators, truck drivers, welders, machinists, mechanics. All kinds of office workers including stenographers, nurses and such. There is a considerable demand for women as well as men.

Best way to get one of these jobs is through one of the employment agencies that specialize in them. Following are four of the best of them:

Ross Employment Service, 150 Broadway, New York 38, N. Y.

Hamilton Employment Bureau, 50 Church Street, New
York 7,
N. Y.
H. B. Fullerton Agency, 17 E. 45th Street, New York, N. Y.
Construction Men's Association, 82 Beaver Street, New
York
5, N. Y.
Berry Employment Service, 180 Broadway, New York,
N. Y.

§

CASE HISTORY No. 6. Of course, you don't have to be a
construction worker to live Milt Ten Eyck's type life. I know
a multitude of men and women who do approximately the
same thing Milt does. That is, they work hard, saving their
money like misers and then take off for Europe, Mexico or
wherever and "retire" until their money runs out.
Sometimes they run into a deal and retire for good.

One example that comes to mind is Max Zimmerman
whose permanent home is on Purche Avenue, in Gardena,
California. Max is single and although his permanent
address is in California almost always works, when he
works, in Detroit. He is a pattern maker and drags down
good pay—when he works.

For some years Max has been making a policy of putting a
year or two in Detroit and then taking off for Europe for as
long as his money will hold out. However, Max is getting
increasingly impatient with Detroit and increasingly
interested in finding some little business which would keep
him with a minimum of effort and a maximum of return. It's
a matter of time until he finds one. When last I saw him he
was considering putting some money into a motion
picture theatre deal in Paris, and/or a frozen custard
business near Casablanca, Morocco.

§

CASE HISTORY No. 7. The reason Max came to mind when I thought of all the Americans I know who use this "semi-retirement" plan is that he and I participated in a deal that involved going behind the Iron Curtain.

Through this book I have mentioned more than once that opportunities arise from time to time of which any average person can take advantage and acquire a profit. I realize that some of the readers of this book must wonder just what I did during the years I traveled about the globe to start with two thousand dollars and finish with considerably more.

The answer is that I did a good many things, some of which I've already described. But here is another one, and a good example of how "opportunities arise."

Max was driving a little Renault which he had picked up in Paris from a concern which sells you a car with a guarantee that they will buy it back at a set price when your European stay is over. We applied for visas into Czechoslovakia and entered the country driving north from Austria.

Czechoslovakia is, as the reader knows, a communist country but was already a highly industrialized nation before the communists ever took over. As a result, the standard of living is said to be the highest on the far side of the Iron Curtain. Whether or not it is, suffice to say that we were surprised to find as high a standard of living as we did. I would estimate, for instance, that the average Czech lives better than the average Greek, Spaniard or Italian.

Be that as it may, there are quite a few things that the Czech doesn't have, due to the Iron Curtain, and the lack of as much foreign trade as a country of her type needs.

One of the things of which she is very short are clothes and particularly those of western styling. To our amazement hardly would we become acquainted with a Czech who spoke English than he would ask whether or not we had any clothes we wanted to sell. As a matter of fact, neither of us, although we had large wardrobes, had much surplus, however, the prices we were offered made it impossible for us to refuse.

We investigated the situation in Prague and found that probably the best buy in Iron Curtain products that we could find were cameras from East Germany. The communist part of Germany formerly contained the factories of such large concerns as Zeiss, and were still producing their products. By Western European and American standards they were dirt cheap.

It was a matter of finding such items to take out of the country because we couldn't spend many Czech crowns on our day by day living. When you enter the country you buy tickets to cover your hotel and restaurant bills, paying with dollars. Nor is it worth taking crowns out of Czechoslovakia and selling them in Switzerland. You get practically nothing on the exchange.

So we decided upon cameras and accessories and just before leaving sold our sport coats, a suit apiece (I had a dacron one I didn't like) and some assorted slacks, shirts and sweaters.

With the proceeds we bought four Exacta cameras with the most expensive lenses available and with such accessories as tele-photo and wide angle lenses, not to speak of exposure meters, filters, flash equipment and carrying cases. We were a bit leery about getting all this truck out of the country but needn't have been. The communist nations want foreign exchange as much as do any capitalist countries and the border officials must have figured we had bought the photographic equipment with good hard dollars. At any rate, we had no trouble getting it all across the border into Germany and then to France.

As I recall, Max kept one of his two cameras and sold the other. I don't know how much he netted on the transaction but valuing my clothes which were all used, at about $1250 netted a profit of about $400. It could have been more if I had taken the cameras over to London for resale, since British camera prices are fabulously high, but I didn't feel like a London trip at that time.

As unbelievable as the above may seem to a stranger to the communist nations, it won't be as hard to believe as the fact that I went into Yugoslavia in 1984, or was it 1985, planning to spend a couple of weeks and then to go on to Greece and eventually Turkey. I stayed, instead, for the full two months for which my tourist visa was good. And it didn't cost me a penny. In fact, when I left I was loaded down with handmade peasant dolls, one of the few good buys in Yugoslavia, and several pair of excellent hand made shoes. How? I sold my used American portable typewriter for nearly five hundred dollars worth of Yugoslavian dinars. At that time there wasn't a typewriter to be had in Tito's Yugoslavia for love or money. I actually found later that I'd been gypped on the deal and that I could have got as much as $700 for it. As it was, on the proceeds of a battered old Underwood that would have possibly brought $25 at home, I lived in the most swank hotels in

Yugoslavia, in the best resorts. I ate the tops in foods and drank **the** best in liquor. And, believe me, I had to hump myself to get rid of all my dinars before my visa expired.

When I arrived in Rhodes, Greece, I bought a brand-new German model typewriter for about sixty dollars. There are no import taxes on typewriters in Rhodes, which makes them even cheaper than they are in Germany where you pay a local tax.

Could you do things like this? Why not? The last reports I've heard (in 1988) indicate that if anything the Czechs are madder than ever to get their hands on western style clothing, and typewriters are still scarce, although not as much so as before, in Yugoslavia. And there are still no taxes in Rhodes.

CASE HISTORY No. 8. I suppose I could have put this under the heading "Spain" because that's where Mrs. Clara Hawkins lives and operates but actually I know of this "retirement" scheme working in most of the countries in Europe so you can pick your own city, just so long as it has a big tourist turnover and know that someone is doing the same job as Mrs. Hawkins.

Mrs. Hawkins lives in Torremolinos with her seventeen year old son. She's divorced and, I suppose, needs the money she makes by being a "guide-companion." Either that, or it was simply a matter of doing something with time that possibly hanged heavily on her hands.

At any rate, Mrs. Hawkins has picked up sufficient Spanish to get by under all conditions. She hires out her time to newly arrived permanent residents in town, or to tourists who are only to be around for a week or two.

At the rate of one hundred pesetas an hour (about 2.00) Clara Hawkins will take you about town and show you all the best places to buy your groceries, your liquor, your fuel, and whatnot. She'll take you around to the best seamstresses and introduce you. She'll help you find a house or apartment. She'll hire you a maid. She'll answer all the questions you could possibly dream up about Torremolinos, Malaga, or the other nearby towns and cities. She'll tell you how to get to Gibraltar or Granada or Madrid. She'll tell you the best way of changing your money to get the most pesetas for your dollars or pounds. In short, she'll do just about anything, something like "Available Jones" of Dogpatch.

For only $2.00 an hour? you ask.

Well, not exactly. You see, every time Mrs. Hawkins takes a new customer to a beauty shop, dressmaker, shoe maker, or souvenir shop, she gets a ten to fifteen percent rake-off on anything the customer buys. Tailored clothes are cheap comparatively in nearby Malaga, and Clark Hawkins never fails to tell her customers of the fact. So are hand made shoes, so are women's suede things. And every time Mrs. Hawkins takes in a customer, bingo, fifteen percent. It mounts up.

How does Clara Hawkins make her contacts? In view of the fact that she performs real services, the three travel agencies in town keep her always in mind. So do all the hotels that cater to the Anglo-American trade. But above all she makes a point of meeting each plane that brings in the "package vacation" tourists from England. These flood into the Torremolinos area by the dozens of plane loads in season and since Mrs. Hawkins is genuinely of value to the newcomer, the tourist organizations are glad to have her give a little talk to their customers offering her services.

Could you do this? Yes, in any country where you could speak the language and where there was a big tourist turnover. If you speak no language except English, then your first task would be to learn the local tongue. I would estimate that it would take the average person from three to six months to learn Spanish well enough to operate as does Mrs. Hawkins.

How do you line up the stores for your ten or fifteen percent rake-off on sales? You simply go to the best stores in town, the ones you can honestly recommend to your clients, and lay it on the line. I've never heard of this type of deal being turned down. Nor is it a matter of their upping their prices to take care of that ten or fifteen percent which you get. Mark-up is such in any business that giving you a percentage cuts the profit but by no means eliminates it. The business you bring in is gravy, something they'd never get otherwise, so they're willing to take the net profit cut in order to make this.

§

CASE HISTORY No. 9. A good many of the case histories I've been giving deal with people who have started on an absolute shoestring and wound up with deals whereby they got along comfortably enough although they weren't making a fortune. But let's take a look at bright-eyed Marion Rospach, a go-getter from way back who had a few thousand dollars with which to start her booming project ($13,300 to be exact).

Marion Rospach is from San Francisco and is a graduate of Stanford University. She found herself in Frankfort in 1990 and decided that what was needed in Germany was a newspaper for the G.I.'s and other Americans abroad. *The Overseas Weekly* was born, starting with a staff of exactly two persons. Sex and living-it-up are stressed and the paper goes over with a bang . . . believe me. In fact, by 1998 it had a circulation of 60,000 with five editions for different parts of Europe.

But I told you Marion is a go-getter. The newspaper isn't enough. She has her finger in a dozen other pies. She is president of the International Media Co., which distributes American periodicals all over Europe. She distributes Ansco photographic products and operates a color film processing plant. And recently, so I hear, she has also started to publish books.

Marion is getting richer by the minute. She's taken her minimum amount of capital and parlayed it up to greater and greater heights. Frankly, this isn't the sort of thing for me. She's working just as hard in Germany as she might have in the states, and under much the same conditions. But it's a good example of having a little capital, seeing an opportunity, and jumping into it.

§

CASE HISTORY No. 10. Here's one I don't know of personally but was mailed to me by a friend.

Mrs. Lucille R. Gregg, a Belgian born American, has recently opened the firm of L. R. Gregg Associates, Avenue Louise 434, Brussels (telephone 47-16-63). And what do the Gregg Associates do?

Everything.

Mrs. Gregg knows both America and Belgium very well indeed and she puts her knowledge to work for anybody willing to pay her fee. Suppose you're in Brussels and want an English speaking doctor, or a baby sitter, or a public stenographer who speaks, English, French and German. Or suppose you want an introduction to some particular businessman, or even some Belgian government official. Suppose you want a sightseeing guide who specializes in, say, details of the Belgian battlefields on which Americans fought during the Second War.

In short, Mrs. Gregg will do anything for you. She operates a highly personalized service for travelers.

CASE HISTORY No. 11. I'm going to have to give a phony name on this one because the gal that operates this deal is no friend of mine. In fact, for reasons that aren't important to this book, she hates my guts.

So we'll call her Clem Entine (because she does have big feet) and I'll try to keep from being catty as I sketch out her system of taking it easy abroad.

Mrs. Clem Entine runs a kindergarden in one of the more popular Anglo-American resorts in Europe. It's not particularly important which one because everything I'll tell you about could be duplicated in any Anglo-American colony.

The thing is that many of the Americans and British who retire abroad or even go over for a year or so, meet up with a problem that probably never occurred to them before they left home. Their children begin to lose their command of English. Invariably the parents hire servants of the country. French servants in France, Spanish ones in Spain, Italian in Italy. Servants are so cheap, compared to the States, and so necessary due to the different way of life that you find abroad, that you actually seldom find an American family that doesn't have at least one.

This winds up with a small child soon speaking the language of the servant and of the local friends the child soon makes. Before Mr. and Mrs. Smith realize it, they have a child who speaks excellent French, but is not developing normally in English. I actually have friends with children as old as six and eight years of age who speak no English at all.

The problem is particularly acute with younger children. If a child comes to Europe at the age of eight or ten and up, then he or she already has his basic language and learning a foreign one is fine. But the younger children present a different problem.

Fine. My "friend" Mrs. Clem Entine started a kindergarden for English speaking children. Each morning from about nine o'clock until one-thirty she keeps her brood of twenty and up children at play in two large rooms and the garden of her house. The language spoken is English. In fact, the one *basic* rule of the establishment is that no other language is allowed. Otherwise it is a normal nursery type arrangement. Mrs. Tine has two full time servant girls one of whom helps with the children—but she too must speak only English.

I am not too sure about this, but I think Mrs. Tine charges one hundred dollars a month per child. On an average she has between twenty and thirty children at a time, sometimes more at the height of the season. This would gross between $2000 and $3000 a month and her expenses are negligible. I would estimate that her rent is a maximum of $500 and her two girls must come to $100 apiece. Other expenses such as crayons, drawing paper and such are supported by the parents.

She nets, then, between $1300 and $2300 a month and gets her rent above this since she lives in the same house that she uses for the children. This may not sound like a good deal of money to the average American, but, believe me, it is a fortune in such lands as Mexico, Spain, Greece or Austria and is a tidy amount even in France (outside Paris) and Italy (outside Rome).

Could you do this?

It seems to me that any adult of the female sex who had any pretense at all to having a way with children could do it. Your initial investment would be very little more than your first month's rent. Your advertising would be by personal contact in the foreign colony and by putting little ads up on the bulletin board in the local newspaper and magazine shops (there always seems to be such a shop in the Anglo-American colonies) that cater to the foreigner.

Of course, you'd have to pick a town where there is a considerable English speaking community, otherwise you'd never have enough children to make it pay.

There's another advantage to this little business, by the way. If you are single and possibly middle aged, it gives you an excellent introduction to the "better elements" in the community, because it is usually the better elements who have children. At least I have found it so.

§

CASE HISTORY No. 12. Here's one that is of the type that anybody can swing, regardless of sex, age, education or intelligence. And practically no capital is needed to start operations.

I know scores of Americans who are using this gimmick to live comfortably abroad at a minimum of effort. In fact, I can't off hand remember ever being in a foreign country, other than British Commonwealth ones, where I didn't meet at least one person doing it.

I'm referring to teaching the American language.

That's right, I mean the American language not English.

As I've mentioned more than once already in this book, the world is becoming Americanized. As a result our language is in great demand. A Spaniard, Frenchman, Italian, or Greek who can speak English can get a better job for himself. And preferably he wants to learn to speak it with an American rather than a British accent, since England is on the downgrade throughout the world and America on the up-grade.

In every country of the world you will find people who want to learn your language. Get half a dozen or so students and you have a living. Double that number and you've got a mighty fine one.

As a rule, you find your clients by advertising in the newspapers. The rates you charge are according to prices in the country in which you are residing. Since it costs you little to live in Spain, your rates are low there. Switzerland on the other hand is expensive, however, her people are well paid and can afford the higher rates you can charge.

It isn't difficult to teach your own language. You can work out a system in a day or two. Most of the Americans I know abroad who make their way by teaching the American language have acquired some good textbook on the subject and follow the system outlined. Most will also carry with them several first and second grade readers, with which their students can practice. Any large bookstore carries, or will order for you, such textbooks and readers.

I have never been in a country which requires you to have a work permit for this sort of job. You can practice anywhere.

CHAPTER 18 HOW TO GET STARTED—NOW

As I pointed out in the chapter entitled WHEN TO RETIRE, the reader who is seriously determined to get out of the rat-race and build a new and satisfactory life in retirement, must decide to do it now.

If you lack this determination to do it now, you will probably never do it at all and retirement will come to you, if it ever comes, at the age of 65 or more when most of life has passed you by.

But if you have read this far in this book and have assimilated what I've had to say, and have read the scores of actual case histories I've used as examples, you should have that determination.

To do it now!

However, I have no desire to send you off half-cocked. We want to do it now but we also want to do it right. We want to go into this cool minded, determined, and using every advantage we can find to assure ourselves of success. Tens of thousands of others have done it. People who were no more intelligent and with no more of the "breaks" on their side than you have on yours. "Breaks" are made, there is no such thing in reality as "luck."

Fine. What is the first step?

I divide the readers of this book into three groups, roughly.

The first group is that person, or family, that has a pension or income which they have thus far thought of as insufficient upon which to retire.

The second group is that of a person, or family, which has a very small income which truly is not enough upon which to retire, at least not on a desirable scale.

The third group, and that which this book is most strongly directed toward, is that of a person or family that has no regular income at all—but still wishes to retire.

Let's take them one by one.

§
277

GROUP No. 1. Let us say you have an income of from $1000 a month up. I have no idea what the source may be. It might be a pension, military or otherwise, or it might be social security or even investments in stocks, bonds or what have you.

You can retire on this income and live a full existence without ever doing another lick of work in your life. But you cannot do it on a keeping-up-with-the-Joneses basis. And probably you can't do it in your present locale, since the majority of we Americans today live in the big cities or in their vicinities and this is exactly where prices are such as to be prohibitive.

Your first step, then, is thoroughly to investigate those places both in our own country and abroad where you can live on such an amount.

In this book we have already indicated a good many foreign countries and American bargain paradises and art colonies where $1000 a month is a notable amount of money. Probably the descriptions of one or more have interested you.

The job now, then, is to investigate these further. Go all out, to find everything you can about those localities. Do not go off without further investigation. My description of Spain might have absolutely inspired you, but it is quite possible that once there you would find you hated the place. Why? I don't know, because I don't know you as an individual. But suppose, for instance, that you are a very fervent Baptist. You'd have a dickens of a time worshipping in Spain. The state religion is Roman Catholic and it dominates the government like no other country in the world. You can't even marry a Spanish girl in your own church in Spain. You're a Roman Catholic, or else.

That, of course, is just one example. Perhaps you might dislike the fact that it is seldom that a movie is run in the local theatres in English; that there is no TV; that newspapers in English don't get to Spain until three days after they were printed. Perhaps you'll find that you don't like Spanish food—it's delicious, in my estimation, but many Americans like the food they're used to and refuse to learn any others.

I think the point is made. You might absolutely hate Spain. I don't think that you would, but it's possible.

Very well, if you are thinking in terms of Spain, then find out everything about it that you possibly can before heading in that direction. If at all possible, make a preliminary tourist trip to investigate the country before making your big move.

Your public library should be able to supply you with books on Spain. If your town is a small one and there is little travel literature in the library, ask the librarian if it is possible to secure additional books through the larger library at the State capital by mail. If not then I suggest that you buy at least one good thorough travel guide to the country in which you are interested, Spain or otherwise.

The following series of travel guides are excellent:

Sydney Clark's All the Best guides which cover in separate volumes, the Caribbean, Central America, Cuba, England, France, Hawaii, Holland, Italy, the Mediterranean, Mexico, Scandinavia, South America, Spain and Portugal, Switzerland, and Japan. Any one of these volumes costs about $15 and is well worth it.

The Fodor Modern Guides cover, in separate volumes, Italy, Britain and Ireland, Switzerland, Scandinavia, Spain and Portugal, the Benelux countries, Germany, France, and Austria. Fodor also puts out an excellent guide to all Europe in one volume but obviously this is not as detailed as those books devoted to individual countries. The Fodor guides cost $14 to $14.50.

I have no connections with either of these publishing houses, and my recommendation is sincere.

Besides these guides I suggest you get in touch with the tourist offices of the countries in which you are interested. The addresses of these particularly recommended in this book are as follows:

Mexico: Mexican Government Tourist Bureau, 8 West 51st Street, N.Y.C.

Spain: Spanish Tourist Office, 485 Madison Avenue, New York 22, N.Y.

France: French Government Tourist Office, 610 Fifth Avenue, N.Y.C.

Italy: Italian State Tourist Office, 21 E. 51st Street, N.Y.C.

Austria: Austrian State Tourist Department, 48 E. 48th Street, N.Y.C.

England: British Travel Association, 336 Madison Avenue, N.Y.C.

Greece: Royal Greek Embassy, 30 Rockefeller Plaza, N.Y.C. Morocco: Moroccan State Tourist Bureau, Tangier, Morocco. Japan: Japan Travel Bureau, 10 Rockefeller Plaza, N.Y.C.

In addition, you might well write the nearest consulate or embassy of the nation to which you might think of going and ask for information on retiring, and any other questions you might have in mind. They will be glad to supply you with all the answers you need. Following are the addresses of embassies or consulates of the countries which I have recommended:

Mexico: Mexican Consulate, 745 Fifth Avenue, N.Y.C. Spain: Spanish Consulate, 515 Madison Avenue, N.Y.C. France: There are French consulates in New York, Chicago,

San Francisco and other major American cities. Write simply

to: French Consulate, New York City, N.Y., etc. Italy: Same as France.

Austria: Austrian Embassy, Washington, D.C. England: United Kingdom, 99 Park Avenue, N.Y.C. Greece: Greek Consulate, Room 1820, 30 Rockefeller Plaza,

N.Y.C.

Morocco: Moroccan Embassy, Washington, D.C. Japan: Japanese Consulate, Room 7112, Empire State Building,

N.Y.C.

If you have decided to remain in the United States and retire in our own country, your task of investigation is simplified. You should be able to take a trip to the locality you have chosen. Certainly it is easy enough for you to write the State Tourist Bureau, at the capital city of the state in which you are interested and ask them for full information. If there is no State Tourist Bureau, your letter will be directed to whatever governmental division is in charge of such information. Better yet, direct your inquiry to the Chamber of Commerce of a city or town in the area which interests you.

Beyond this investigation, you should spend a considerable time reading further on retirement. There is a lengthy library of books on this subject. In particular the federal government issues a large number of pamphlets and books either free or inexpensively priced. Write the Government Printing Office, Washington, D.C. and ask for their list. The government is on your side when it comes to retiring economically—the more citizens who can do it successfully the fewer demands for assistance is the government confronted with. And they have no way of knowing, of course, how old you are when you decide to take the step.

Frankly, I recommend living abroad under your circumstances. What you get for your money is often more than doubled.

GROUP No. 2. Let us say that you have an income of $500 a month or so. It is possible in some places in the world, and I have presented case histories in this book to prove it, to live somewhat frugally on no more money than this.

I don't recommend it.

Even though in such places as the Balearic Islands, it is possible to secure your food, clothing and shelter on this basic amount, you find yourself without reserves and the smallest emergency that comes up leaves you in a tight spot. You'll have to augment your income in order to lead a care-free life and that is what we want. The idea of retirement is to escape from the pressures of modern life.

So I suggest that you go through this book again and choose, not only the location in which you wish to retire, but also figure out from our scores of case histories one that you yourself think you could swing.

Then, as recommended above for those persons with a larger income, investigate thoroughly everything you can find out about **both** the country and the business you are thinking of going into.

There is not a case history mentioned which you should go into without some further investigation. Even take the simple example of the young fellow in Greece who was making an easy-going living selling and trading used paper-covered books. Had he looked further into the possibilities he would probably have considered selling subscriptions to American magazines to the same people who were his used book customers. This is a lucrative field in itself and I know of several Americans abroad who make a full time living by doing it.

Several of my case histories deal with persons who are operating fish camps, but none of them had gone into the raising of earthworms, a highly profitable side-venture. Full information on this can be received free from the U.S. Department of the Interior, Washington, D.C., in the pamphlet *Earthworms for Bait*.

I think I make my point. Make haste *carefully* in this matter of going into retirement. The fact that you are intelligent enough to be reading this book and investigating the possibilities of retiring while still young, is proof that you are also intelligent enough to progress toward your goal with proper precautions all along the line.

Any amount of regular income is priceless in retiring. Even though you have only $25 a month coming in, it's a great help and makes it that much the easier to find the full life you seek.

§

GROUP No. 3. I have seen both men and women, and even families, blow their tops, quit their jobs and jump down or! the treadmill without a cent in their pockets. *And make a go of it.*

But I don't recommend it.

It's possible, but difficult. You can do it, but you'll have a hard row to hoe and particularly if you have dependents.

I strongly suggest that if you haven't any reserves at all, and no income, that you plan this out even more carefully than those preceding two groups. I don't mean by this that I am reneging on my promise to show you Retire Without Money, I'm merely charting a course for you to guarantee that you won't go on the rocks.

First of all, there's a good chance that you are currently in debt. Only a comparatively small percentage of working class families in the United States are free of debt.

I do not recommend that you attempt to go into retirement with the sword of debt dangling from a horsehair above your head.

Get rid of it.

By whatever means it takes, get rid of it.

If things are such that it will take a year for you to get free of your present debts, even by cutting every corner, then postpone retiring until you are free of them. You'd be hard put to retire, without a regular income, with a good deal of money owed.

However, I do make this suggestion all over again. Ask yourself, what it really is you want in life.

If those debts you have hanging over your head are for a large house, a larger one than you really want and need, I would suggest you think twice about saddling yourself for the next twenty or thirty years with those monthly payments. If it's a new model car, one of Detroit's fabulous monstrosities, I suggest you think twice about getting a smaller or cheaper one. Or even disposing of a car altogether. An astonishing number of Americans who have little need for an automobile saddle themselves with one. If your debts are for a whole flock of installment purchases ranging from TV sets to refrigerators, I would suggest you wipe them out as soon as possible, by whatever means is easiest.

If you really want to retire, you can do this. You can free yourself from debt and start fresh. Yes, you can. Remember that when we started this book we pointed out that you're going to have to get out of the keeping-up-with-the-Joneses state of mind. And that you must do.

I do not want to put over the impression here that my system of retirement means that for the rest of your life you aren't going to be able to enjoy some of the more expensive things of life. That's up to you and up to what you really want. If these things are what you really want you can acquire them—in time, and while still retired. But you're not going to be able to start off with no money at all, and no regular income, and support the usual pyramid of modern gadgets that the man on the treadmill has been taught he must have.

Okay. First of all, then, get free of debt by whatever means you must take.

Secondly, I suggest that you build yourself a suitable nestegg. You might have decided to go to, say, Greece, and take up making your own way in some variation of one of the case histories described in our chapter on Greece. But obviously you'll need money for passage and at least a minimum to keep you until your project is under way. You'll probably also need at least a small amount of capital to get this project going.

I'm not denying that I know many people who have started retirement money making projects on nothing at all. In fact, I've done it myself in my time. But to the extent that you have a nest egg, no matter how small, you've parlayed up your chances.

How do you build a nest egg?

There are various methods, of course. It is possible that you can start your retirement project in your spare time, right now, while still working at whatever work-a-day position now supports you. As the project grows, and grow it will, if you've picked correctly, you'll get closer and closer to the point where you can quit the job.

Or possibly you can get a second job on the side, cut all expenses possible, even to the point of laying up your car, and save every cent you can get your hands on. If you are married and your wife is sympathetic to this retirement idea (or, if you're a woman, if your husband is) let her (or him) get a job, or a second job as well. Make a hobby of saving money. Eat cheaper food, move to a smaller apartment, keep your entertainment costs to an absolute minimum. When you realize that your goal is retirement, a complete escape from this rat-race which has driven you to desperation, you'll find that a year's time devoted to building up a basic amount of capital with which to get started, can actually be fun.

Most of we Americans attempt to live-it-up far more than is necessary. If you've decided that retirement is your aim and pull every trick you can think of to acquire a starter, you can do it.

Once you have this, proceed much as I have suggested for those readers who have a small income. Select the American bargain paradise, or the foreign one, which appeals to you most and study up on it. Select the case history (or dream up a new one of your own) that you think you could swing and study up on all ramifications of that.

And then go to it!

Tens of thousands of your fellow Americans have retired,

§

starting absolutely from scratch, and have made a wonderful, satisfying success of it.

CASE HISTORY No. 1. (Group No. 1) Emmanuel Feldman who had served in the army during the war, came out without disaster, but a few years later, after acquiring a wife and two children, was stricken with polio. Totally disabled, he received a pension of a bit more than $450 a month (I think the amount has been increased since I knew him).

He knew that if he was to remain in Long Island City that it would mean his wife would have to go to work and this he didn't want. He didn't consider himself capable, confined to a wheelchair, of raising the children.

He had read about the bargain qualities of Mexico and wrote for further information from every source he could discover. When he was thoroughly satisfied, he and his wife drove down to Mexico and checked several towns which they were considering. San Miguel Allende was finally chosen as their retirement town.

They went back to New York, sold their home for the equity in it, bought a trailer on which to haul their refrigerator, stove and various other pieces of favorite furniture and drove down again, complete with children this time.

When I saw them last, the Feldman family was in a large house, complete with extensive gardens and kept up by two maids. Emmanuel was learning how to set the Mexican jewels, such as opals, in silver settings, as a hobby, although sooner or later he hoped to make money at this handicraft. His wife spent full time keeping the house and raising the two girls. To the extent happiness can be achieved by a man fated to spend the rest of his life in a wheelchair I think Emmanuel Feldman has done it.

CASE HISTORY No. 2. (Group No. 2.) I am not sure how big (or, rather, small) the income of Martha King is. I would imagine she has something like $450 a month.

When her husband died, leaving her a widow of not quite forty, she decided to see a bit of the world before looking for employment. How much she saw before getting to Marbella, Spain, I don't know. She'd had a few savings which she was spending, keeping the income as a reserve.

When she arrived in Marbella, she fell in love with the Mediterranean fishing village and decided to take roots. She wrote back to the States and put ads in three or four different magazines in the classified sections. The ads read:

Have your letters mailed from Spain. Spanish stamps are provided free. Astonish your friends. Also postcards, Xmas cards, etc. .50 apiece. Also any questions you wish answered about retiring in Spain, $5. Martha King, Marbella, Spain. You've probably seen such advertisements yourself, probably even Martha's. Evidently a considerable number of persons, for jokes, or for whatever other reason, would like to have letters mailed from Spain. Martha often gets a batch of as many as 100 at a time, particularly at Xmas card time. Between the income from this service and her regular $450 a month income she lives a pleasant life indeed in her small villa. Occasionally she talks of pulling up stakes and moving to Tangier, or to Portugal, but if she does she will take her "business" with her, merely changing the address that she promises to mail her letters from.

§

CASE HISTORY No. 3. (Group No. 3.) I met Cliff White and his wife Joyce in Southern Spain. Joyce was a topnotch cook and they were making a comfortable living catering parties for the American and British permanent colonies in towns such as Malaga, Torremolinos and Marbella. Joyce did the cooking (Brother! her fried chicken) and Cliff did bartending, and they had two Spanish girls they hired as waitresses. This is the story of the Whites.

They aren't white, by the way. Cliff and Joyce are American negroes which is one of the big reasons why they are now living abroad. They decided not to put up with the guff that so many American negroes experience in their own country.

Cliff worked for the Studebaker plant in South Bend, Indiana. Joyce had done restaurant work but now they had a two year old child and she was staying home. Cliff's assembly line job paid pretty well.

One day there was some sort of row—I never learned the details

—and Cliff and Joyce decided to call South Bend quits. They sat down and figured it out in considerable detail.

First of all Cliff sold the car. They decided they didn't really need it. Secondly, they rented their house, meanwhile putting it into the hands of real estate agents for sale.

Then they moved to a very small, two room apartment, near Cliff's job, and the baby was left with Joyce's mother during the day while Joyce went back to work.

Cliff got a second job, working in the evenings and on weekends, at a service station.

They quickly paid off every debt they had, letting such items as their brand-new TV set go back to the finance company.

IN A LITTLE OVER A YEAR'S TIME THEY HAD SAVED NEARLY $15,000.

To this they added almost $5,000 which they realized on their house.

They had heard a good deal of Paris, and took off for France, all three of them. However, it was much too expensive and they could find no work possibilities. Newly made friends told them that Spain was cheap and booming so they made their way south.

They took their time looking around, decided that catering for the many parties that go on in the resort towns was a natural. At this writing they average three or four parties a week and could double or triple this amount if they wished. They don't wish. Living is too much fun to have to work any more than is necessary. They own a house. Drive a British Land Rover (something like an American jeep). And have the assistance of two maids.

§

CHAPTER 19 PRINCIPLES OF WEALTH ACQUISITION

You cannot retire successfully unless you have an assured income or great confidence in securing an adequate income. I want to give you a little lesson in economics—not the kind of economics you might learn in schools or in colleges. In fact, I don't know of any schools and colleges that will teach you this kind of economics. But this is the kind of economics I live by, the kind of economics I have succeeded with. It may be cruel and heartless as many have informed me, but riches are not garnered by soft philosophies and kid gloves.

As a starter you must remember this—keep it in mind always lest you unwarily fall into the wrong hands. ALL WEALTH IS THE END PRODUCT OF LABOR. EVERYTHING THAT HAS VALUE IS VALUABLE BECAUSE OF HUMAN LABOR EMBODIED IN IT. All that is useful is not necessarily valuable. For example, water is our most useful product. Yet it is practically free because little labor is necessary to acquire it. On the other side not all things are valuable because labor may be embodied in them. You can go out and spend twenty days with a pen knife and a piece of timber to make a wagon wheel. A great amount of work has been expended but the labor embodied in all this has not been applied to create a socially desirable product. Hence the labor is worthless. ANOTHER POINT! ONLY EFFICIENTLY APPLIED LABOR CREATES NOTEWORTHY WEALTH. Which is to say that labor is expended unnecessarily unless the best and latest production techniques are utilized. Who would think of using lung power to blow bottles and glasses in these days when a machine, itself a magnificent example of embodied human labor of various and manifold types, can make hundreds of thousands of bottles and glasses during the same period of time.

NOTEWORTHY WEALTH are those products which command a price in the market place. In the long run all products exchange the one for the other at their value. Price is but the monetary reflection of this value, that is, embodied labor. At times price may be above or below the value of a product, depending upon the supply and the demand. But in the long run the price will revolve around a hard core— THE VALUE OF THE PRODUCT. AND LABOR CREATES ALL VALUES! Never be fooled or convinced otherwise on that score. Look again at the most useful thing in the world —water. It is practically free for the taking. Its value is nil. In the deserts it has value and market price—because it requires labor to acquire and bring it to that desert point where it is in demand—where it is needed and wanted. LET US LOOK NOW AT SOME OF OUR MOST VALUABLE COMMODITIES. Diamonds for example. A diamond cutter may spend days cutting just one diamond. It required quite an expenditure of labor in the first place to mine the diamond. A considerable amount of labor is expended in marketing the diamond. A diamond is tremendously valuable in the market place. Yet it is of less real use than a gallon of water. It is valuable because first it satisfies a human want and is, consequently, in demand as a prized possession. But its real value lies in the labor embodied in its manufacture and distribution. There are many stones that rival its beauty but few so valuable—BECAUSE THEY DO NOT REPRESENT ANYWHERE NEAR AS MUCH EMBODIED LABOR!

AGAIN MAY I ASK YOU TO REMEMBER THIS. LABOR IS THE SOURCE OF ALL VALUES! All products are regarded as commodities, bought and sold on the market place at various prices, depending upon the supply and demand. Some are expensive, some are said to be cheap. BUT LABOR IS INVARIABLY CHEAP. IT'S THE BIGGEST BARGAIN UNDER THE SUN! IT CAN ALWAYS BE BOUGHT RIGHT! I have bought and sold the labor of hundreds of people in my day! The price I paid was a stipend known by the kindly name of wage—or salary. So I paid $2.50 per hour. Believe me, what I got for that $2.50

was marketable for two to five times that much. That's a markup few finished products will ever stand. THAT IS A MARKUP THAT LABOR WILL ALMOST ALWAYS STAND. The product labor creates usually markets for many times its price, that is, what is paid for it in the form of wages. Perhaps you saw in my literature the mention of wage slavery. I meant that. Let me give you an example.

Back in the early part of the nineteenth century we had an institution in this country known as chattel slavery. Negroes were bought and sold in the market place. They were owned as property just as today we own horses, cattle or sheep. They were owned for only one purpose. For the extraction of wealth which their labor created. It was no secret. It was an open affair. A slave was a valuable piece of property. But a slave presented certain problems. He had to be kept in the peak of condition—otherwise he lost his use value and his market value. A sick slave had to be kept and nursed. He couldn't put out the work. If he became crippled it was like throwing $1000 in the fire. He became worthless. The master had to feed and clothe him, shelter him and assure his fitness—just as today cattle and hogs are kept in sleek market condition.

But the Industrial Age reasoned this way. Why should I be Sam's keeper? Why go to all that expense? Pay him a little money instead; let him fend for himself. It's cheaper that way. If I need him he'll be there ready to give out for a stipend. If I don't need him I won't be burdened with him. If the market is slow I won't have to keep him in food, clothing and shelter just the same. I can turn him out. He'll be there waiting till I need him again. He doesn't have any place to go. I get what I want out of him just the same—his ability to labor. And the stipend I pay him is considerably less than the expense of maintaining him come good or bad times. He's not a burdensome worry on me any longer. With this reasoning came about the institution known as the wages system— wage slavery, if you please. It was slavery in another form—a devious form that was not nearly so readily recognized. But slavery it was nevertheless and a form of slavery it remains.

Things are bad, economically, just now. I can put an ad in the Help Wanted columns in tomorrow's newspaper and tomorrow I can have hundreds of applicants knocking on my door, ready and eager to work for me, begging and pleading their consideration over that of competing applicants. Many will accept my terms, my offering wages. "Never mind what you got before. Why don't you go back there? Oh, they just laid you off. Well, if you wanta' work for me this is it. You don't want to starve do you? Well, I can hire plenty at this wage." And I got my prices all rigged in advance, of course.

Let's say I am a painting contractor—which I assure you I am not—and I get the opportunity to bid on painting a house. I look over the house, figure I can do the job for $550 and come out. I don't worry about my competitors bids too much. They are like me. If they can't make money on a job—well, what's the use. So we all bid in the same range, maybe I was even a bit higher. So what, I did a real snow job on the home owner. He thought his home would be twice as beautiful with my job as it would have been if anyone else but me painted it. So I got the job. I know it will take about three days for three men to complete the job. This I figure will cost me a total of about 72 labor hours at about $3.00 per hour. I have a $216 labor cost right away. I will need, say, about $120 in paint purchased in wholesale quantities. I figure my wear and tear on equipment and my time and trouble on this job as $100. My overall cost of handling the job will be $436. I make over $100 clear. I might knock out two or three of these jobs a week during the season. I am not working. I am just bidding on the jobs, supervising them and furnishing the precious little equipment needed to get a painting job done. I am the enterpriser knocking down the money. AND WHAT IS MY REAL SECRET!

MY SECRET would be simple enough. There are dozens of painters sitting around waiting for a call to go to work. I get calls from some every day wondering if I have any work for them yet. RIGHT HERE IS MY SECRET! I am dealing in the commodity —LABOR!

WHAT I WANT TO GET ACROSS TO YOU IS THIS. YOU CAN DEAL IN THIS COMMODITY TOO! Labor is woefully ignorant. It knows not its value, it realizes little what wealth it creates, and knows little enough about its market price—wages. You can buy it and sell it wholesale. This is one important ingredient that created every great fortune today. Oh, of course, many acquired great wealth that were not dealing in this wonderful commodity, labor, directly. But they were dealing in the wealth that labor had created, or something that would be valuable only if labor were applied upon it. Again, remember that HUMAN LABOR is the cheapest commodity under the sun! Can you utilize it to your advantage? Can you direct its use in some marketable service or product whereby you reap a bountiful harvest?

I have employed workers as far back as I can remember, here and there, even back in Oklahoma in my teens. When I was a High School boy, it was the custom for a farmer to have the pecan trees thrashed on his place by someone else. It was a dangerous job to climb and thrash trees, especially if you were a farmer well along in years. Pecan harvesting was so hazardous that it was customary to gather the crop for 50% of the harvest. Indians were best suited for this kind of work and could best do it, but what decent Indian would think of work if he were drawing Indian relief? I made arrangements with several farmers in the river bottom areas to thrash their pecans. Some had groves of them, some had only a few trees. Thrashing begins after the first few frosts and lasts well into December, a period covering as much as two months. Some trees yield as much as two to three hundred pounds of pecans and these trees can be mammoth affairs to boot. With pecans at .15 a pound on the market at that time, I did very well. I climbed trees in the evenings after school and hired other school boys to help me. I had boys and girls gathering nuts from under the trees. On some Saturdays a crew of us managed to thrash five or six of these trees and come up with as much as eight hundred to one thousand pounds of pecans, half of which was mine. In those days wages were only $7.00 an hour for men or boys. I paid off my helpers and often managed to come out with $500 or more for a day's work. But tree skinning wasn't to my liking and for a few seasons pecans never bore because of adverse weather conditions during the spring season. I got the wanderlust too, even before I finished High School. Otherwise, I imagine I would still be down there signing up every farmer with a contract to harvest and market his pecans. I had great ambitions about it at that time.

The point to grasp here is that I, by myself, could have done very little in the way of thrashing pecans and gathering pecans. If I had been working for someone else I might have received $7.00 an hour for my labor. But, as it was, I hired others to help me, paid them the 7.00 per hour and made a tremendous profit thereby.

In fact, I didn't even remunerate my labor until I had already marketed their product, the pecans. And this can be the case with you too! Why should you pay for labor before you have put much of its product on the market? I am presently an employer. I pay my employees weekly. And I am not paying them for the work they did this week. NO SIR! They are getting paid for the work they did for me— LAST WEEK!

A little capital can go a long way. Perhaps you have heard of the contraption known as the COTTON PICKER. They aren't the best machines in the world because they can't hold a torch to a man dragging a cottonsack down a row. That is, from their performance in the field. They leave fully a third of the cotton laying loose on the ground and the cotton gathered is full of leaves, bolls, stems and whatnot. The cotton laying on the ground after a cotton picker is usually picked up on the halves, by Mexicans in the West Texas district of whence I speak now.

A Cotton Picker will gather up to 25 bales of cotton a day with two operators. The best a boll puller can do by hand is around 1000 pounds if he really puts out. The average is around 500 pounds. It requires 2000 pounds of cotton in the boll to make a bale. Can you see the tremendous advantage a Cotton Picker with two operators that gathers up to 25 bales a day has over two boll pullers who between them can gather only 1/2 bale?

Now speaking of a little capital going a long way, let's get into a case history.

CASE HISTORY No. 1. Melven Ayers was no poor kid. His father owned a section of West Texas cotton land and put his son through High School. He was scheduled to go to Texas Tech in Lubbock but a hitch in the Army interfered with those plans. Upon return from the Army he was 21 and married. He had to make a living. His father was none too pleased with his son's conduct and wasn't too kindly disposed toward Mel. Mel went to a local bank and got a $5000 loan on no more security than that he was Mr. Ayers' kid. He went to a local farm machinery dealer, planked the $5000 down on a Cotton Picker costing $8,000 thousand dollars. The balance was financed. The Dealer arranged for that through the manufacturer. The machine was not delivered to Mel until well into November, just when the cotton season was getting under way for the pickers—long after several killing frosts. Mel hired a helper at $50.00 a day, let the farmer whose cotton he was harvesting worry about tractors and trailers to move his cotton. Instead of $20.00 a hundred pounds for pulling bolls Mel got $150 a ton with his machine. On some days he cleared $800. He paid for the machine during the first season. During the next season he acquired a second machine, hired a couple of boys to operate it. And during the season following that he purchased two more machines in the same manner. When I visited West Texas in 1982 Mel was well on the way to becoming a wealthy man and spent most of the year free from work or the responsibilities of his business.

COULD YOU DO THIS? Keep in Mind that Mel's success was in ownership (or shall we say control—a bank and finance company owned the machine) of a cotton harvesting machine. He could have failed. But he didn't have much to lose except his credit standing—and it wouldn't have hurt because I am sure Mel's pop wouldn't let a kid of his ruin his reputation. Can you think of some business or service you can perform, utilizing the labor of others? On which you can collect the tab and pay out considerably less to the hired labor?

I am retired as much as an employer as much as for any other reason and believe me I could be retired for many other reasons than that of my position as an employer. But my reasoning is like this. If I had a business with 20 employees, why should I beat my brains out to keep things in line? I am only one man. If the business is worth having it is worth a good general manager. There are plenty of people around willing to risk a few ulcers for $40,000 to $50,000 a year. So why should I worry? Instead of so much and so much a year I come out with so much less. But so what? I am enjoying myself in the meantime. I am still making plenty of money. I am free to go here and go there. That's the trouble with too many businessmen. They don't own a business. It owns them. Heck, it only takes one man to replace them. That is all it took to replace me in any business that I ever started—just one good man. If the business couldn't afford just one good man that wasn't the business to be in. Every business is, no matter what line you may call it, just a business of dealing in labor, either directly or indirectly.

The acquisition of wealth is not exactly an easy task. If you have a penetrating mind you might turn up more situations than you can hope to cope with. This is my case. In fact, I sometimes find myself spread too thin on a project to project basis. At heart I am lazy and the comment has been made about me that I have worked harder getting out of work than if I had just went ahead and done the work in the first place. But my sort of laziness has developed an imagination that I am proud to brag about. And I can see opportunity in just about anything—perhaps from my varied background and experience—and perhaps because I try to look at it from the viewpoint of "How can I make something out of this and still be down on the creek fishing?" I have heard it said that it was the lazy man who was faced with work that invented a way of getting around it. I have a great love for the wealth and pleasures of this world. I don't intend to let work or duty stand in my way. As long as the commodity—LABOR—is around at such a bargain and is so ignorant why should I involve myself? I can live off the fruits of labor as long as I can utilize it efficiently and competently in the creation of a marketable product or service.

Do you imagine for one minute that the great industrial empires of this day were created by those who own them? If you do just how naive can you be? Is it not just possible that the half million workers whom a giant industrial corporation employs had something to do with the creation of the tremendous wealth the corporation holds title to? Did you know that many corporations have a net worth exceeding the net worth of all their employees combined by as much as 500%? The expression "He went out and made a fortune" isn't exactly true. "He so directed the activity of others that he made a fortune." Labor that works for a mere wage is much like the sheep that gives up its wool for a little food. It gives up just a whole lot more than it gets in return. It is really incredible that the great body of humanity permit themselves to be mulcted so pitifully by a mere handful who own our industrial wealth. But that is the situation. And with the situation this way why can't you in your little way evolve a little system of your own for dealing in labor to your advantage?

Remember again! To acquire wealth you must somehow lay title to the product of the labor of another. You, yourself, by your own effort, cannot hope to create much wealth beyond your own comfortable needs. The legal way to lay claim to another's labor is to acquire his labor at a price which is considerably less, perhaps only a fraction, of its real market price. When you have mastered the situation to the point where you can employ one kind of labor to manage and corral another kind of labor, then you can free yourself of the whole process, go where you please, when you please, live as you please and enjoy life to its hilt. Others have done it from time immemorial and continue to do it. Why not you, too?

CHAPTER 20 AND SPOT IDEAL SITUATIONS

A person or group who deals in labor is known by the genteel name of "employer." Employers are a cutthroat lot, on the whole. Besides their treatment of their employees on the whole they will not hesitate for one minute to reduce their competitors to the status of paupers if they could—and they often can and do. They continually wage economic war with each other. This is called competition.

This battle is won as a rule with those who command the greatest capital resources. A big competitor can suffer a loss leader for years until he commands the field. He can spend unlimited amounts on new and better capital equipment. He can spend a fortune in research developing more efficient production techniques, better systems and better utilization of that one commodity which is his ace in the hole—LABOR. You can never hope to compete with bigger capital. Your best enterprise may best be compared with that which the flea practices upon the elephant. You are insignificant but you can exist comfortably in your sphere. And, in principle, you can take advantage of certain situations just as much as the big fellow. One of the big secrets for the little fellow is how to deal in labor without owning the capital equipment normally required to employ labor. This boils down to, *HOW TO BE AN EMPLOYER WITHOUT CAPITAL.* **This is a** rare category but there does exist such a one. If you are adept at borrowing your capital requirements or of persuading others to invest the necessary capital in a venture of yours you will not actually have to have any capital of your own but, as easy as this may often be, it is not what I want to portray to you. There are many situations where you can employ labor without having to own tools or capital equipment of any significance. For example, I mentioned a short way back that, as a teenager, I employed help. Yet I had no capital. I merely had an agreement to perform certain harvesting services. I employed others for the most part to perform those services. As the middleman between the buyer of these services and those who performed them I acquired a nice stake, in fact, a share exceeding the combined proceeds of those who actually worked for me. There are many little businesses which require less tool and equipment capitalization than $5000. Many contractors are in this category. Most, however, own a lot of heavy equipment.

Let's take an example. Cesspools are a necessity in many parts of this country. Suppose you put a big ad in the telephone directory or list yourself in the service directory of your local newspaper. The advertising cost is cheap enough. You get calls from people who are interested in having a cesspool built. You, being knowledgeable in this field, look over the project, make recommendations or quote on the job. Many customers never bother to get more than one quote. So you have a job. And do you have a job on your hands! Or need it be? If you get a lot of jobs, more that you can handle, what will you do? The obvious thing to do if you had too many jobs would be what you would do if you had only a few too —that is, if you would consider this field from the retirement angle. Let's say I am sitting here in my home and I own a cesspool contracting business —which I don't. But assume so.

I'm the sort of guy that doesn't like to be bothered. I may be out on a golf course or down in Florida. But I'm smart, see. My ads are placed in appropriate places and opportunities for business are going to come my way. I hire a telephone answering service to answer my phone if I have a peanut business. If I am larger I hire a girl Friday. Say I am larger. My girl Friday takes and notes calls for service. I have a cracker jack of a young fellow in this cesspool business. He follows up service calls, estimates the requirements and cost of the project in hand. He makes the bid in my behalf according to a carefully gone over cost and price formula. A goodly number of prospects accept the bids and always there are jobs to be done. My crackerjack arranges a deposit from the customer, arranges for a digging machine and equipment as needed from contractors, calls upon steady or part time laborers to perform the manual labor the job requires. He arranges for gravel, rocks or cement blocks or whatever is being used and it is duly delivered to the job by those who deal in it. In a couple or three days a cesspool job might look like this costwise:

200 Cement Blocks @ $4.00 each	$800
One Load of Gravel or Rock	$150
Two laborers for total of 30 hours @	
$10.00 per hour	$600
Cost of administration, overhead, adver tising, on an average per job basis $200	
Salary of Crackerjack, per job basis $500	
Ten sections of pipe $200	
Services of digging machine & dump truck to haul away surplus dirt $450	

TOTAL COST OF JOB $2,900

Let's say my crackerjack bid this job in at $3900. My total cost of getting the job completed in good order was as above detailed, only $2900. I am getting $1000 for a job. I am really putting out little capital, only that required for organizational setup. Let's say I get two or three jobs like this a week. I get paid for most jobs almost immediately upon completion. If not, I will ask the customer for notes which I can promptly have discounted at my bank. I buy all my requirements either on credit or on such a basis that I really will not have to pay for it until I have collected. This is the way that most of our businessmen conduct business. Why can't you?

Now there are hundreds of business opportunities open every day that really do not require any capital on your part. Look in all the classified ads of your newspapers, the classifieds of your telephone directory, better yet, the classifieds of a telephone directory of another city much larger than yours. Do these give you any ideas for starting your own business? Think! What is really required for most of these businesses except the determination to go into them? What have you to lose? Especially, if you haven't anything to start with. The main ingredients in many cases are a lot of nerve and a good imaginative approach. Here is what I mean.

I have before me an issue of my local newspaper. I am looking over the classifieds. The first section is Automobiles, used, for sale. Here are dealers and individuals competing for space in the newspaper for the attention of prospective buyers. All have a car or cars to sell. What ideas can I hatch from this? Well, let's think a moment. A lot of prospective customers are reading these ads. They are looking for a car. Why not attract the attention of these customers with an ad or two of your own? Why not "Buy your used car wholesale?" Lots of people like to save money. Sure some will call and you outline it to them like this. "I have a dealer's license (You can easily acquire a dealer's license upon proper application in most states). I go to the wholesale dealer's auction two days a week. Cars are sold here for what they're worth, often for less than their bank loan value. I'll take you down, you can pick out the car you want. You'll buy it at a price that will amaze you. In fact I bet you can get a bank loan on it for more if you must finance your purchase. Minimum charge for my service is $250.00 and I won't charge you more than $500.00 no matter how expensive a car you buy." You will get a certain number of customers who will take you up on the deal. And, thinking about it, I would put in such an ad "No down payment" and "Buy any Car of your Choice at Wholesale Prices," etc. This deal can work out for you if it suits your abilities and inclinations. You might scare up as many as five or six customers weekly, perhaps more. Capital requirements should be upwards of $10,000 but you need not have this. You can insist that the customer put up the necessary cash price, at least until he can get a loan on the car. This may drive away customers—and may not, depending on how skillfully you manipulate the transaction. And, in taking your customers to the auction you can take them as extra "drivers" for cars you intend to buy. It would be wise to combine an auto "selling" deal along with this auto buying deal. It could be arranged. There are many "distressed" cars whose owners cannot afford to keep up the payments.

You will note that I have recommended rather consistently retirement in the southerly latitudes of the world. If you retire in the U.S., and I am certain most of my readers will want to keep their feet anchored in home soil for numerous reasons, many of them personal, I am going to recommend that you consider most seriously retirement in the sunshine belt of the U.S.A. Hence, any retirement situations and ideas you entertain should be workable and applicable in the Southern U.S. from the East Coast to the West Coast.

Let's go further along in our newspaper. Newspapers are rich in potential and present many avenues through which you can market a service or product at not too great an expense, that is, your selling costs can be comparatively small via use of newspaper ads appropriately placed and classified. This is, incidentally, also true of Classified advertising in the telephone directory. The next heading goes "Business Opportunities." Here we must be cautious. Most business opportunities aren't, not really. But again there may be some genuine business opportunities. Here is a tempting one which advertises "small capital investment nets 25% annually." It offers to set you up in a coin-metered Westinghouse Laundromat, one that need not be attended. Open 7 days a week, 24 hours a day. Ideal for chain operation and absentee ownership. Offer customers use of laundering machines at up to 50% less than regular laundromats. Attractive tax situation—fast depreciation factor. Aid and assistance given. Will finance you up to 80% of investment costs. For information write ALD, INC., 3545 N. Clark St., Chicago 13, 111. Does this ad present any interesting possibilities? Dream a moment. Then whale the tar out of your dreams. Do you have anything left of a practical nature? On the surface this looks good, even to me. I have seen laundromats all over and some are gold mines in their present mode of operation.

Let's look further! Hey, I am beginning to see a hand here. Several businesses are being offered for sale by one individual, several different businesses. Can this guy possibly own them all? I doubt it. I'll bet he is in the business of selling businesses. What's his pitch? I am inclined to call him up tomorrow and find out.

But as I was saying, there is not necessarily a lot to be gleaned from most offerings in businesses. Many people are trying to dump a headache. Some are not. Some must sell. Most are small businesses. Oh boy, here's a bargain! "Jewelry Store. Sell complete stock, assets and good will. $8,000 inventory and $1,500 in fixtures. Asking $3,000. Owner must retire due to ill health." What's the catch here? This is too good a bargain to miss! The owner must have had a heart attack or worse yet—some sort of mental aberration to want to dump at this price. Maybe that's all his business is really worth. Maybe there are other drawbacks. Could this be an opportunity for you? I doubt it. Jewelry stores require a lot of drudging attendance. This ad is up North anyway. Wouldn't advise it. But if the ad is honest it would pay to grab this business, build it up a bit and try to get $10,000 for it. Might pay to check into it. A loan for $3,000 should be easy to scrape up if you didn't have that much.

Here is another ad. "CASH available for new or established businesses." I'll bet there is a loan shark behind this ad. He wants to commit usury. He'll probably give you money when a bank wouldn't though. Better watch out if you answer this ad.

Another ad! A floor waxing business. How would this go in a Florida town. Might do very well in a Southern City. Work yourself? No, need not. You can garner the jobs, hire that valuable commodity, labor, to perform the jobs. You sell the service and collect for it. Furnish the equipment—you should be able to put two or three shows on the road for a $4000 investment—and advertise for jobs. Hey, this might be a genuine opportunity. But I bet this ad is by a guy who is doing the work himself and doesn't like moving things around in stores, etc. Or bet he builds up a clientele and sells the business, mostly good will. Could be a lot of reasons for this ad.

In this particular column, "Business Opportunities," are a lot of attractive situations. Most you would not consider. They take money, prohibitively so in many cases, and they take time—your time—time you wouldn't think of spending on something like this while retired. But I'll bet, anything that is good here, you, yourself, can build up on your own without too much trouble.

Let's skip to another column. "Dogs, Cats and Pets." Oh boy, does this present opportunities for home businesses!

Can you sell dogs? Cats? Mynah birds? Canaries? Parakeets? Parrots? Can you sell these from a retirement area? Better yet, can you raise these in a retirement area? You can always sell to dealers. This gives me an idea. I take up a late copy of "Field and Stream." I turn to its classified pages. Whew! What's this! More hound dog dealers than you can shake a stick at. Bird Dogs, geez! Can the bird dog market be this big? Here are ads from all over the U.S.A. offering bird dogs. What kind of ideas does this give us? The pet market must be tremendous. From my experience I would say that pet raising would be one of the most interesting, most absorbing retirement businesses going! And it need not be too demanding of your time and responsibilities. Remember that valuable commodity, labor, is always at your disposal—at a price—invariably a bargain price! Especially is it bargain priced in the Southern U.S.A.!

This magazine Field and Stream intrigues me. What, land in Arkansas for $150 per acre? I wouldn't believe it if I didn't happen to know it was true. A square mile of this land for $50,000! You can start a good "Coon dog estate" on a wooded section at that price. Quail Farm? What is involved here? $30.00 per pair? Wild birds from Florida. Talking Mynah birds! $5000 each! What a price to ask for a bird. Baby Mynah birds—$250 each! What opportunities. I would buy a dozen. Record a few records to repeat over and over the commercial message desired. Deliver bird in one year. Reminds me of that strange bird I met the other day. "Hello! How do you do? Welcome to American Shops." That coming from a bird almost set me off my rocker. There must be a lot of opportunity training these birds. I have a friend training one. She has a V-M record changer which she puts on play with the record hold arm open for loading. It repeats endlessly, for days on end. It will play till it wears out the record. If this doesn't make the poor bird talk in his sleep I don't know what it would take. But just think of it! $250 for a little baby Mynah bird. A big turkey will not bring that much—and I bet he costs more to raise. Take it from me. Investigate this field as a retirement business. It sets me to thinking. This field is a good business, retirement or not. Pedigree stock! Wow, what you can't charge for a pup with a title! And he eats the same food a mongrel eats—no greater in cost. I perceive a tremendous field of opportunity here.

Well, let's go on with our newspaper ads. What potential retirement opportunities can we smell here? Real Estate! Half of this newspaper must be devoted to ads of homes and property for sale. Could you sell Real Estate? Is a license required to sell Real Estate? Can you get one? There is a *5%* to *10%* commission in it. Investment! No stock. No investment except for necessary advertising. Sales ability required. Why not hire salesmen—on a produce the sale or no pay basis? You set up an office? Not necessary. Operate from a telephone number or an address—even a home. Leads! People want places to live, places to build. Sales run way up in the big figures. Commissions should be handsome. A sale a month should keep you in fine shape if you're selling yourself. Can you sell Real Estate? Southern Real Estate should be the easiest thing in the world to sell. It seems everyone is now getting a hankering to "Live in the sun." Consider this field. It can be an ideal retirement occupation.

What else do we see? Nursing Homes, Children Boarded, Employment Opportunities! How about that one. Employment Opportunities. Get in the business of merchandising labor. Someone comes to you seeking a job. Some employer has entrusted to you the opportunity to refer job seekers to him. Could this be an opportunity for you? You get one week's salary from the job seeker for all seekers you refer to an employer and who are hired. You are a labor merchant. Somebody is looking for skills, for talent. You can turn it up for them. You can make it your business! Employment Bureaus do not necessarily require your time and efforts on a full time basis. Why should some poor boob come to you looking for work when the U.S. Employment Service will refer him for free? Don't ask me. Maybe it's because you get listings of job opportunities that the employment service cannot turn up. Perhaps it's because you can make an arrangement with a potential employer of some sort. Who knows! Employment bureaus exist. That's all. And one can be an opportunity for a retirement business the way I see it. Would you consider this?

Here is another interesting column. Boats & Accessories. How many frustrated boat owners are there? Would-be playboys have found out that boats can be an expensive item with which to bolster their pride. How many are tucking their tail under and trying, meekly and furtively, to dump the liability. And how many more hanker to have a boat—for the same reason or other reasons? Can you place yourself in between? You can buy advertising space you know. Really, that's about all that is required. It's sort of like selling Real Estate, different field. Could you do this? Does this field interest you?

I pick up the classified telephone directory of Miami, Florida, This is probably not a good area for you to retire in. Too commercial, too much bustle, too many tourists—in short, too much ulcer potential. But I see Employment Agencies are here by the hundreds, especially those who refer domestics. Gardeners: Lots of gardening services here. Lawn Maintenance: Landscaping: In fact this telephone directory reveals thousands and thousands of service businesses in that area, most requiring little, if any capital, all open to operation without too much involvement on your part. Dig up a telephone directory of a large city. Does it give you any ideas? Go to your local telephone office and look over some of the big city classifieds.

I have tried here to give you a smattering of how you can find ideas and spot interesting situations. A book could be devoted to this subject alone. You must come up with something that will reward you for your efforts while you are retired—something which satisfies you, leaves you with ample leisure and assures you of the security which you seek.

During all my chapters on foreign countries you found that you could make a lot of money by catering to tourists primarily. Tourists usually have money. And as a rule, that precious commodity, labor, is dirt cheap, extraordinarily so. You have seen hundreds of instances where others have successfully exploited an idea. It would pay to train your eyes for situations—NOW! Learn how to spot them. Use your imagination literally—let it run rampant. Never mind that it's a ridiculous dream. Boil it down with practical considerations. You will be surprised that you'll come up with something worthwhile on many occasions. Try it for yourself and see.

CHAPTER 21 ODDS & ENDS

How to Use Your Imagination. Imagination is a dream searching for fulfillment. You will find it wise to dream. Dream magnificent dreams—the wildest dreams. Incorporate your ambitions and wants into these dreams. What would make you happiest in the whole world? Well dream about it. Picture this dream. Fix it in your mind. Now just how impossible is it? What would you have to do to make it come true? What can you do? What have you that will help you in the way of realizing this dream? What does it really take? Imagine yourself taking every step to realize your dream's fulfillment. Do any embryo plans begin to present themselves? Does any idea come to you that you can use to bring this about?

Dreams are the stuff ambition is made of. Dreams beget interests and pursuits. Dreams are the basic raw material for ideas, plans and, eventually, a course of action. Dreams are easy. They spring from desire. But putting dreams on the drawing boards— and thence to a material reality is beyond the average person. A thousand miles of dreams will draw them only a mile along the road. Better mileage any worthy dream deserves.

Don't be afraid of being labeled an idle dreamer. If you use your imagination enough sooner or later you'll give birth to a dream desirable enough and practical enough for you to undertake its realization. I subscribe to being a dreamer. During my younger years my dreams ran into fantasy. They were not practical by any stretch of the imagination. But of these impossible beginnings were laid the groundwork for mental projections of a more realizable nature. My tastes began to become definite and cultivated along certain lines. I began to find things I liked well enough to have in this world. My fantastic dreams gave way to the realization that every want we really have can be satisfied fully in this world we have in hand. I still, on occasion, dream on an astronomical basis.

309

But I manage to boil something little and something worthwhile out of them. Little inventions are the practical stuff of big dreams. Personally, I do not limit my dreams to this or that.

Whatever strikes my fancy or interest I delve into. How does a dream—or an imaginative project—like this sound to you. Let's try to create an engine that operates directly upon the heat of the air! I have heard a hundred persons say it was impossible for every one who thought it was practical. But I have had no one to tell me why it couldn't be done. That is impossible too! If it can't be done there must be reasons why. If it can be done there must be reasons why. Can't you just imagine such a machine—a machine where fuel costs were no consideration? The heat of the air is ever renewed by the Sun. Why can't it be extracted or captured? We humans feel we utilize tremendous amounts of power but our power use is minuscule comparatively. I, personally, have had a lot of fun with this particular idea among others. It would be a great dream to have such tremendous energy that oceans of fresh water can be pumped to great deserts and be turned into Edens of plenty. But in some of my encounters with unimaginative engineers I have come across arguments against it on the basis that it was perpetual motion, etc., etc. In fact, the impossibility of the idea was so stressed that I confess I made fools of some of them. What is not— is impossible. But many educated men cannot see this idea—when such is no longer just an idea. The heat pump is an embryonic beginning of just such a development.

The difference between great men of accomplishment and impractical fools is not so great as you might think. Dreams that are boiled down on practical premises can materialize. Dreams that are based falsely produce disappointment and despair.

Getting back to our subject in hand, that of retirement, put your dreampower to work on it. Have you nerve enough to try to realize your dreams—just one good one? The steps you take to realizing your dream will not only net you happiness in their realization and fulfillment but in the engrossing activity along the pathways they lead you.

A negative way to approach the subject of ambitions and dreams is to take out of your life all that you DON'T LIKE! What are you dissatisfied with? What makes you unhappy? What misfits your tastes and comforts—your mental ease? What are you hopelessly hooked with? Are you not free? Why can't you chuck it all? Is your misery so important to the world? To you? Do you owe the world a miserable temperament? Must you reflect its ills in yourself? Do you feel you're going to live more than once—that you will have a second chance? It's about time you woke up! Happiness is worth going after—NOW!

The problem arises as to HOW. Here is where I have tried to help you. Courage are you lacking in? Will you listen to those who say it can't be done? Will you insist on being tied down? Can't you take a bold step and ACT? NOW? Start your dreams on the basis of WHAT YOU WANT TO GET AWAY FROM! When you start your dreams and pursue them consistently, plans for their fulfillment will evolve. Human nature has some "DO" in it and I think you have some "DO IT" in you, otherwise you wouldn't have bought this book.

Take my advice and dream, dream, dream. When you mentally traverse the road to the pinnacle of your dreams you will bring it down to the pathway of achievement.

WHY RETIRE YOUNG? I think I have stressed this throughout my book. Why waste your life? It's yours and you're going to live it only once. Why not get all the mileage you want out of it while you can? What this might mean in your particular case depends on your tastes and bent. But whatever it is, as long as they are worthwhile human motives you should not defer their realization until you can no longer enjoy them should you be able to. With advancing age we are able less and less to appreciate many of the physical activities of life through participation. What you can enjoy as an older person is far removed from what you can enjoy now. Don't dream of your old age in the terms of present wants. If you want something now—

better try to enjoy it now. There is no reason in the world why you should not retire at 25 instead of 65, if, in so doing, you do not shirk your social obligations—or at least —prove a drag upon society. In my own opinion the world should be filled with happy fun-loving people. Don't permit your life to be so harsh that you are denied happiness now—and in your later years.

§

HOW TO CHOOSE THE RIGHT CLIMATE. I am not in the health field. But there are climates which are better from the standpoint of health, happiness and pursuits in which we find pleasure. As a general observation it is said that cold changeable climates make industrious people and warm climates make indolent pleasure loving people. Fortunately, because man can control his climate indoors wherever he may be, no longer need heat put a damper on our ambitions or industriousness, nor a cold climate prod us along the byways of dreariness. On the whole the right climate depends 'In what you seek. Health, sport, outdoor life or what do you want? As a retired person you are not necessarily tied down to a particular climate or locale. But if you want to settle down you should choose the one you like best and one that likes YOU. Keep in mind that the healthier areas of this country are in the South—Florida, Texas, Arizona, and other southerly states. Before you settle, travel a lot. It even pays to move around a bit. The people you settle among will be more of a consideration than the climate. And you will find all kinds of people somewhere in the great "retirement belt" of the Southerly states. In choosing your retirement area definitely consider the climate factor. It has a lot to do with human happiness.

§

WHAT? WORK IN RETIREMENT? Work need not be boring. I get a great pleasure out of writing. I can write effortlessly into the wee hours of the morning. Doing the work that you like is not work at all—it is activity that accomplishes and satisfies.

Idleness, especially for younger people, is the worst thing in the world. We have to have a sense of belonging in the world, a sense that we are contributing something to it, that we are "getting somewhere," that we are accomplishing something. This urge varies with the various parts of this country and with various parts of the world. You can lose your social consciousness altogether—if your associates in your area have also lost or never had such a social awareness.

Work while in retirement is healthful just as is exercise and recreation. But the work must be wholesome, interesting. You must be free to do the work or not to do it. It must not demand of you— in better words you are the master of the work; it does not own you. It can be no more than a work project or a hobby. It can or cannot be the source of your income, depending on your circumstances. If you must work and it is unpleasant, it may be little gain over your present circumstances.

By all means, if you retire, find some useful and soul satisfying activity to absorb your hours. Few people I know could really be happy while completely idle. For you, I would say, there are too many useful and soul satisfying pursuits to follow in this world while living in a retired or semi-retired state to let idleness bore you.

PARADISES FOR MEN. On this subject I will address myself to young unmarried men—men who have no wife or family responsibilities. I am married myself and have several children. I was a young unattached wanderer myself prior to my marriage. I visited many parts of the world and, from an American man's viewpoint I found many places literally a paradise for men. Many young American men find Japan a paradise for themselves. I will not give an opinion here as it might be highly controversial. I was in Japan during my younger years. I regarded that country as a real paradise — bargain-wise—for retirement purposes and because of Japan's remarkable womanhood. Japanese women are positively the most feminine creatures on earth. But I wish to say that I have considerably revised my opinion with my years about living in Japan myself. My background unfits me for that kind of life. It is something personal. With you, young man, it may be different! I still have a very high respect for young Japanese womanhood.

In all my travels I have never been more impressed by women anywhere as much as by the women of the Scandinavian countries (Holland, Denmark, Norway and Sweden), Austria, Germany and Czechslovakia. If you want women on the naughty side I will not make recommendations here as I do not appreciate this kind of womanhood. There are many countries where women are definitely more on the naughty side than normal, unashamedly so. But I don't mean to recommend a man's paradise from an adventurer's standpoint. I mean it solely from the viewpoint of seeking a lifetime companion who would probably prove superior and more compatible to our tastes in womanhood than to those we are, as Americans, accustomed. In my mind there is little question that in this country more than any other women are on the spoiled side. Some of the nicest women I have ever met were our own American women. But there are some qualities developed in women of the countries I mention above that do not but rarely exist in women here. We say we have "charming" women here and we have. But I daresay you'll revise your whole conception of the word "charm" if you meet with women from these countries. In these countries, especially in Germany and Austria, there exists a rather unwieldly surplus of women, literally millions who can never hope to have a husband. Some of the finest women in the world live there. More intelligent women you'll meet nowhere. They have an "alertness" and "energy" of personality that will surprise and amaze you. The average American is "deadpan" and uninteresting by comparison. Their beauty is unsurpassed anywhere in the world. They are industrious and hardworking. They are extraordinarily clean. They have many physical and cultural interests. And they understand a man as a man wants to be understood. On the whole they are extraordinary women. I would never worry about fine women from these countries being up to my standards. Rather, I would be concerned if I were up to their standards! They are of strong moral fiber —few of them decay under the American influence, although some do.

Women from these countries are not puritanical in their outlook or social conduct. Especially is this so in Germany, Austria and Sweden. In their home settings you will find them not too restrained. If you should meet them on their vacations—when they are out for recreation and fun and have only a week or two to realize it in—in Southern

Spain, North Africa, Italy, Greece or other female tourist havens, you'll meet exciting women at their most exciting! And believe me, these are the fine young women you'd be proud to take home and introduce to your mother and father as your wife. As far as I am concerned women in these countries are unspoiled and appreciate a well balanced view of life.

They look upon life's pleasures with dignity and liberality that is wholesome. If you are a young man visit one or more of these countries by all means. They are truly a man's paradise.

§

BUY YOUR TWO BEDROOM RETIREMENT HOME FOR ONLY $10,000. If you can raise $10,000 now you can retire in ten years in a beautiful two bedroom home free and clear. How is this done? Many builders in Florida and Texas will build a home for you and sell it to you for $5,000 down plus closing costs. The payments will run about $750 per month on a 10 year mortgage. You can find these offers in almost any newspaper in retirement areas that attract you. The secret of ownership is digging up or borrowing that $10,000 NOW! When you purchase the place you promptly rent it out for $1000 a month or MORE! With the general inflation trend you raise the rent as prices go up. But your payments remain the same. At the end of the ten years you own a property worth perhaps $100,000 or more which you bought high at a price tag of say $7,500.

Another angle to this, perhaps an even better one, is to buy acreage or a lot for a price of $3000 to $6000. The builder will build your home for no down payment and take a mortgage on the home and property. This is a profitable operation for him as he makes a profit on the home. He discounts the mortgage with a bank or with a loan company. He may have to endorse the mortgage with a guarantee if it exceeds the appraised value of the property. This is no problem to most builders if it should prove to be a thorn in making the sale. They merely increase the price of the property a bit, take out a 1st and a 2nd mortgage and discount the 2nd mortgage more than the first. Second mortgages, if discounted enough, make attractive investments for many firms and individuals. On your end it is like owning a home for $10,000 as you need put up NO MONEY after the down payment. The rental which exceeds the payments for financing, insurance, taxes, repairs and maintenance may give you some in pocket money. In the "Retirement Belt" there is little difficulty in renting homes as the population is growing there by leaps and bounds.

If you want to cut your retirement say, to five years, and can raise $3,000 to $6,000 NOW you can buy citrus land, put it in citrus and expect a retirement income in the future. Citrus juices are being consumed by diet conscious Americans like milk and the demand is steadily increasing. You'll never have to perform a day's work in the field in the citrus grove business. You can contract to have all work performed. The sum of $15,000 to $30,000 will buy and develop 10 acres of good citrus land. In five years its value will have tripled and the market price will have kept pace with the inflation factor. In five years you will have a producing grove that should net you from $20,000 to $30,000 per year in income. Again I wish to stress that you need not involve yourself in work. All kinds of maintenance, management and harvesting services exist at very reasonable prices. Labor is cheap in the citrus areas.

If you are a dextrous financial manipulator with a good credit standing you can raise the necessary money by careful borrowing and make this investment. By the end of the FIRST YEAR you should have ALL your outlay in hand and in ten years you will have free and clear a property worth at least $27,000 and on which you will have realized already an income of over $100,000. In other words you can, by manipulation of credit, invest nothing and come out with a tidy fortune.

Let us look into a possibility. Outside McAllen, Texas there is citrus land for sale. In its raw state it is priced at $325 per acre, more or less. Ten acres will cost $3,250. You purchase the land outright with the money you raise. You contract with a builder to build you a nice two bedroom brick veneer home. Builders in McAllen are quoting $4,500 to $6,000 for a neat little two bedroom brick home. This is about 50% less than in most areas of the U.S. It will cost you about $1,500 to have the land set out with citrus trees. This would be oranges or grapefruit. Your total outlay might come to $11,000 on paper.

It is well to consider that citrus groves require pruning, fertilizing and irrigation each year. This could cost you $500 a year more before there is any return from citrus production. But you can get around this too. Citrus trees are so spaced that, in their first years, truck crops can be raised among them without impairing their growth and development. You can have truck croppers use and irrigate the land. As a condition of using your land you can make a deal that they have the trees pruned, watered and fertilized. By renting the grounds to truck croppers and the home to a tenant you can either equal or beat your outlay on mortgage, insurance, tax and maintenance.

Your retirement "situation" in South Texas might look like this. In five years your citrus grove is worth about $1,000 an acre. Your home was really a $7,000 market value from the moment it was built. At the end of five years it will certainly be that value or greater, especially if you consider the inflation factor. You will have a property worth $17,000 and it will begin citrus production that will probably net you a very minimum of $2,000 annually. At the end of ten years your home and property will undoubtedly be a greater value and you will have realized a gross income exceeding $10,000 during this time. All this for an original outlay or a loan of say only $5,000 for a period of six months or a year. Let us recapitulate on this transaction.

In the beginning you raised $5,000. You spent it like this. You laid out $3,250 for land and $1,500 for citrus grove development. A home was built for you that was charged on paper at $6,000 with closing costs. The moment your package is finished it is valued like this: Fully developed virgin citrus land @ $500 per acre—$5,000. Home— $7,000. This is an immediate value before you are set to make a single mortgage payment. Now comes the financial trick of the trade, getting your $5,000 back and still holding effective title to the property.

By way of mortgage manipulations you can take out one or two mortgages amounting to a face value of $12,500. You can discount these (through the builder or a third party) so that you come out with $11,000 in cash. With this $11,000 you can pay off all costs and have your original $5,000. You will then have no cash in the transaction. But you will have heavy payments. On a 10 year basis you might find yourself paying $130 a month on this package. During the first five years you can trim this down to a net outlay of $30 a month or perhaps nothing at all by renting your home and by having your acreage used by truck croppers. After the fifth year your revenue from the citrus will more than pay the mortgage payments and put money in your pocket—perhaps enough to retire on! If you manipulate the transaction carefully in this manner you may actually have to put out less than a penny! You would have to borrow $5,000 or loan your funds to the transaction for about six months to a year.

Keep in mind that as your citrus grove grows and develops you are making money by property appreciation. And your property insures that your investment beats the inflation factor. At the end of five years as pointed out your ten acres of citrus land will be valued at around $10,000 and your home at $7,000 or more, a total of at least $17,000. This appreciated value will more than exceed your outlay in purchase price and interest. And, if you are careful in management you will not have a penny tied up in your property when the transaction is only six months old or at the end of ten years when it is finally paid for. In fact, I repeat, you should have realized a net income of at least $10,000 during the five years over and above other revenues which went to retire the mortgages. You very well could have moved onto your property at the end of the first five years and met mortgage payments out of revenue from the citrus—and met a good part of your living expenses on the income left over. Anything you earn on the side through other activities will be strictly bonus income for you. Keep in mind that your citrus grove will probably outlive you, hence it will be a good retirement income for life.

If you carry this to a logical conclusion you will not, however, be satisfied with just one transaction. No need to depend on only ten acres of citrus grove when, if you don't tie any money up for more than a year in creating these packages, you can go on and on until you have four or five homes and forty or fifty acres of citrus groves. You can go on repeating the process by acquiring other acreage and building other homes on the same basis. You can rent the property and manipulate your financing as you did in the first case. This may be known as "shaky financing" but you risk losing little if you are extraordinarily careful in your management. As you can well imagine it does not take many transactions like these to assure you of a secure retirement income—for life!

CHAPTER ^^U LAST WORD

ALL right, that's it. You can do this thing. You can retire, starting right now, as of this minute. Before you is the road to *real* life.

The treadmill, the rat-race, the carrot-on-the-stick chasing existence, the workaday world; all these you can forget. It's up to you.

Good luck!